INTERNATIONAL POLITICAL ECONOMY SERIES

General Editor: Timothy M. Shaw, Professor of Political Science and International Development Studies, and Director of the Centre for Foreign Policy Studies, Dalhousie University, Nova Scotia, Canada

Recent titles include:

Pradeep Agrawal, Subir V. Gokarn, Veena Mishra, Kirit S. Parikh and Kunal Sen
ECONOMIC RESTRUCTURING IN EAST ASIA AND INDIA
Perspectives on Policy Reform

Solon L. Barraclough and Krishna B. Ghimire
FORESTS AND LIVELIHOODS
The Social Dynamics of Deforestation in Developing Countries

Jerker Carlsson, Gunnar Köhlin and Anders Ekbom
THE POLITICAL ECONOMY OF EVALUATION
International Aid Agencies and the Effectiveness of Aid

Edward A. Comor (*editor*)
THE GLOBAL POLITICAL ECONOMY OF COMMUNICATION

Paul Cook and Frederick Nixson (*editors*)
THE MOVE TO THE MARKET?
Trade and Industry Policy Reform in Transitional Economies

O. P. Dwivedi
DEVELOPMENT ADMINISTRATION
From Underdevelopment to Sustainable Development

John Healey and William Tordoff (*editors*)
VOTES AND BUDGETS
Comparative Studies in Accountable Governance in the South

Noeleen Heyzer, James V. Riker and Antonio B. Quizon (*editors*)
GOVERNMENT–NGO RELATIONS IN ASIA
Prospects and Challenges for People-Centred Development

George Kent
CHILDREN IN THE INTERNATIONAL POLITICAL ECONOMY

Laura Macdonald
SUPPORTING CIVIL SOCIETY
The Political Role of Non-Governmental Organizations in Central America

Gary McMahon (*editor*)
LESSONS IN ECONOMIC POLICY FOR EASTERN EUROPE FROM LATIN AMERICA

Juan Antonio Morales and Gary McMahon (*editors*)
ECONOMIC POLICY AND THE TRANSITION TO DEMOCRACY
The Latin American Experience

Paul Nelson
THE WORLD BANK AND NON-GOVERNMENTAL ORGANIZATIONS
The Limits of Apolitical Development

Ann Seidman and Robert B. Seidman
STATE AND LAW IN THE DEVELOPMENT PROCESS
Problem-Solving and Institutional Change in the Third World

Tor Skålnes
THE POLITICS OF ECONOMIC REFORM IN ZIMBABWE
Continuity and Change in Development

John Sorenson (*editor*)
DISASTER AND DEVELOPMENT IN THE HORN OF AFRICA

Howard Stein (*editor*)
ASIAN INDUSTRIALIZATION AND AFRICA
Studies in Policy Alternatives to Structural Adjustment

Deborah Stienstra
WOMEN'S MOVEMENTS AND INTERNATIONAL ORGANIZATIONS

Larry A. Swatuk and Timothy M. Shaw (*editors*)
THE SOUTH AT THE END OF THE TWENTIETH CENTURY
Rethinking the Political Economy of Foreign Policy in Africa, Asia, the Caribbean and Latin America

Sandra Whitworth
FEMINISM AND INTERNATIONAL RELATIONS

Cuba in the International System

Normalization and Integration

Edited by

Archibald R. M. Ritter
Professor, School of International Affairs and Department of Economics
Carleton University, Ontario

and

John M. Kirk
Professor of Spanish
Dalhousie University, Nova Scotia

St. Martin's Press New York

CUBA IN THE INTERNATIONAL SYSTEM

For information, address:

St. Martin's Press, Scholarly and Reference Division,
175 Fifth Avenue, New York, N.Y. 10010

First published in the United States of America in 1995

Printed in Great Britain

ISBN 0–312–12653–0

Library of Congress Cataloging-in-Publication Data
Cuba in the international system : normalization and integration / edited by Archibald R. M. Ritter and John M. Kirk.
p. cm. — (International political economy series)
Includes bibliographical references (p.) and index.
ISBN 0–312–12653–0
1. Cuba—Foreign relations—1959– 2. United States—Foreign relations—1993– 3. Cuba—Relations—United States. 4. United States—Relations—Cuba. 5. Cuba—Economic conditions—1959–
I. Ritter, Archibald R. M. II. Kirk, John M., 1951– .
III. Series.
F1788.2.C8 1995
327.7291073—dc20 95–1328
CIP

This book is dedicated to all those who seek an authentic, equitable and peaceful reconciliation between the United States and Cuba. May their goodwill, commonsense and continuing efforts prevail quickly.

Contents

List of Tables

Acknowledgements

This book, *Cuba in the International System: Normalization and Integration*, is the outgrowth of a symposium held in September 1993 at Carleton University, in Ottawa, Canada.

The objective of the Ottawa symposium was to examine Cuba in the context of the Inter-American and international systems. It was designed to rethink the processes and issues which constitute the main elements of Cuba's relations with the Western Hemisphere, including the Cuba–United States conflict and perspectives for its normalization. In the symposium, economic issues, security considerations, political democracy and human rights, as well as Cuba's international relations, were reanalysed.

The symposium brought together analysts mainly, though not exclusively, from universities and research institutes in Canada, Cuba, the United States and Latin America. Unfortunately, only a selection of the many valuable papers presented formally at the symposium could be included in this volume, owing mainly to a limitation on the length of the book.

We would like to express our gratitude to a number of organizations which provided financial support and made possible both the symposium and the preparation of this book. Included among these are the Co-operative Security Competition Program, Ottawa; the MacArthur Foundation, Chicago, United States; the Social Sciences and Humanities Research Council of Canada; and Carleton University, Ottawa. We would like to thank the members of the advisory committee for the symposium whose wise counsel helped us to maintain what we believe was an appropriate 'balance' in the design of the symposium. This committee include: Professor E. Dosman, Director, FOCAL, Ottawa; Professor H. Klepak, Director, Centre for Research on Latin America and the Caribbean, York University, Toronto; F. Léon, UN Economic Commission for Latin America and the Caribbean, Santiago; P. Monreal, Centro de Estudios sobre las Américas, Havana; Professor D.H. Pollock, Norman Paterson School of International Affairs, Carleton University, Ottawa; Dr J.L. Rodríguez, Ministro de Finanzas, Havana; and Dr L. Suárez, Director, Centro de Estudios sobre las Américas, Havana.

We would also like to express our gratitude to our institutional sponsors, namely Carleton University, Centro de Estudios sobre América and Centro de Investigaciones de la Economía Mundial, of Havana, and Dalhousie University, Nova Scotia.

There are many individuals who provided encouragement and assistance for both the symposium and the preparation of this book. Of these, we would like to thank in particular Mónica Lee of Simon Fraser University and Diane Richer of Ottawa who provided administrative support for the organization of the symposium and prepared the manuscript for publication.

Finally, our thanks go to our respective wives and families for putting up with us during this venture, including our absences, and our continuous preoccupations with this project and the issues on which it focuses.

List of Abbreviations

ACP	African, Caribbean and Pacific (countries associated with the European Union)
ACS	Association of Caribbean States
ALADI	Latin American Integration Association
ANPP	National Assembly of People's Power
ASCE	Association for the Study of the Cuban Economy
CAIC	Caribbean Association of Industry and Commerce
CANF	Cuban American National Foundation
CARICOM	Caribbean Community
CBI	Caribbean Basin Initiative
CBM	Confidence-building measure
CCC	Caribbean Council of Churches
CDA	Cuban Democracy Act
CDR	Committee for the Defense of the Revolution
CEA	Centre for the Study of the Americas
CECE	State Committee on Economic Collaboration
CIDA	Canadian International Development Agency
CIS	Confederation of Independent States
CLAPTUR	Latin American Confederation of Tourism Press
CMEA	Council of Mutual Economic Assistance
COMECON	Soviet Bloc Common Market
CSBM	Confidence- and security-building measure
CSCE	Conference on Security and Cooperation in Europe
CTO	Caribbean Tourist Organization
EC	European Community
ECLAC	Economic Commission for Latin America and the Caribbean
ECOSOC	Economic and Social Council (United Nations)
EU	European Union
FAO	Food and Agriculture Organization
FCSC	Foreign Claims Settlement Commission
FOCAL	Foundation for Canada and Latin America
GATT	General Agreement on Tariffs and Trade
GDP	Gross domestic product
GLACSEC	Group of Latin American and Caribbean Sugar Exporting Countries

GRULA	Coordination of Latin American Governments in the UN System
GSP	Gross social product
IAEA	International Atomic Energy Association
IAI	Inter-American Institute (for Global Research)
IBEC	International Bank for Economic Cooperation
IBRD	International Bank for Reconstruction and Development
ICAO	International Civil Aviation Organization
ICSID	Internationl Centre for Settlement of Investment Disputes
IDA	International Development Association
IDB	Inter-American Development Bank
IDRC	International Development Research Centre
IFAD	International Fund for Agricultural Development
IFC	International Financial Corporation
IICA	Inter-American Institute for Cooperation in Agriculture
ILO	International Labour Organization
IMF	International Monetary Fund
IMO	International Maritime Organization
INIE	National Institute for Economic Research
INTUR	Tourism Institute
IOC	Intergovernmental Oceanographic Commission
IRELA	Institute for European–Latin American Relations
IRS	Inland Revenue Service
ISO	International Sugar Organization
ITU	International Telecommunications Union
Juceplan	Central Planning Office
LDC	Less developed country
LIC	Low intensity conflict
MIGA	Multilateral Investment Guarantee Agency
MINCEX	Ministry of Foreign Trade
MININT	Ministry of the Interior
NAFTA	North American Free Trade Agreement
NAM	Nonaligned Movement
NATO	North Atlantic Treaty Organization
NGO	Non-governmental organization
OAS	Organization of American States
OFAC	Office of Foreign Assets Control
OLADE	Latin American Energy Organization
PAHO	Pan American Health Organization
Parlatino	Latin American Parliament

PCA	Panama Canal Authority
PCC	Communist Party of Cuba
PNM	People's National Movement (Trinidad/Tobago)
PTIA	Protection of Trading Interests Act
SDPE	Economic Planning and Management System
SELA	Latin American Economic System
UBPC	Basic unit for agricultural cooperation
UNCTAD	United Nations Conference on Trade and Development
UNESCO	United Nations Educational, Scientific and Cultural Organization
UNICEF	United Nations Children's Fund
UNIDO	United Nations Industrial Development Organization
UPU	Universal Postal Union
VOA	Voice of America
WCL	World Confederation of Labor
WFTU	World Federation of Trade Unions
WHO	World Health Organization
WIPO	World Intellectual Property Organization
WMO	World Meteorological Organization
WTO	World Tourism Organization

Notes on the Contributors

Carlos Alzugaray, a veteran Cuban diplomat, is now Ambassador to the European Union and the governments of Belgium and Luxemburg at Brussels. He has been posted permanently in Tokyo, Sophia, Buenos Aires, Montreal and Addis Ababa. He is also a professor at the Instituto Superior de Relaciones Internacionales Raúl Roa Garcia in Havana, and was Vice-Rector for Research and Post-graduate Studies from 1988 to 1991. He has published numerous works on Cuba's international relations and is the author of *Sistemas políticos: poder y sociedad, estudios de casos en América Latina* (1992).

H. Michael Erisman is Chair of the Political Science Department at Indiana State University. He is the author of many books and articles on Cuba's foreign relations and editor of other books. Among his publications are *Cuba's International Relations: The Anatomy of a Nationalistic Foreign Policy (1985)* and *Cuban Foreign Policy Confronts a New International Order* (1991).

Julie M. Feinsilver is at present a consultant on health issues with the Pan-American Health Organization. She is the author of a variety of works on Cuba, including *Healing the Masses: Cuban Health Politics at Home and Abroad* (1993).

Edward Gonzalez is Professor of Political Science at the University of California, Los Angeles. He is co-author of *Cuba Adrift in a Post-Communist World* (1992).

Gillian Gunn is Director of the Cuba Project at Georgetown University, Washington and has written extensively on Cuba. Her most recent work is *Cuba in Transition: Options for US Policy* (1993).

Rafael Hernández is a senior analyst at the Centro de Estudios sobre las Américas (CEA) in Havana. He is co-editor (with J. Domínguez) of *US–Cuban Relations in the Nineties* (1991).

John M. Kirk is Professor of Spanish and Latin American studies at Dalhousie University in Halifax, Nova Scotia. His publications include numerous edited books on Cuba, as well as authored works such as

Between God and the Party: Religion and Politics in Revolutionary Cuba (1989).

Hal P. Klepak is Professor of Political Science at the Royal Military College, Kingston, Canada. He is author of a variety of works on Latin American and Caribbean security and strategic issues.

Francisco León Delgado is a senior analyst at the Economic Commission for Latin America and the Caribbean in Santiago, Chile and is author of numerous studies and reports on Cuba and Latin American development issues.

Carmelo Mesa-Lago is Distinguished Service Professor of Economics and Latin American Studies at the University of Pittsburgh. He founded and edited the journal, *Cuban Studies/Estudios Cubanos*. The most recent of his 13 books and numerous articles on Cuba is *Are Economic Reforms Propelling Cuba to the Market*? (1994).

Pedro Monreal is an analyst at the Centro de Estudios sobre las Americas (CEA) in Havana, and was recently Visiting Professor at the University of California (Berkeley). He has written extensively on the Cuban economy and is a co-editor of *Cuadernos de Nuestra América.*

Marifeli Pérez-Stable is a professor at Old Westbury College of the State University of New York. Among the most recent of her many works on Cuba is *The Cuban Revolution: Origins, Course and Legacy* (1993).

Donna Rich Kaplowitz is Director of Cuba Research Associates, an organization that specializes in USA–Cuba trade issues. She served as editor of *CubaINFO*, a fortnightly publication on Cuba published by John Hopkins University, Washington, DC. She has written extensively on Cuban foreign policy and the US trade embargo of Cuba and is editor of *Cuba's Ties to a Changing World* (1993).

Archibald R.M. Ritter is Professor of Economics and International Affairs at Carleton University, Ottawa. He has written extensively on Cuba's economic experience as well as on Latin American development issues, and recently co-edited *Latin America to the Year 2000: Reactivating Growth, Improving Equity, Sustaining Democracy* (1992).

Manuel Rua del Llano is a senior economist with the Chamber of Commerce of the Republic of Cuba and a research associate with the Centro de Estudios sobre las Américas in Havana. He has written a number of studies on the Cuban economy.

Luis Suárez Salazar is Director of the Centro de Estudios sobre las Américas in Havana and editor of *Cuadernos de Nuestra América.* He is author of many works on Cuba's international relations.

Andrew Zimbalist is Professor of Economics at Smith College, Northampton, Massachusetts. He has published numerous books and articles on comparative economic systems and economic development as well as on the Cuban economy. His most recent book is *Baseball and Billions: A Probing Look Inside the Big Business of our National Pastime* (1992).

The Caribbean

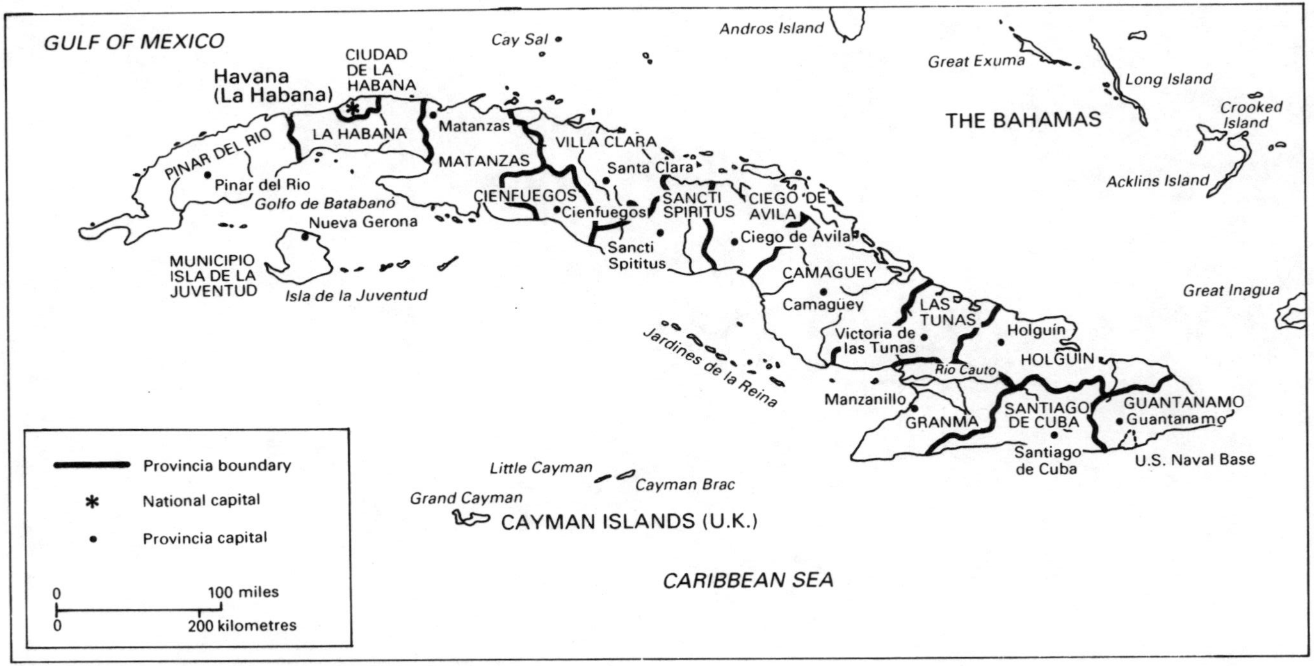
GULF OF MEXICO
Cay Sal
Andros Island
Great Exuma
Long Island
THE BAHAMAS
Crooked Island
Acklins Island
Great Inagua
Havana (La Habana)
CIUDAD DE LA HABANA
LA HABANA
PINAR DEL RIO
Pinar del Rio
Golfo de Batabanó
Nueva Gerona
MUNICIPIO ISLA DE LA JUVENTUD
Isla de la Juventud
Matanzas
MATANZAS
VILLA CLARA
Santa Clara
CIENFUEGOS
Cienfuegos
Sancti Spititus
SANCTI SPIRITUS
CIEGO DE AVILA
Ciego de Avila
CAMAGUEY
Camagüey
Jardines de la Reina
LAS TUNAS
Victoria de las Tunas
Holguín
HOLGUIN
Rio Cauto
Manzanillo
GRANMA
SANTIAGO DE CUBA
Santiago de Cuba
GUANTANAMO
Guantanamo
U.S. Naval Base
Little Cayman
Cayman Brac
Grand Cayman
CAYMAN ISLANDS (U.K.)
CARIBBEAN SEA
Provincia boundary
National capital
Provincia capital
0
100 miles
0
200 kilometres

Cuba

Introduction

Archibald R.M. Ritter and John M. Kirk

By the mid-1990s, Cuba's economy, society and polity were confronting intensifying challenges which were unprecedented in depth and breadth since 1959. A major element in resolving the multidimensional crises facing the country involves Cuba's international relations. Cuba has achieved considerable success in reintegrating itself into the international system following the ending of its special trade and aid relationships with the countries of Eastern Europe and the former Soviet Union and the demise of the latter country itself. Indeed, Cuba now has normal trading relations with virtually all countries with the exception of the United States. This international reintegration has been useful in terms of helping to reorient and to expand trade as well as to increase tourism and, to some extent, foreign investment. By mid-1994, however, there had been no progress in normalizing relations with the United States which continued to be locked in a worsening paralytic and deadening embrace, with little apparent interest demonstrated by the United States in dialogue with Cuba.

The objective of this book is to analyse Cuba's international relations, focusing on Cuba's strategies of diversifying and strengthening its bilateral and multilateral linkages as well as on Cuba's relationship with the United States. The first part of this volume examines the domestic political and economic context for Cuba's international relations. Chapter 1, by Marifeli Pérez-Stable, analyses the political dimensions of the crisis of the 1990s. The next three chapters then focus on the economy, with Andrew Zimbalist sketching the general economic situation as of early 1994, Pedro Monreal and Manuel Rua del Llano outlining the institutional reforms introduced in the economy, and Carmelo Mesa-Lago analysing the monetary policy changes introduced in 1993, notably the liberalization of dollar remittances from Cubans abroad.

Part II explores Cuba's broader international and inter-American relations, emphasizing the reorientation and redesign of Cuba's policy approaches. To begin this part, the chapter by Julie Feinsilver stresses the degree to which Cuba is already integrated into the international system, but also notes the problems involved in entering the Organization of American States, the Inter-American Development Bank, the International Monetary Fund and the World Bank. Luis Suárez Salazar then provides a broad analytical survey of the changes which have occurred in Cuba's international relations. Francisco León Delgado analyses and evaluates three general approaches to Cuban 'reinsertion' into the international system, namely (1) 'plural' or broad multilateral; (2) Latin American; and (3) Inter-American, concluding that, at present, the Latin American option is the most feasible and desirable, and is complementary to the longer-term Inter-American option. Michael Erisman and John Kirk explore Cuba's successful relations with the Caribbean countries (which in July 1994 entered a broad trade agreement which included Cuba) and Canada, respectively.

The third and longest part of the book explores Cuban–United States relations. The two chapters from a Cuban perspective, by Carlos Alzugaray and Rafael Hernández, emphasize the security dimension and problems of resolving the impasse, respectively. These are followed by the chapters of Gillian Gunn and Edward Gonzalez, both of which seek to explain the paralysis in the current relationship and some of the factors and policies which could lead to movement towards reconciliation. Hal Klepak presents some important insights concerning 'Confidence-Building Measures' and practical steps by which both Cuba and the United States could move beyond paralysis towards resolution of their current symbiotic and pathological relationship, now a relic of the Cold War. Donna Rich Kaplowitz examines the impacts of the Cuban Democracy ('Torricelli') Act on the trade of subsidiaries of US enterprises, concluding that significant losses are imposed on US subsidiaries, almost no harmful impacts are felt by Cuba and yet the Act further discredits the USA diplomatically and continues to be counterproductive to US objectives. Finally, Archibald Ritter analyses an aspect of the US–Cuban relationship that will be difficult to resolve, namely the demand on the part of the US government for compensation of those who were US nationals in 1959 and whose properties were seized; the hope of many Cuban émigrés for compensation (if not restitution); and the counterclaims for damages arising from the US embargo which may be made by the government of Cuba.

Before we conclude this introduction, a summary of the causes, character and consequences of Cuba's multidimensional crises of the first half of the 1990s is necessary in order to outline the context and indicate the urgency of the ongoing renewal of Cuba's international relations.

While a number of causal factors are responsible for the current crises, including dysfunctional economic architecture and the character of the political system, the central cause is the decline in the foreign exchange available for the purchase of imports, which fell from around $US 8.0 billion in the latter 1980s to perhaps $US 1.7 billion by 1993.[1] This reduction was generated by the demise of the former USSR, the ending of special relationships with the countries of Eastern Europe, the blockages produced by the US embargo and the failure of Cuban policy to diversify the structure of exports prior to and after 1990.

The collapse of foreign exchange earnings has contributed to a set of interlinked crises: an energy crisis, an agricultural food–nutrition crisis, a general macroeconomic crisis, a crisis of the 'social safety net' and a political crisis. The main feature of the *energy crisis* is the reduction of petroleum imports from an accustomed level of about 13 million metric tons in the 1980s to about 4 million in 1993 and perhaps 6 million for 1994. This has led to cutbacks in electrical supply, shortages of fuel for agriculture and industry and impaired transportation. Second, a major problem has arisen because a large proportion of food and agricultural inputs have been imported in recent decades. The decline in foreign exchange earnings has reduced agricultural production, including both food for domestic consumption and export crops. (The sugar harvest of 1994 was 4.0 million tons, even less than that of 1993.) *Food availability* has diminished seriously: a recent study by the Spanish Aid Agency reported large reductions in the production of 11 of 15 major crops, and a decline in average daily caloric consumption from 2550 in 1970 to 1780 in 1993 compared to the 2600 level recommended by the World Health Organization.[2]

Third, reduced imports of raw materials, intermediate inputs, replacement parts and machinery, together with fuel shortages, electrical blackouts and labour problems arising from a dysfunctional structure of incentives (to be discussed later) have led to reductions in levels of economic activity by 50 per cent to 55 per cent in per capita terms from 1987 to 1993 – a decline unequalled this century.[3] This economic collapse has also led to problems of a social and societal nature. Despite efforts to maintain the coverage and quality of the educational, health, nutritional and social security systems – perhaps the major achievements of the revolution – their deterioration has been unavoidable in view of the supply constraints arising from the economic contraction. Open unemployment, hidden 'unemployment-on-the job' (people being paid but not producing anything), high absenteeism and a shift to legal or illegal, registered or unregistered small-scale economic activities, have all increased sharply. A proportion of these activities include prostitution, 'black market' operations of various sorts and petty crime – all of which have increased sharply and visibly.

Moreover, the general structure of incentives eliciting human energies for economic activities has become deformed and dysfunctional. In the 'internationalized' part of the economy (including the tourist sector and all those who have access to foreign exchange or 'dollars' from any source) prices are in dollar terms (or pesos at the 'black market' rate) and the rewards for economic activity are correspondingly high. In contrast, in the 'socialist' part of the economy and society, prices and the wage and salary scale are in pesos. With an unofficial exchange rate of 50 pesos per US dollar (Feb 1995), the real incomes of people working exclusively in this part of the economy are low and have declined sharply owing to the reduced availability of goods and services in the official price-controlled economy and the need for people to make purchases in the black market.

An important consequence of the coexisting internationalized market plus black market economy on the one hand, and the domestic socialist economy on the other, is a growing social divide – with accompanying domestic frustration and polarization – between those Cubans with access to foreign exchange or involved as sellers in the 'black market' and those outside this part of the economy. The former are able to purchase imported goods in special dollar stores while the latter must eke out a living on the ever-decreasing rations. The second consequence of this duality in economic structure is that large volumes of resources and particularly human resources are induced out of socially valuable activities in the socialist economy and into the highly remunerative 'internationalized' sector. This can be seen clearly with the diversion of qualified academics or other professionals to service jobs in the tourist sector: the real economic compensation available from the latter far exceeds the real incomes of salaried professionals in the socialist economy.

The political consequences of the economic and social crises are of intensifying significance and visibility. Falling real incomes, worsening nutrition, a weakening social safety net and the blockage of the survival strategies of some people whose small-scale enterprises have been recriminalized, all generate discontent which ultimately has political implications. The absence of any convincing new 'vision' as to where Cuba's economy and society are going and how they are going to get there also has a debilitating and dispiriting effect on the citizens of Cuba, who can see no way out of the current situation. A vigorous policy response to the crisis and a new 'vision' are vital. So far, however, the policies adopted are hesitant, insufficient, inconsistent and credibility-destructive, while the implicit vision is essentially that of the old status quo. Hopelessness, despair and anger arise from this situation for many Cubans. But because of the monopoly role of the Communist Party in Cuban society, these sentiments can have no direct impacts towards renewal and reform within the political system. The result of this situation was visible with the first anti-government demonstration in Havana on 6 August 1994, and with the escalating refugee crisis of summer 1994. It is unlikely that such chaotic actions will change the government or public policy in the short run, but they may signal an important change in the political landscape, namely the beginning of a period where frustration and anger can no longer be easily repressed.

Adding fuel to the fire is the attitude of the Clinton administration, which has misread the nature of the current situation in Cuba. In this it is no different from its eight predecessors. What marks Clinton's approach, however, is the way in which he has amended 28-year-old legislation (which previously had welcomed Cuban Exiles to US soil). Moreover, his government has ignored the 1984 migratory agreement (allowing up to 20 000 Cubans per year to migrate to the United States). Indeed Cuban government sources indicate that, while 80 000 exit visas were granted by Havana, less than 2000 entry visas were issued by Washington. The current policy, which has tightened the economic blockade around Cuba, severely reduced remittance payments by exiles to their families on the island and engaged in sabre rattling, is designed to increase pressure on Havana, or to 'put the hammer down on Castro', in terms used by President Clinton.

Whether the current political regime in Cuba can survive in the longer term will depend ultimately on its ability to weather the current economic and social crises and reorient and reform the economy successfully in the context of the international market-oriented economic system. Any predictions as to whether significant economic reform and recovery will occur in the near future seemed impossible to make in mid-1994.

The central features of Cuba's current survival strategy in 1994–5 included: (1) intensifying and diversifying diplomatic and trade relations with all parts of the world; (2) opening the economy increasingly to foreign investment and tourism; and (3) introducing some domestic economic reforms. The first strategic element has been implemented pragmatically and diligently both bilaterally and multilaterally, as this volume seeks to illustrate. Cuba's efforts to be a responsible trading partner and international citizen in recent years have borne fruit, as exports have increased to countries other than the former USSR and Eastern Europe. The second element – expanded tourism and foreign investment – has also been implemented with some success since 1990. Tourism has indeed expanded rapidly, and will continue to do so. Foreign investment in the form of joint ventures has also increased, with 146 such ventures involving companies from 28 countries, established by June 1994.[4] A further 130 new joint ventures are in various stages of negotiation. While foreign investment is significant, it is less significant than hoped for. Moreover, both tourism and foreign investment are highly vulnerable to political instability: any scent of such instability can quickly sour tour operators and foreign investors as regards a particular country, leading to rapid cut-offs of both tourism and foreign investment.

The third element – some internal economic reforms – includes a number of policies to absorb the excess money created and poured into the economy each year (through wage and salary payments far in excess of the value of goods and services available for purchases) in order to relieve the extreme (suppressed) inflationary pressures and to reduce the resultant disincentives to productive effort.[5] Other policy changes included some liberalization of small-scale enterprise (partly reversed in May 1994), the creation of a new type of cooperative in the agricultural sector, and the legalization of the holding and use of foreign currencies, notably the US dollar.

From a Cuban perspective, these economic changes constituted an expansion of the acceptable range of policy initiatives and reforms. Who would have predicted in 1992, for example, that Cuba would partially privatize its telephone system and permit foreign payments to be made through the mechanism of a debt for equity swap?[6] The inauguration of several stores in the Benetton chain in 1993, the visit of Pierre Cardin in 1994 and the influx of European investment all indicate Havana's welcome to foreign capital. Behind this approach is a clear strategy by Havana to diversify foreign investment.

On the other hand, many analysts argue that this is too little and too late; indeed, Cuban policy making appears to be close to paralysis. According to this view, the decline in real per capita income from 1987 to 1993 has made a variety of institutional reforms, policy reorientations and structural transformations urgent. These would include an exchange rate policy change, basic changes in monetary policy, tougher action to reduce the fiscal deficit, major changes in the scope for the private sector, reform of the regulatory environment within which the private sector operates, price liberalization, financial system reform and the establishment of the legal foundation for a more decentralized and more market-oriented economy. Especially worrisome from this perspective is the fact that Cuba's economic contraction has preceded significant transition, in contrast to Eastern Europe where the transitional processes were accompanied by simultaneous contraction. Would further structural and institutional reforms generate further economic contraction in Cuba's case? That said, the comparison with the former Soviet Union and former socialist bloc is of course inevitable. Cubans are not unaware of the weakening of fundamental social programmes, and the economic problems in the wake of the simultaneous introduction there of rapid economic restructuring and political opening. Cuban concerns about what would happen in Cuba if similar reforms were to be introduced cannot be readily dismissed. The essential dilemmas, it would appear, are complex.

While Cuba has successfully normalized its relations with virtually all countries of the world, its relationship with the United States has continued largely unchanged, though the diplomatic frigidity and economic embargo were intensified by the 1992 'Torricelli' Act and the policies imposed in August 1994 (the cutting off of financial transfers by Cuban-Americans to their relatives in Cuba, and the placing of refugees in special camps). US policy towards Cuba has been singularly unsuccessful in forcing a change of government, or in promoting the adoption of a multi-party democratic system or in stimulating a process of economic reform. Indeed, US policy probably has impacts which are the opposite of its intentions, in that it probably strengthens support for President Castro and the economic and political status quo, because it permits him to adopt the mantle of champion of Cuban nationalism against the aggressive intentions of the United States.

The impacts of the economic embargo are paradoxical at the present time. The embargo has undoubtedly hurt the material levels of living of the Cuban people, though it has probably been of political benefit to President Castro. On the other hand, the embargo is less significant as a source of Cuba's current economic woes than it is often made out to be by the Cuban leadership, media and some analysts, who attach blame to the embargo for almost all Cuba's problems. While a normalization of relations is inevitable and will be of immense economic benefit in the long term, in the short term an ending of the embargo would in fact have significant political costs to the Cuban leadership and economic costs as well. The short-term economic costs would be incurred largely because Cuba is unprepared for what could be a tidal wave of entrepreneurship, financial inflows, managerial knowhow, direct foreign investment marketing expertise, and tourism coming from the United States and especially the Cuban-American community. Having virtually abolished the private sector from 1968 to 1993, and only allowing a gradual re-opening at present, Cuba remains with minimal defences facing a possible economic 'take-over'. Little thought has been given and no significant policy initiatives have been proposed or implemented with respect to confronting or managing a lifting of the embargo.

It is indeed difficult to comprehend why the United States has persisted in so counterproductive and foolish a policy towards Cuba, an approach with which virtually no other country agrees. The proximate cause, of course, is the influence of the Cuban American National Foundation (CANF) in domestic US politics. But that successive US presidents, and especially President Clinton, have been so beholden to CANF, and so fixed for 35 years on a policy approach that has failed so dramatically is bizarre. It would appear to most of the world that a nation which can ignore human rights abuses in China (while denouncing shrilly the lesser violations in Cuba) and which can reopen diplomatic ties with Vietnam (where more than 50 000 Americans lost their lives) while denouncing Cuba surely defies logic. Indeed, the official policy for some 35 years has revolved around the idea of waiting for Fidel Castro to die. Meanwhile the Cold War has ended everywhere except for the Washington–Havana axis, apartheid in South Africa has been overturned, Israel and the Palestinians are establishing a modus vivendi, and peace negotiations have prospered in Central America.

One hopes that the analysis of the US–Cuban impasse on the one hand, and on the other the evidence that most countries have come to terms with the Cuban revolutionary process, will pose some logical questions as to why Washington's approach has been so different and so anachronistic. Perhaps some of the contributions here will encourage a reconsideration of policy towards Cuba on the part of some US citizens and help to promote a normalization of the relationship between the United States and Cuba. Common sense surely demands it.

Notes

1. Economist Intelligence Unit, *Country Report: Cuba*, 2nd quarter, 1994, p.4.
2. Ibid., p.14.
3. Ibid., p.4 and authors' calculations.
4. 'Joint Ventures' *CubaINFO*, 6:9, 1 July 1994, p.10; 'Investment Approaches Critical Mass', *Cuban Business*, 8:5, June 1994, p.1.
5. *Granma International*, 1 June 1994, p.4.
6. 'Joint Venture', *CubaINFO*, p.9.

Part I

The Domestic Context: Economic and Political Challenges

1 Cuban Nationalism and Political Democracy Towards the Twenty-first Century[1]

Marifeli Pérez-Stable

Cuba is facing a political crisis. With the downfall of Eastern European communism and the disintegration of the Soviet Union, the Cuban economy lost the network of trade, credits and aid which had sustained it against the US embargo. Cuban leaders have reluctantly recognized the economic predicament of such dramatic proportions that it requires of them a response antithetical to their history: however gradually, they must implement reforms, the logical conclusion of which is the restoration of a mixed market system. The political crisis, however, is no less dramatic: to address it, the Cuban government must move to constitute political democracy. In part because the leadership has yet to acknowledge the second crisis, the prospects for a successful political transition are even more uncertain than those for an effective economic transformation. Simply stated, a successful confrontation of the political crisis ultimately entails holding free and open elections that could well end the tenure of Fidel Castro and the Cuban Communist Party (PCC), an option that the current government has not so far seriously contemplated.

The origins of the political crisis lie largely in the course of post-1959 domestic developments and, therefore, democratization should be a response to the exigencies of Cuban society. However, US policy deflects whatever impulses (at best, only a flicker) Cuban leaders might have towards opening the political system. In the post-Cold War world, the United States has conditioned the normalization of relations to the establishment of political democracy on the island. Because nationalism was the driving force of the Cuban Revolution and still constitutes the government's last bastion of legitimacy, the current leadership is loath to implement reforms that appear to be concessions to the United States. Because US policy, especially the Cuban Democracy Act of 1992, is an affront to Cuban sovereignty, it unintentionally buttresses the Cuban government's hold on the nationalist mantle. Indeed, with the exception of the Carter administration, the United States has never had normal relations with Cuba – before or after 1959. And that reality is an essential component of the Cuban dilemma of the 1990s.

Thus the issue of political democracy is caught in the convolutions of Cuban–US relations. On the one hand, Cuban leaders are the bearers of a more sovereign nation whose citizens are more equal; they consider national sovereignty and social justice to be the substance of democracy, their rule a mandatory safeguard. On the other, the US government defines democracy in terms of its political forms: civil liberties, separation of powers, contested elections. Undoubtedly, in the world of the 1990s, a political system that does not guarantee the rights of a peaceful opposition and offer it the opportunity of competing for public office cannot be reasonably considered democratic. Nonetheless, 35 years ago, when the Cuban Revolution came to power, the idea of alternate forms of democracy seemed plausible. Then the revolutionary government rejected representative democracy and embraced the search for a new democracy. After more than three decades, however, Cuban leaders are no closer to forging alternative democratic forms: the search is poignantly over. The balance sheet of revolution and socialism has unequivocally unmasked the myth of an alternative to political democracy. And thus, largely because of domestic considerations, the Cuban government ought to move in that direction. Indeed, history will ultimately judge the Cuban Revolution and its leadership on the basis of how the current government manages (or fails) to bring about a peaceful and democratic transformation of socialism and one-party politics.

THE SOCIAL REVOLUTION OF 1959 AND THE ESTABLISHMENT OF A NEW POLITICAL SYSTEM

The Cuban Revolution was the most extraordinary event in the island's history. Its roots lay in the long struggles for independence against Spain in the nineteenth century, the intimate and often traumatic ties with the United States in the twentieth, and the peculiarities of Cuban society – a monoculture economy marked by jarring contrasts of modernity and backwardness; a complex social structure and interactions among social classes; and a political system of feeble institutions. When, on 1 January 1959, Fidel Castro proclaimed, 'This time the revolution is for real!', the Cuban people responded with a groundswell of will, energy and passion. The revolution awakened in ordinary Cubans a new sense of empowerment that allowed them to imagine a new Cuba of greater sovereignty and equality. Even when, at the height of the Cold War, the new government turned to the Soviet Union and embraced communism, the call of nationalism and the commitment to social justice proved to be stronger in most Cubans than the anti-communism to which they had until then subscribed. Could there have been a more powerful testimony to the authenticity of the revolution than the relative ease with which the overwhelming majority of the Cuban people relegated the prevailing sentiments of the time and supported the new Cuba?

Thus the Cuban Revolution's greatest strength was the remarkable popular consensus that it elicited. That the Cuban people so intensely supported it was, moreover, Cuba's best defence against the United States. After 1961, when the revolutionary government thwarted the Bay of Pigs invasion, its primary political challenge was to translate the effervescence of the social revolution into an institutional infrastructure, political practices and cultural norms that consolidated the new Cuba. Essential to that effervescence were, on the one hand, the interaction between popular support and the leadership of Fidel Castro and, on the other, the identification of his authority with the revolution and *la patria* (the homeland). The rallying cry of *con Cuba o contra Cuba* (with Cuba or against Cuba) which so compelled the Cuban people became tantamount to *con Fidel o contra Fidel*. Thus the new politics was born in an ambience of national unity which rendered treacherous the expression of dissent. That the revolutionary government left to opponents no options but jail, death or exile certainly did not augur well for political democracy. That same government and its programme of national sovereignty and social justice, however, enjoyed an impressive degree of popular support. And, indeed, the challenge was to institutionalize a political system that would permanently consolidate and renew it.

Since the early 1960s, the Cuban government has offered four responses to that challenge: a modest institutionalization (1961–5); the radical experiment of mass mobilizations and unorthodox economic strategies (1966–70); a more full-fledged institutionalization (1971–85); and the rectification process (1986 to the present). Although these responses and their domestic and international contexts differed in important ways, the institutions of state socialism – a centrally planned economy and a vanguard party-led political system which, until the 1980s, appeared to be viable alternatives to those of capitalism and representative democracy – were at their core. At the same time, Cuban politics also hinged on the identification of Fidel–*patria*–revolution as the magnet aligning popular support and elite unity. Over the course of 35 years, these two models (state socialism and Fidel–*patria*–revolution) have tensely shaped the political system: the first has emphasized the role of institutions such as the PCC and the central planning system, the second that of Fidel Castro and popular mobilizations. Five crucial premises have underlain the Cuban leadership's efforts to establish a new political system.

First and most important is the nationalism embodied in the struggles for a sovereign Cuba launched in the nineteenth century and concluded by the Cuban Revolution. Independence from the United States is its weathervane: maintaining it has been the raison d'être of the Cuban government and the primal consideration of many Cubans in continuing to support it. Second, and intimately tied to national sovereignty, is social justice. Socialism allowed relative equality in the satisfaction of basic needs. Because Cubans are more equal, they are united, and national unity is the *sine qua non* of standing up to the United States. Thus a strong commitment to policies that enhance social justice and minimize divisions among Cubans has been a central characteristic of post-1959 Cuban politics. These two premises – national sovereignty and social justice – constitute the crux of the 'permanent revolution' that the Cuban government claims as its mantle.

The other three guiding principles followed logically from the first two: the concept of *las masas* (the masses); the creation of a new *conciencia* (consciousness); and the maintenance of elite unity. The Cuban leadership consolidated its rule on the basis of extraordinary mobilizations. Overwhelming popular support substantiated the idea of alternative forms of politics. Consequently, a central aim of Cuban politics has been to institutionalize that support and, because of it, the creation of a new popular *conciencia* has been crucial. Indeed, ordinary Cubans manifested this remarkably in resisting the invaders at the Bay of Pigs, participating in the literacy campaign and rallying around the government during the missile crisis. However, only if they continued to value in their daily lives collective 'goods' such as national sovereignty and social justice over the individual pursuit of material interests would this consciousness blossom. The effort to bolster an appreciation of these collective 'goods' in part explains the leadership's long-standing resistance to market-oriented reforms that emphasize individual gain. Finally, Cuban leaders have likewise deemed elite unity to be an integral component of the new politics. If they were divided, whom would the people follow? And if *las masas* heeded different leaders, how could *la patria* withstand the United States?

These five principles emerged in the course of the social revolution. They were clearly incompatible with representative democracy and its fastidious insistence on checks and balances, separation of powers and individual rights. Nonetheless, these principles seemed – in 1959 and for a good part of the past 35 years – to constitute the core of an alternative form of politics, one relentlessly driven by the ideals of nationhood and social justice. That such single-mindedness of purpose left little room for the expression of diversity seemed rather inconsequential in the face of the formidable consensus that the Cuban Revolution commanded. That, in addition, commitment to *la patria* and the revolution quickly became indivisible from loyalty to Fidel Castro did not seem to trouble most Cubans. Fidel, after all, was a revolutionary of epic dimensions, and his leadership had indisputably been vital to the creation of the new Cuba. For a long time, his exceptional qualities seemed to outweigh the other equally undeniable reality evident from the outset: that Fidel was also Castro, a *caudillo* and an autocrat.

After three-and-a-half decades, Cuban leaders find themselves in a dead-end because they never really moved beyond the politics of revolution. The four responses they gave to the challenge of establishing a political system capable of consolidating and renewing the extraordinary support they had initially mustered failed. On the one hand, the experiences of the Soviet Union and Eastern Europe have definitively discredited state socialism. On the other, the model of Fidel–*patria*–revolution no longer conjures up the legitimacy it once did. Moreover, although the five premises underlying the often tense interaction of these two models are exhausted, or nearly so, Cuban leaders continue to insist upon them. And therein lies the heart of the political crisis.

POLITICAL PITFALLS OF THE CUBAN REVOLUTION

First, the Cuban Revolution is history. While the idea of the revolution is very much alive, the revolution itself has been over for quite some time. Social revolutions do not last forever: after a relatively brief period of radical transformations, they begin an institutionalization which attempts to secure the stability of the new order. In that sense, the Cuban Revolution came to an end in 1970, when the failure of the 10 million ton sugar harvest forced the Cuban leadership to desist from the radical experiment and accept more fully the orthodox models of state socialism. During the 1970s and 1980s, the reality of socialism slowly gained ascendance over the effervescence of revolution. Thus revolution (until 1970) and socialism (after 1970) have imbued Cuban society with distinct, if also overlapping, dynamics: the first emerged in the demise of the old Cuba and forged a popular consensus in support of a programme of national sovereignty and social justice; the second became the conduit for realizing that programme and consolidating the new Cuba.

Nonetheless, although the dynamics of state socialism has increasingly defined Cuban society, the idea of the revolution has retained relevance because of three important factors. First, the current leaders of Cuba are basically the revolutionaries of 1959. The memory of their once phenomenal popular support and the belief that their rule is indispensable to the safeguarding of *la patria* renders them recalcitrant in the exercise of power. Second, a significant percentage of the population has strong emotional ties with the social revolution because of a lifetime of conviction and dedication. If they acknowledged the end of the revolution, they would have to seek a different compass to their lives. Third, even though the Cold War is over, US policy remains unchanged, reinforcing the view of the United States as Cuba's unrelenting antagonist. In short, the presence of Fidel Castro, a degree of popular support and US policy have extended the life of Fidel–*patria*–revolution. That model, however, is at the root of the political crisis, and the Cuban government's continued reliance on it is an unequivocal sign of weakness.

While iron-clad unity around Fidel Castro, *la patria* and the revolution initially allowed the Cuban government to survive against the United States, its politics imposed a regimentation of public life that is today undermining the revolutionary legacy. In preparing the PCC Congress of 1991, Cuban leaders admitted that too often *la doble moral* (duplicity) dictated the boundaries of public discourse: people were afraid to speak up because the political system only permitted the expression of unanimity behind the leadership for the sake of *la patria*. Indeed, the politics of Fidel–*patria*–– revolution created a second society outside the confines of official Cuba, the reality of which a popular observation has caustically recorded: in reality, there are 22 million Cubans – 11 who walk the streets, 11 who go home every night. Moreover, as was the case elsewhere, one-party politics in Cuba was not conducive to political pluralism. Thus neither model gave much recourse to the second society. Although in the early 1990s the Cuban government obliquely recognized an important element of the political crisis, it remained as intransigently bound as ever to the tenets that originated *la doble moral*. Unless Cuban elites found the courage and the wisdom to break new political ground that permitted the second society to express itself freely, history was not going to judge them kindly.

The economy is a second pitfall of post-1959 Cuban politics. Without doubt, socialism rendered Cuban society more just. Indeed, Cubans have had better and fairer access to basic needs such as health, education and social security than most other Latin Americans. While the social successes of the Cuban government are generally recognized, its economic record has, at best, been mixed. Over the past 35 years, systematic growth has eluded the Cuban economy: only during the 1970s did it register real per capita growth. Although the government made modest strides in diversifying the domestic economy, it only slightly reduced dependence on sugar exports which, in part, accounts for chronic trade deficits and continued vulnerability to the world economy. Post-1959 Cuban development, moreover, depended on the network of trade, credits and aid that the Soviet Union and Eastern Europe provided; without it, the Cuban economy has virtually collapsed. Thus Cuban leaders failed to create a sound economic basis to sustain the nation. Moreover, like state socialism elsewhere well before its demise, Cuban socialism has long provided evidence of the weaknesses of central planning. In the 1990s, economic reality was inescapable: the long-standing second economy (the black market) has so flourished that the value of its goods and services may be significantly larger than the official economy. Ultimately, then, Cuban socialism failed to consolidate an economy capable of permanently upholding the revolutionary ideals of national sovereignty and social justice.

A third political pitfall is the concept of *las masas*. If the social revolution genuinely animated the concept, the achievements of the past three-and-a-half decades have decidedly rendered it obsolete. In the 1990s, Cubans are more urban, healthy and educated than they were in 1959. Present in Cuban society is a critical mass of professionals and skilled workers. Contemporary Cubans are thus citizens not *masas*, and neither the politics of a single party nor the dynamic of Fidel–*patria*–revolution can adequately accommodate the individuality and the diversity in the concept of citizenship. These new generations of Cubans, moreover, have not developed the *conciencia* that Cuban leaders so needed at the core of the new politics. Although ordinary Cubans have often been capable of extraordinary heroism, fortitude, and dedication, they have not generally incorporated that *conciencia* into their daily lives. In short, everyday concerns have loomed larger in the actual consciousness of citizens than the historic visions of the Cuban leadership. That the selfless, heroic *conciencia* manifested during times of crisis turned out to be a chimera in daily life and work is the fourth political pitfall.

Cuban leaders have proved themselves to be quite adept at reconfiguring the coalition of governing elites. From the outset, they have shown an impressive capacity to rotate elites, maintain consensus among them, and prevent significant ruling group divisions. In the 1990s, the Cuban leadership once again gave evidence of its talent. At the 1991 PCC Congress, membership in the new Central Committee showed remarkable turnover (more than two-thirds) and a broader social and geographic representation of the Cuban population than those of earlier Central Committees. Similarly, the profile of deputies elected to the National Assembly in 1993 reveals more extensive turnover (more than 85 per cent) and more widespread representativeness than those of the previous Assembly. Nonetheless, Cuban leaders have yet to meet the decisive challenge of elite renovation. They have not seriously contemplated the imperative of meaningful contestation for public office and thus the possibility of turning the reins of government over to another coalition of elites. Again, neither one-party politics nor the Fidel–*patria*–revolution dynamic permits true elite renovation or the public consideration of opposition platforms. And that is the final pitfall of post-1959 Cuban politics.

Without doubt, then, Cuba is facing a political crisis. In the 1990s, the political system has been at odds with Cuban society. It is, moreover, unable to safeguard the revolution's achievements of nationhood and social justice into the twenty-first century. Cuban institutions seem incapable of incorporating the creative energies – political and economic – of new generations of citizens whose input *la patria* desperately needs. Cuba, however, is also at a political impasse. Although the dimensions of the crisis are daunting, the Cuban government is likely to remain in power for the foreseeable future. Why?

THE CUBAN POLITICAL IMPASSE

The principal obstacle in confronting the political crisis is that it has yet to climax: Cubans have not actively challenged the government. Their quiescence, however, is misleading. It certainly does not indicate majoritarian support or even the public's willingness to listen to the leadership, giving it the benefit of the doubt. In contrast, for most of its tenure, the Cuban government has elicited a combination of support and sufficient goodwill that rendered its rule, if not democratic, at least politically viable. Of course, Cuban leaders maintain that their rule continues to be legitimate and the only alternative to safeguard the homeland and social justice in accordance with the heritage of 125 years of struggle. This notwithstanding, they have also provided evidence of a more precarious sense of security than their defiant rhetoric might indicate. In 1991, the PCC Congress passed a resolution empowering the Central Committee to take whatever steps necessary to uphold the government. In 1992, the revised constitution included two new articles: one establishing a National Defence Council and the right to declare a state of emergency; another sanctioning the people's resort to armed struggle in defence of the government if other recourses failed. More recently, civilian and military leaders have alluded to the possible use of violence to quell dissent. Clearly, quiescence does not quite mean that a majority supports the government, and apparently the leadership knows it.

The current stability is, nonetheless, real even if it hinges on a rather delicate balance: the continuation in power of Fidel Castro; a critical mass of genuine support; the fear, apathy and sense of impotence of wide sectors of the population; and the appeal to nationalism that US policy substantiates. Even though much diminished, the leadership of Fidel Castro is still the magnet aligning elite unity and whatever popular support the government still possesses. That sufficient numbers of citizens – even if not a majority – continue to endorse the government to the point that many would put their lives on the line to defend it is, indubitably, a powerful element of the political impasse. By the same token, that a good many Cubans – most likely a majority – are paralysed in their discontent is a recognition of a complex reality: repression is effective; the exigencies of daily life leave little energy to engage in other matters; a viable, credible alternative is not yet in sight. Thus their silence is also a crucial component of the status quo. Finally, US policy, especially the Cuban Democracy Act of 1992, fuels nationalism and allows the Cuban government a credible pretext to resist meaningful reforms.

We have come full circle. The political crisis certainly originated in the exhaustion of Fidel–*patria*–revolution and the bankruptcy of one-party politics as viable models to renew popular support and renovate elites. In spite of this, Cuban leaders continue to insist on both because it is the only way they know how to govern. The alternative is to move towards political democracy and accept the possible outcome of losing their grip on power. Although the US government makes a change of policy conditional upon the execution of political reforms, the principal reason for instituting them is Cuban society itself. The United States did not cause the whole political crisis; mostly, the course of domestic developments did. Clearly, the two dimensions are closely intertwined: a change in US policy would relieve the siege mentality that in part sustains the dynamic of Fidel–*patria*–revolution; changes in Cuban domestic politics might prod the Clinton administration into engaging the Cuban government in serious negotiations. Unfortunately, US policy appears immovable for the time being. So Cuban leaders need to ask themselves how long they are willing to wait before they acknowledge the political crisis and begin addressing it responsibly.

Officially, the Cuban government attributes the crisis to the economic collapse and is hoping that even bottoming out will gain time. Whether the economy has reached its trough and, more importantly, whether it can – however modestly – rebound is a matter of considerable debate. Even if it does both, the political crisis would not significantly recede. Cuban leaders cannot forever govern on the terms of Fidel–*patria*–revolution and a single party. In the first place, Fidel Castro – one way or another – is going to pass from the scene, and then the first recourse will be definitively exhausted. Second, the Cuban Communist Party will not be able to defend its exclusive right to uncontested power indefinitely. Third, and most important, the Cuban people are no longer willing to be governed in the same ways as in the past. A majority no longer responds to the premises that inspired post-1959 politics. Today the political system is incapable of renewing popular support or even the willingness of the majority to listen to the leadership for credible guidance out of the nation's predicament. The logic of Cuban politics, however, likewise impedes the emergence of another elite coalition and the formation of alternative platforms for the citizens of Cuba to consider in deciding their future.

Thus, even in the unlikely event that the economy will soon recuperate, Cuban leaders will still confront a political dead-end. Do they have the time to postpone until that uncertain moment of economic recovery the hard but ultimately unavoidable political decisions? Their inaction so far indicates that they have answered this question positively. How long they have for the course of events to prove them right or wrong is the crucial issue. When and how will they cross the threshold of political transformation? Will a popular revolt force them over it? Will they then thwart the popular will with the use of tanks? Under those circumstances, would they continue to insist so intransigently on their rule that important sectors of Cuban and international public opinion would call for some form of outside intervention? Or can Cuban leaders still marshal the courage and the acumen that so often characterized them in the past to break the stranglehold of the current impasse without the use of force?

If events in Cuba unfold precipitately and violently, the democratic character of the transformation would be very much in question. Unfortunately, as time passes without substantial changes in Cuban domestic politics or in US policy, the likelihood of a violent outcome increases significantly. The best prospects for a successful political transition lie precisely with the gradual movement away from the dynamic of Fidel–*patria*–revolution. To start with, Cuban leaders need to recognize the political dimension of the dramatic crisis they are facing. They will then be compelled to make concessions to the second society in much the same manner that they have made modest, reluctant compromises with the second economy. Just as the government recently legalized (within strict limits) the behaviour of citizens engaged in private enterprise, it needs to acknowledge the political rights of the second society. The crux of the matter is that recognizing the second society carries with it the possibility – perhaps the certainty – of a governmental turnover. That, in fact, is the only reasonable litmus test of meaningful reforms: establishing rules of the political game that give opponents the opportunity to compete – fairly and freely – for public office.

The Cuban government and its supporters ought to recognize that to oppose them is not tantamount to betraying *la patria*. A trustworthy opposition is, moreover, absolutely imperative for the peaceful transformation of the status quo. Giving those citizens who now form an inchoate opposition (and the human rights activists are but the tip of the iceberg) the freedom to organize themselves and present their platforms to the public is thus a precondition if such a transformation is to happen. Consequently, the Cuban Communist Party should relinquish the claim that it has a historically given monopoly on power. Sooner or later, Cuban elites will face the absence of Fidel Castro. Without him, they will have to modify the political system to allow political contestation. By then, however, unless reforms had been previously instituted, it might well be too late, with the outcome being the complete disavowal of the revolutionary legacy. They should therefore initiate changes now, with Fidel Castro at the helm, even if ultimately they are voted out of office. If the Cuban government moved in that direction, it would undoubtedly force a change in US policy. Far from being a concession to the United States, however, democratization is the only genuine response to the political crisis brought about by the bankruptcy of one-party politics and the exhaustion of Fidel–*patria*–revolution.

CONCLUSION

In their struggle against Batista, and for the better part of their tenure in office, Cuban leaders have almost always emphasized the supremacy of political factors in dealing with what often seemed to be intractable realities. It is thus rather ironic that they are so adamantly insistent on the primacy of the economy in diagnosing the current crisis. Nevertheless, the crisis is also political, and only a political response will encourage a peaceful transformation of the status quo. Whatever their rhetoric, Cuban leaders know that, sooner or later, a transition from their rule will take place. What they ultimately need to decide is whether they will maintain the present course indefinitely and risk firing upon their own citizens, or whether they have the wherewithal to launch a political reformation and accept its consequences. In the end, history will condemn or absolve them according to the way they meet the political challenges of the current crisis.

Note

1. For a full exposition of the arguments presented in this chapter, see: Marifeli Pérez-Stable, *The Cuban Revolutin: Origins, Course, and Legacy* (New York: Oxford University Press, 1993) and Marifeli Pérez-Stable, 'Legislative and Electoral Dynamics: Reforms and Options', in *Transition in Cuba: New Challenges for US Policy*, pp.39–65. Concluded in May, 1993, the latter, a project of the Cuban Research Institute of the Latin American and Caribbean Center at Florida International University, was sponsored by the US State Department and the US Agency for International Development.

2 Cuba, Castro, Clinton and Canosa*

Andrew Zimbalist

Cuba's place in the world has changed dramatically over the past five years. With the collapse of the communist states in Eastern Europe and the Soviet Union, Cuba is now little more than an isolated anomaly. All of Cuba's troops have left Africa, and it no longer supports revolutionary movements in developing countries. It is a threat to no country.

Does it still make sense for the United States to pursue a Cold War Cuba policy in a post-Cold War world? If President Clinton continues the Reagan–Bush strategy of tightening the US embargo, will it succeed in forcing the fall of the Castro government? And when the Castro regime at last does come to an end, will the US embargo have been the best prelude for promoting democracy, political stability, economic growth, human rights and popular welfare in Cuba? The answer to each of those questions is a resounding 'no'. Present US policy toward Cuba – as epitomized by the escalating economic warfare of the 1992 Cuban Democracy Act endorsed by both the Bush and Clinton administrations – is anachronistic, inconsistent and counterproductive. To formulate a constructive US policy towards Cuba, it is crucial to get beyond the fact that Castro is a dictator. American policy makers must understand the political dynamics that have allowed Castro to survive the last five years, even though during that period Cuba lost its most important political allies and its national income fell over 50 per cent.

Never before under the revolution has the Cuban economy been in such a crisis. After strong economic growth between 1970 and 1985, the Cuban economy stagnated between 1985 and 1989, declined approximately 4 per cent in 1990, fell another 25 per cent in 1991 and dropped an additional 15 and 13 per cent in 1992 and 1993, respectively. The decline's proximate cause is clear enough. Cuba has a small and heavily trade-dependent economy. With the US embargo, Cuba came to depend on the old Soviet trade bloc (COMECON) for more than four-fifths of its imports. With access denied to the US market and restricted in others, and with imports from the former COMECON countries slashed by more than 90 per cent

* An earlier version of this chapter appeared as 'Dateline Cuba: Hanging on in Havana', in *Foreign Policy*, 92, Fall 1993.

between 1989 and 1992, Cuba's economy and people are now struggling to survive.

The Cuban government's response to the crisis has been deliberate but inadequate. A number of reforms initiated before 1989 are being continued, others are being accelerated, and some new programmes are being put in place. The current emphasis on foreign investment and tourism, structural reforms in the operation of foreign trade, creeping fiscal austerity and the impossibility of central planning in the presence of pervasive supply uncertainties have combined to transform the nature of Cuba's economy. Yet the needed and more concerted introduction of a broader market mechanism and enlarged private sector has not been forthcoming.

The US embargo, of course, attacks the Cuban economy at one of its most vulnerable points. Cuba has always been dependent on foreign trade. Indeed, from 1987 to 1989, Cuba's imports as a share of its estimated gross domestic product (GDP) averaged more than 35 per cent. By contrast, in other small, medium-income Latin American countries, imports constituted around 25 per cent of GDP.

Cuba's reliance on COMECON trade greatly aggravated the country's import dependency. During 1987–9 an average of 84 per cent of Cuba's imports came from Eastern Europe and the Soviet Union. Beginning in 1990, that link, with its preferential prices, began to collapse. By 1992 the value of total trade turnover (exports plus imports) between Cuba and the former Soviet bloc countries had fallen to only $830 million, or roughly 7 per cent of its 1989 level. The import of certain key commodities dropped precipitously as well: oil imports from Russia decreased from 13.3 million tons in 1989 to 1.8 million tons in 1992; fertilizer imports plunged from 1.3 million tons to 0.25 million tons; and animal feed imports fell like a stone, from 1.6 million tons to 0.45 million tons.

Adding to Cuba's economic woes has been a shift in its terms of trade. Between 1989 and 1992, the prices Cuba paid for imported wheat, chicken, milk and petroleum rose between 16 and 40 per cent, while the prices of Cuba's two most important commodity exports, sugar and nickel, fell by 20 and 28 per cent, respectively.

As Cuban dependence on the capitalist world market has increased, the long-standing US embargo has become more costly than ever before. President George Bush's tightening of the embargo during the last two years of his administration increased the pain. Overall, the value of Cuba's imports fell from $8.1 billion in 1989 to less than $3 billion in 1992. That massive shock sent the Cuban economy reeling, undermined its labour markets, spurred the rapid growth of an underground economy and cut national income by about 45 per cent between 1989 and 1992. In the face of economic collapse, the Castro regime has responded with an even tougher political line. Repression has increased despite Cuba's new policy of direct elections for the National Assembly and other perfunctory political reforms that came out of the Fourth Party Congress in October 1991. Acts of protest and opposition remain isolated and mostly individual in nature; there are virtually no signs of a substantial political challenge to Castro's continued rule.

BATTLE OF WILLS

Since the beginning of its embargo in 1960, the United States has sought to depose the Castro government by imposing heavy economic costs on the Cuban people. That policy has been a failure for 34 years. Indeed, as most Cuba experts and political leaders outside the United States recognize, the aggressive US policy has only served to bolster Castro's legitimacy as a national leader, justifying his heavy hand on the populace.

Today, despite the tightened embargo and Cuba's greater vulnerability, the policy remains a failure. The Castro government is succeeding in navigating a course that has thus far avoided the shoals of starvation and rampant unemployment while maintaining, albeit with increasing difficulty, its commitment to free health care and education. Moreover, the Cuban economy has, by now, already absorbed its worst hits. After the further decrease in national income of 13 per cent during 1993, occasioned in part by the devastating storm of 13 March and a 40 per cent reduction in the 1993 sugar harvest, the economic downturn will probably level off during the second half of 1994, with the possibility of a gradual turnaround thereafter. If Castro has been able to maintain his grip on power during the crises of the last five years, then there is little prospect for his political demise as the economy begins to stabilize and slowly improve.

It is time for the Clinton administration to produce a new Cuba policy – one that returns to the course of reconciliation that President Jimmy Carter began to chart in the first years of his administration. In 1977, the Carter administration opened discussions with the Castro government on a wide range of bilateral issues. Each government established interest sections (proxy embassies) in the other's capital. Carter lifted the ban on travel to Cuba by US citizens and halted reconnaissance overflights. A fishing agreement was negotiated. The air of rapprochement led the Castro government to release 4000 political prisoners and to begin a dialogue with the Cuban exile community. Washington and Havana reached agreements allowing exiles to visit their families in Cuba. The incipient normalization was soon sidetracked, however. Carter had to contend with a conservative backlash after the Panama Canal treaties; and Castro sent troops to Ethiopia to repel a Somali invasion, leading US strategists to fear another outburst of radical internationalism. Normalization was frozen and then reversed with the presidency of Ronald Reagan, who helped to spawn the Cuban American National Foundation (CANF), reimposed the travel ban and provoked an intensification of tensions.

The National Institute for Economic Research of Juceplan (Cuba's central planning board) is now evaluating the economic impact of the US embargo. The study seeks to analyse the costs sector by sector, considering only direct costs from lowered production, higher costs for obtaining goods and lower prices for some foreign sales. Though preliminary, its estimates give some sense of the magnitude of the loss. From 1960 to 1990, the total cost of the embargo approached an estimated $38 billion, roughly 20 per cent higher than Cuba's GDP in 1989. Another study, conducted by the Johns Hopkins School of Advanced International Studies, suggests that the total trade turnover between Cuba and the United States could reach $6.5 billion annually after a few years of trade. Having lost most of its trade with the former Soviet bloc, and all of its aid, Cuba suffered all the more acutely in 1991 and 1992 from the US embargo.

Cuba's only option, apart from modestly increasing trade with China, has been to increase trade with others in the West. Cuba's problems with that approach are manifold: Cuba's industrial park is built overwhelmingly with COMECON technology and equipment; Cuba's export products are geared for COMECON in their selection, specification and quality; Cuba lacks the market contacts, information and skills to enter Western markets; with its debt overload and scant foreign currency reserves, Cuba has difficulty obtaining trade financing; Cuba cannot trade with its natural commercial partner in the West, the United States; and Washington applies pressure and formal restraints on other countries and their companies to limit trade with Cuba.

The transition from protected trade within COMECON to competitive trade in world markets would be difficult even if the considerable political and commercial restraints were absent. Still Cuba's particular export role within COMECON left a product mixture that is assisting Cuba's penetration of Western markets more than those in most other former COMECON countries. Cuba mostly exported primary products – sugar, nickel, tobacco, citrus and fish – that are with few exceptions competitive in world markets. By contrast, the manufactured consumer and capital goods exported by most other COMECON countries are not. Further, despite the absence of important political change, Cuba has already been adapting its foreign trade institutions and management training to facilitate a reorientation to world markets. Thus Cuba's transition to the new international economy could have been accomplished with considerably more grace and celerity than the others – were it not for Cuba's heavy trade dependency and the tightening US embargo.

STRANGLING CUBA

Cuba's efforts to enter the 'free trade' of world capitalism have been blocked not only by its inability to conduct commerce with the United States, but also by US efforts to prevent Cuba from trading with companies from other countries. US attempts to create a de facto blockade take several forms. First, the US government prohibits the importation of goods into the United States that contain even trace amounts of Cuban input, whether or not that input has been thoroughly transformed in the course of manufacture. Thus, for example, the French conglomerate Le Creusot Loire was told that it could not sell steel containing Cuban nickel in the United States. Understandably, the company then cancelled its contract with Cuba to build factories transforming bagasse into hardboard in exchange for Cuban nickel. Even foreign confectionery companies are affected by the policy. In principle, at least, they are not allowed to export chocolate bars made with Cuban sugar to the United States.

Second, companies operating outside the United States are not allowed to sell goods to Cuba that contain more than 20 per cent US inputs or that are based on a US technological design. In addition, foreign companies wishing to sell goods to Cuba that contain between 10 and 20 per cent US inputs must apply for a licence from the US Treasury Department. Under that restriction, the Swedish company Alfa-Laval was prohibited from exporting filtration equipment for the Cuban sugar industry in May 1991 because a component filter membrane was of US origin.

Third, the US government prohibits foreign banks, which are fully owned by foreign nationals and operate solely on foreign soil, from maintaining dollar-denominated accounts for Cuba or from conducting dollar-denominated commercial transactions involving Cuba. Fourth, US nationals who are directors of companies operating outside the United States are prevented from dealing with Cuba. Fifth, ships docking at Cuban ports are not allowed to enter US ports for six months. Although that restriction was part of the October 1992 Cuban Democracy Act, it was actually put into practice by presidential decree in April 1992.

Sixth, threats and other pressure have been employed against other countries to deter economic relations with Cuba. Sometimes the threats are embodied in legislative initiatives that call for sanctions to be taken against countries that engage in certain types of transactions with Cuba. Sometimes the pressure takes the form of letters or phone calls indicating that the United States would look unfavourably upon Cuban participation in certain commercial activities. Thus, for instance, Tabacalera, S.A., of Spain was induced to withdraw from a major investment in developing tourist facilities on Cayo Coco, off Cuba's north coast. In November 1991, Ricardo Alarcón, the Cuban ambassador to the United Nations, gave a speech to the General Assembly in which he cited 27 recent cases of trade contracts interrupted by US pressure.

The British journal *Cuba Business* claimed that British Petroleum was keenly interested in investing in offshore oil exploration in Cuba until seemingly dissuaded by US authorities. The *Petroleum Economist* reported in September 1992 that the State Department 'vigorously discouraged' foreign firms like Royal Dutch Shell and Clyde Petroleum from investing in Cuba, and France's Total allegedly was told that the offshore oil block it was exploring had been sold to US interests before 1959. On 17 October 1992, Cuba signed a textile joint venture deal eventually to be worth $500 million in foreign capital to Cuba with two Mexican businessmen. According to an article in the Mexican newspaper *El Financiero*, the US ambassador to Mexico, John Negroponte, travelled to Monterrey to visit the two businessmen after their return from Cuba. This démarche fell on deaf ears, however; not only did the Monterrey businessmen proceed with their textile investment, they went on to invest in a new joint venture dedicated to the separation of cobalt from nickel and to serve as a liaison between Cuba and other Mexican investors. Each of the aforementioned extraterritorial applications of the US embargo predated the signing of the Cuban Democracy Act.

Since 1975, subsidiaries of US companies operating in foreign lands have been allowed, subject to certain restrictions, to conduct commerce with Cuba. However, they first need a special licence from the US Treasury Department. Until the Cuban Democracy Act, the number and value of licences showed slow but constant growth. The total number of licence applications grew from 164 in 1980 to 321 in 1990, with the authorized value of the subsidiary trade turnover increasing from $292 million to $705 million. In 1991, according to the last figures available, the authorized total reached $718 million; $383 million of that amount was Cuban imports, and 91 per cent of those imports were food. With the prohibition of subsidiary trade established by the Cuban Democracy Act of October

1992, licensed subsidiary trade turnover fell sharply to $499 million in 1992.

With Cuba's increased dependence on Western trade, there should be new opportunities for Western companies. Grain previously imported from the Soviet Union (often shipped in trilateral trade via Canada), for instance, now could be purchased directly from the West. Cuban sugar sales to the former COMECON that exceeded 5 million tons a year must now find world markets. One large player in both the grain and sugar markets is the US-based agribusiness, Cargill. In 1990, Cargill subsidiaries in Switzerland and Canada obtained five US Treasury licences to sell grain products to and import sugar from Cuba. Left unencumbered, this and other subsidiary trade could probably expand very rapidly. Sugar sales alone, at present world prices, could come to more than $1 billion.

But now, US policy toward Cuba has blocked such developments. Even though all US administrations since 1975 have recognized that restricting subsidiary trade impeded the sovereign trade policies of foreign countries and hence violated international law, the Bush administration reversed its earlier position by supporting the Cuba Democracy Act, which bans third-country US subsidiary trade.

The key issue now is how and to what extent the act's prohibitions are implemented. If the act is strictly enforced along with the other extra-territorial restrictions, then Cuba will have even more difficulty selling its raw materials on the international market. Foreign companies afraid of losing unfettered access to the US market might join US subsidiaries abroad in avoiding Cuban products such as sugar, citrus, tobacco, coffee, fish, nickel and cobalt.

Should the Clinton administration try to carry out the act's provisions, however, it will face stiff resistance from the international community. In November 1992, the United Nations General Assembly voted 59 to 3 to condemn the extraterritorial provisions in the Cuban Democracy Act as attempts to violate trade sovereignty and international law. Even the closest US allies object. In October 1992 the Canadian government issued a blocking order, imposing fines up to $8500 on companies complying with the new US law and threatening executives with up to five years imprisonment. The British government followed with its own blocking order, including potential punitive action. The European Community has denounced the act and is studying countersanctions. Mexico and other Latin American countries have also joined the chorus of condemnation. And in November 1993, the UN General Assembly passed another resolution to condemn the US embargo by a still wider margin, 88 to 4. Meanwhile, Cuba has signed several new trading pacts with its neighbours and Cuba's readmission to the Organization of American States (OAS) is being actively discussed.

WHO BENEFITS?

As in previous US Cuba policy manœuvres over the past decade, it is clear that the chief aim for American politicians in the Cuban Democracy Act was to appease the rich and influential members of the Cuban American National Foundation (CANF) and its outspoken director, Jorge Mas Canosa. Although the Treasury Department will enforce the legislation nominally by not issuing new licences, it can also choose to look the other way when foreign subsidiaries trade without a licence. To the extent that the act is implemented at all and succeeds in intimidating a few companies, Cuba should not have great difficulty in finding alternative supply sources. Hence the incremental economic damage to Cuba of the Cuban Democracy Act will be minor.

In the meantime, the act annoys US allies while it bolsters the Castro government's propaganda campaign against the United States and justifies increasing repression in Cuba. One outspoken Castro critic, former Costa Rican president and Nobel Peace Prize recipient Oscar Arias, said about the act: '[Measures] that tend to impose more sacrifices on the Cuban people are arguments one gives Fidel Castro to continue living in the Cold War'.

The Cuban Democracy Act also contains a provision that could end all aid and special commercial arrangements for countries that offer Cuba preferential trade. Thus Mexico and Venezuela may be shut out of the preferential access to the US market granted by the Caribbean Basin Initiative (CBI) or the General System of Preferences statutes if those countries sell oil to Cuba below world market prices, as they now do to other Caribbean countries. So far, the US government has succeeded in preventing such a deal for Cuba.

ECONOMIC PERFORMANCE AND PROSPECTS

There is little question that the Cuban economy is a mess. Although central planning was abandoned long ago, the value of trade on the black market easily surpasses official retail trade. Labour markets function sporadically at best, and for the bulk of the labour force the incentives to work remain weak. Most of Cuba's production capacity goes unused because of shortages of raw materials and spare parts. With few exceptions, new productive investment has virtually ceased over the past three years. The country's transportation and communications infrastructure is a shambles. Inadequate supplies of pesticides, fertilizers and petroleum, as well as poor weather, made Cuba's 1993 sugar harvest the smallest in 30 years. The 'storm of the century' that wreaked havoc along the US East Coast in mid-March 1993 also brought heavy damage to Cuban crops and tourist facilities in Havana. The chief of the United Nations Development Programme office in Havana estimated the damage at $1 billion. For these reasons, some observers expect economic activity to continue to plummet. That, however, is unlikely.

Cuba's economy, especially its foreign sector, has been transformed over the past three years. Some 500 enterprises are self-financing in their foreign trade and are unencumbered by most central rules and regulations. Dozens of trading companies, some domestic and some foreign, have sprung up. More than 140 joint ventures are now in operation; they are allowed to contract independently with local producers. Some Cubans are even allowed to own private enterprises. Foreign investment has surpassed $500 million in the last two years, and much more appears to be on the way. Western management consultants are teaching Cuban managers the techniques of market research, product design and promotion, quality control, packaging, finance, negotiation, human resource development, intellectual property protection, and so on. In February 1993, a French management school opened a Havana branch as a joint venture. Cuban managers have embraced their new skills and are becoming agents for change. In short, a new dynamic of institutional change has emerged from the economy's desperate circumstances. The structural and psychological momentum towards a mixed economy is strong. Indeed, one of the aforementioned investors from Monterrey declared that the Cuban economy 'is in a frank transition toward capitalism'. Castro's 3 July 1993 announcement that Cuba would soon remove penalties on the holding of dollars provides a further fillip to this trend. Exile dollar remittances will boom and social tensions and inequalities will grow. Incentives to work within official labour markets will be further undermined, while those to work within informal markets will grow.

Further, Cuba's external economic shock has run its course. Unfavourable commodity price swings are beginning to reverse themselves. The US blockade and its extraterritorial application have been devastating, but the impact has already been absorbed. In fact, the US tactics have unleashed a backlash of blocking orders and sympathetic trade deals from other countries. Cuba has striven to establish new trade contacts and develop marketing skills.

Little by little, those efforts are beginning to pay off. Nickel production is due to rise from 35 000 metric tons in 1992 to almost 45 000 tons in 1994, and prices have rebounded from their lows below $4200 per ton to above $6000. With the opening of new processing plants, Cuban nickel output is expected to grow to 80 000 tons by 1996. Similarly, although the 1993 sugar harvest fell to a reported 4.28 million tons (a 40 per cent drop from 1992) and the 1994 harvest remained around this level, world market prices jumped from an average of roughly 9 cents a pound at the end of 1992 to above 12 cents (a 33 per cent increase) by mid-1994. Thus export earnings from sugar sales should fall only modestly.

Despite massive inefficiencies in the sector, tourism revenue has been growing at more than 30 per cent a year and should continue its rise. A new 1993 commercial agreement with Russia reverses the trade declines of previous years, improving the market for Cuba's fresh citrus, cigarettes, and some pharmaceuticals and medical equipment. Oil shipments from Russia are scheduled to increase from 1.8 million metric tons in 1992 to 3 million in 1993. The pact also called for a $350 million line of credit intended to aid the completion of various infrastructural and manufacturing projects. These contractual agreements, of course, may not be fully achieved if political instability in Russia further disrupts the country's productive mechanism, or if the unexpected decline in Cuba's sugar harvest prevents full deliveries to Russia.

Meanwhile, biotechnology and medical product sales to developing countries are increasing and there are prospects for modest growth in fish, citrus (buttressed by new Israeli investment), textiles and microelectronics. Import substitution possibilities in medicine and other sectors are good. Even domestic oil production has grown, from 550 000 tons in 1991 to 880 000 tons in 1992, to 1.1 million tons in 1993. Offshore oil prospecting by Total, Petrobras, Talisman and Sheritt Gordon of Canada may yield significant discoveries. One find was announced in May 1994 from a well off the Matanzas coast. It is expected to yield over 200 000 tons of light crude per year. Significant offshore production is several years away, but if testing proves encouraging, Cuba's access to international credit should improve rapidly.

New foreign investments in mining, biotechnology, tobacco and telecommunications, *inter alia*, are also promising. In June 1994, Mexico's Grupo Domos announced an accord to spend $1.5 billion over the next several years to purchase 49 per cent of Cuba's telephone monopoly and to overhaul Cuba's decrepit telephone system. The Cuban economy is certainly not out of the woods, but there is a good chance that Cuban national output will bottom out in mid-1994, with a gradual turnaround commencing thereafter.

WHAT NEXT?

Given that Castro has held on to power while the economy plummeted, it is not likely that any incremental damage from the Cuban Democracy Act will shake him from office. If anything, the act reinforces his raison d'être and prompts him to be more intransigent amid calls for reform. As Cuban political leaders explained to former US Senator George McGovern and Wayne Smith, former US chief diplomat to Cuba, during their trip to Havana in December 1992, showing greater flexibility after an act of aggression by the United States (the Cuban Democracy Act) would show weakness on Cuba's part, sending the wrong signal to the US government.

But suppose the act were to deal further blows to the Cuban economy and the Castro government were somehow destabilized. The Clinton administration must consider very prudently the likely effects of that improbable scenario. More than half of Cuba's population consists of blacks and mulattos who have made significant social and economic gains since the revolution. They are not about to accept a vision of their country's future from white, right-wing Cuban exiles in Miami. The United States spends tens of millions of dollars every year to beam that vision into Cuba via *Radio* and *Television Martí*. As long as the Miami exile leaders are seen as the US government's preferred alternative to Castro, there will be no political consensus in Cuba for change, no matter how much legitimacy Castro loses. Since large numbers of Castro supporters have access to firearms, an uprising against Castro would probably produce tremendous and sustained violence, along with years, if not decades, of political instability and tens of thousands of deaths. That path could well prove uglier than the last decade of turmoil in El Salvador and Haiti. Humanitarian concerns aside, the United States would face an influx of refugees far more taxing than the Mariel boatlift in 1980 or the Haitian exodus since 1992.

The intensifying US embargo also hurts American businesses, which are increasingly anxious about losing Cuban trade and investment opportunities to foreign competitors. More than 200 US businesses attended the *Euromoney* seminars on investment opportunities in Cuba during 1992–3 and additional seminars held by other trade organizations have been well attended. At the August 1992 Senate hearings on the Cuban Democracy Act, a number of executives testified against the bill, citing serious damage to their companies. At least one large US company obtained special permission from the US State Department in 1992 to make a business trip to Cuba on the pretext of discussing compensation for its expropriated assets. Several other companies travelled to Cuba during 1993 and early 1994.

The United States chose a policy of engagement with the former Soviet bloc, and it paid off. Academic and scientific exchanges, as well as tourism and trade, gradually opened up the intellectual and political landscape in those countries, contributing to their ultimate economic and political transformations. The United States has also preferred engagement with China. If anything, the US government can be more effective in Cuba. Ending hostilities would immediately challenge the assumptions beneath Castro's policies. Encouraging tourism would draw tens of thousands of US visitors to the island – bringing their ideas, money and ways of life. Freer academic exchanges and more open telecommunications would release potent forces for liberalization.

The impact of economic normalization, with the ensuing billions of dollars of US trade and investment, would further bolster the supporters of progressive reform. Cuba's push towards a mixed economy would be reinforced and the pace of reform would be accelerated. Most important, normalization would offer a forum for political dialogue and gradual, peaceful change. That would be in everyone's interest. It is no mystery why Cuba's two leading dissidents and human rights activists, Elizardo Sánchez and Gustavo Arcos, have been calling for an end to the embargo and an initiation of dialogue. Similarly, 1992 reports on Cuba by RAND, the Inter-American Dialogue and one in 1993 by the Center for International Policy all called for a policy of engagement, not estrangement.

Policy making in the post-communist world is proving to be more difficult and perilous than had been anticipated. Enlightened US leadership is needed. Yet Washington still pursues an anachronistic, hypocritical and ubiquitously scorned policy towards its island neighbour. During last year's presidential campaign, CANF sold Clinton a bill of goods based on the premise that Castro was about to fall and that all he needed was a little nudge. That nudge was to be the Cuban Democracy Act. But CANF has anticipated spending Christmas in Havana ever since 1989; they have seriously misread Cuban reality.

It is unseemly in a democracy as strong as America's for a single pressure group to dictate policy, especially one that is so wrong-headed. Yet that is precisely what has warped America's Cuba policy since the early 1980s, when, with the aid of Reagan administration functionaries, CANF was launched. Although CANF can claim only minor support in the Cuban–American community, its political strength goes way beyond its popularity. Through tight organization, successful fundraising, extensive campaign contributions, key political connections, and terrorist tactics within the US Cuban community, CANF has now grown to the point where it believes it has the right to veto the Clinton administration's original choice for the top State Department officer for Latin America.

Rather than reaffirming the strength of such a reactionary – and counter-productive – group, the Clinton administration should repudiate it. By now the premise that CANF fed Clinton has proved false. It is time to reappraise America's failing Cuba policy and start down the path of normalization begun by the last Democratic president of the United States.

3 'Apertura' and Reform of the Cuban Economy: The Institutional Transformations, 1990–93*

Pedro Monreal and Manuel Rua del Llano

The year 1993 saw the consolidation of a process of economic *apertura* in Cuba, one of the most important components of a general policy adopted to confront the worst economic crisis experienced by the country in the last 35 years. This process embraces three simultaneous and inter-related phenomena: the accelerated development of international tourism, the re-orientation of Cuban foreign trade and the exposure of the economy to foreign investment.

The *apertura* which has taken place in these areas represents a partial market-oriented reform, which now coexists with the former economic system, known as the *Sistema de Dirección y Planificación de la Economía* (SDPE – The Economic Planning and Management System), that remains applicable in most sectors of the economy. This coexistence of such obviously contradictory economic models is what has brought about the present existence in Cuba of a dual economic system.[1]

As in almost all processes associated with drastic changes resulting from crises, the conceptualization of this partial reform has been left behind by the real advances of the Cuban economy. Little academic analysis has been published concerning the institutional transformations associated with the *apertura* or the partial reform of the economy.[2]

The central hypothesis of this chapter is that what began as the selective liberalization of the Cuban economy has been transformed into a partial economic reform, characterized by important, market-oriented institutional modifications. This process is capable of generating its own

* This chapter is a synopsis of a larger, unpublished work under the same title. The authors would like to acknowledge the valuable comments provided by Luis Suárez Salazar, Juan Valdés Paz, Tania García, Julio Carranza, Luis Gutiérrez and Rafael Hernández, researchers of the *Centro de Estudios sobre América*.

evolutionary tendencies, which could transform it into a wider economic reform with the potential of overcoming the present dual nature of the Cuban economy.

This chapter does not attempt an exhaustive analysis of the subject, or advance all-embracing proposals. Rather, its aim is to stimulate debate about the recent economic changes in Cuba by emphasizing a crucial angle which has remained insufficiently analysed until this moment – the institutional transformations occurring during the period 1990–93, and their implications.

In terms of methodology, the chapter tries to avoid a common problem in the analysis of economic reforms, namely the adoption of a teleological focus, that is to say the perception that social processes (in this case the reform itself) follow linear trajectories which more or less drive them towards final goals commonly considered to be optimal solutions.[3] In fact, real history is much more complex and less linear, and there seems to exist no basis upon which to reject or affirm a priori the idea that the general reform of the Cuban economy could orient itself towards the market. This article will attempt to prove and explain its hypothesis without the necessity of its being considered as the only or the ultimate solution.

TRANSITIONS, REFORMS AND INSTITUTIONS

One of the most important areas of interest in the social sciences of the late 1980s and early 1990s has been what is referred to as the study of 'transitions'. In general, the term is used rather imprecisely in recent literature to identify not only those processes of social change seen in the former socialist countries of Eastern Europe, but also those of other areas, especially Latin America. The specific form taken by studies in this area has been that of the analysis of 'economic liberalization' and 'political apertura'.[4] At the same time, there has been a decrease in interest within the social sciences in the issue of transitions from capitalism to communism, a subject which for years was considered an important area in studies of 'transitions'.

So-called economic transitions have received special attention perhaps because, following the initial euphoria accompanying many recent processes of social change, the crucial part played in them by economic variables has become evident. The definition of economic transition adopted by this chapter is that of a relatively radical process of transformation from one economic structure to another. The adoption of this fairly simple definition corresponds with the more general level of analysis used in the concluding section.

The first thing to keep in mind is that the majority of recent studies do not examine conventional processes of economic reform: that is to say, relatively stable transitions from one scheme of economic organization to another. Strictly speaking, economic reform is a particular type of economic transition. However, the majority of economic transitions studied in contemporary literature go beyond conventional economic reforms, in that they do not merely represent changes in a scheme of economic organization, but rather are part of larger sociopolitical transformations. Certainly, distinction between different types of economic transition may become a complicated exercise, as major economic transitions (like those which have occurred in Eastern Europe since 1989) are often followed by other transformations which fit within the definition of economic reform. In the same way, processes which begin as economic reforms (such as 'perestroika') may be converted in time into much larger processes of economic transformation more appropriately associated with radical sociopolitical changes.

Despite the fact that much has been written in recent years about economic transitions, the fact is that the dynamic of these changes is still not well understood. In contemporary literature on the subject there appear to exist more discrepancies than points of agreement, a phenomenon which has both theoretical and practical implications. For example, the conceptual promotion of radical and immediate models of transition ('shocks' and 'big bangs'), while displaying the existence of a certain consensus, appears frustrated by the lack of available knowledge about the dynamic of economic transitions. Such theoretical impasses are resolved through the negation of the object of research – that is, of the transition itself. As a result, the premise – as yet not validated through practice – has been adopted that it is possible to achieve a new social and economic structure without the mediation of a process of transition. This follows the logic that, 'if you are going to cross a pond, it is better to cross it in a single leap'. In reality, however, the application of 'shock' or 'big bang' schemes has less to do with theoretical considerations and more to do with the political tactic of rapidly implementing economic changes before the most affected sectors of society have time to organize political opposition.

However, there exists another perspective that simultaneously recognizes both the necessity of transitions and the difficulty of understanding their dynamics, while rejecting the notion of the immediate replacement of an old structure with a new and 'final' structure. Conceptually, it partially supports the idea that, during a process of change, those who support it will possess limited information, making it difficult for them to know the real effects of their policies. This is based on the belief that such policies also alter the economic structures from which originally arose both the adopted policies and available information. If we add to this the complicated learning process which must be endured by the various political and economic actors with regard to new economic structures, it becomes easy to understand why the practical effect of this alternative conceptual current is the adoption of a cautious focus for reform, more in line with the description given by the Chinese to their own reform process: 'Crossing the river, feeling the stones beneath one's feet.'[5]

Additionally, there exists a second question of interest, that of the so-called 'sequence problem', or more precisely, the order in which economic and political changes are produced.[6] This has taken the specific form of the study of the relation between 'democracy' and 'market economics'. Beyond the extensive discussion that would be necessary to clarify the meaning and implications of both concepts – a discussion which is not relevant to the more limited objectives of this chapter – what is significant about the recent literature is that it appears to correspond to the type of 'optimistic' theoretical constructions which currently proliferate in many sectors of the social sciences. These constructions, seen in historical perspective, offer a 'pendular' interpretation of the existent relationship between 'political democracy' and the 'capitalist market'. In 'hard times' (depressions and crises) the approach to this relationship is pessimistic, while in times like the present – considered 'normal' times for capitalism owing to the combined effects of the lack of significant systemic challenges to capitalism and the 'defeat' of the European socialist system – the focus on the relationship is essentially optimistic: 'political democracy' and 'market economics' are processes which, by their own natures, seem to reinforce one another.

However, a careful analysis of contemporary literature on the 'sequence problem' would reveal at least three questions which should be taken into account in the analysis of transitions. First, the present debate over the relationship between 'democracy' and 'market economics' should not be presented as the only relevant debate, as it is only one of the specific forms which could be taken by the more general debate concerning the relation between models of economic and political organization. Second, there is lack of consensus concerning the precise relationships of determination between the contemporary processes of 'economic liberalization' and 'political apertura'.[7] Finally, a thesis developed by certain authors concerns the apparently contradictory logic between the processes of 'economic liberalization' and 'political apertura'. This thesis states that, while the latter process by definition implies the distribution of political power, economic reform implies a process of transformation of state structures of such magnitude that, to be initiated, it requires a certain concentration of power in the hands of the promoters of reform. Such a concentration of power is necessary in order to initiate reform and advance it through its first stages, although the development of reform itself will produce a relative distribution of power. The argument is controversial, but undoubtedly touches on the central relationship which exists between the true content of all economic reforms (structural transformations) and the political premises necessary to make them take root. Based on the premise of economic reform, the concentration of state power can involve two processes: (1) the expansion of the power held by the state to the level of complete control of society, and (2) the concentration of power in determined areas of the state machine. It is worth emphasizing at this point a note of caution introduced by some analysts concerning the contradiction that could exist in some political undertakings that initially favour the initiation of transitions, but which could turn into impediments to the later development of this process.

Another possible explanation for the contradictions between 'political apertura' and 'economic liberalization' is the presumed effect of mutual weakening produced among the two processes. This is because 'political apertura' impedes the implementation of 'economic liberalization' by opening up political opportunities to the opponents of the latter, while 'economic liberalization' creates a series of social costs which mitigate against the stability necessary for the process of 'political apertura'. This argument undoubtedly reflects the problems of the real world of politics, although it is difficult to prove its general validity. For this reason we find the argument noted in the preceding paragraph to be more theoretically all-embracing because of its treatment of the contradictory logic stemming from the very content of each process ('economic liberalization' and 'political apertura') rather than from their possible political implications.

These considerations bring us to a second theoretical question – the role of institutions in economic reform or, to be more precise, the role of institutional transformations. The concept of institution has traditionally been the object of controversy in the social sciences, a circumstance which explains the diversity of definitions for it. Without wishing to deepen this debate, the nature of this chapter demands that there be at least an operational definition of the concept. An institution is here defined as a series of conventions which regulate the relations between individuals or social groups. This definition includes informal as much as formal organizations, as well as explicit and implicit norms and rules. Institutions are historically determined social phenomena.

Institutional transformations constitute the central element of economic reform. In reality, reforms do not simply represent transitions from one mode of economic management to another, but are essentially processes of institutional construction and reconstruction which embrace two larger spheres of action, the organizational and the normative.[8] Even so-called processes of 'economic liberalization' are basically institutional reforms, despite the fact that the neoclassical theories which inspire them erroneously consider the market to be the paradigmatic expression of a spontaneous order, not subject to institutional regulation.

The reality, however, is rather different. In order to function, the market, as a decentralized form of social cooperation,[9] requires the construction of what certain authors term 'explicit institutional instruments'.[10] As a result, 'market reforms' consist precisely of transformations in the artificial conventions which give rise to markets and control their operation.

The modification of state structure by way of institutional transformations determines one of the most important consequences of economic reform: that is, its impact on the process of political domination. In this manner, all economic reform is, initially, a programme of consolidation or entrenchment of political power. For this reason, no economic reform can be explained simply as a 'technocratic' process. Economic reforms are, from their conceptive stages, political processes. These reforms are 'sub-optimal' economic programmes precisely because of their own conditions as political processes. The very fact that, on certain occasions, economic reforms have ended up undermining the political power bases of the same sectors which promoted them is not explained by errors in the technical design of the reforms themselves. Rather, this displays the true complexity of the implementation of processes of social transformation which, like economic reforms, depend to a high degree on the evolution of the more general political context in which they develop.

There exists another relevant theoretical aspect related to the existent relation between economic transitions and institutional transformations – that of the relative weight assigned by policy makers to the initial and final structures of the transition. This relation is conceived of in different ways, which are expressed in two distinct notions of the transition, each having different practical effects on the processes of transformation. In one case, the emphasis is placed on the modification of the initial structure, as policy makers define the aspects of this structure they hope to change and the political action necessary to do so. In this type of transition, the initial structure determines the policy of institutional transformation. In the other variant, emphasis is placed on the final structure, which is considered as the goal of transition. Policy makers elaborate a prefiguration of the desired final structure and then decide on the type of methods which could bring them to it. In this type of transition, goals determine policies. What is important to note is that, depending on the adopted notion, an economic reform can be incited taking as its reference point either transitional structure (initial or final).

Finally, some brief considerations should be noted concerning the relevance of the theoretical points indicated above to the Cuban case. Firstly, we should emphasize the pertinence of the concepts of economic transition and economic reform to the country's present situation. Cuba is at present moving from one economic structure to another, but this transition could continue to develop along a number of diverse lines, only one of which is economic reform.

However, it should remain clear that economic reform is not some type of gradual change in economic policy. It is, above all, a means of facilitating the transformation from one economic structure to another. This is a key point because, whatever its specific form, all reform begins with the recognition of the necessity of overcoming an initial structure, and of the relatively radical nature of the change necessary to achieve this. For this reason, the debate on reform seems linked to the issue of economic models.

In the case of Cuba, the discussion of the economic model issue is often presented in an incomplete manner. What is genuinely important is not so much the ideological connotation that a new model could have, but what could be called the 'political economy' of the model – that is, the evaluation of it as a phenomenon of causal relationships established by socio-economic processes.

The economic model – understood as an analytical abstraction useful for explaining the functioning of a specific pattern of accumulation which could serve as the basis of economic policy – does not fundamentally express a phenomenon which is directed by the decisions of policy makers. Occasionally, models 'emerge' without having been previously planned. Specifically, in the case of Cuba, the new economic model has been 'emerging' beyond anyone's aspirations because the conditions of economic accumulation in the country have been substantially modified in recent years.

THE ECONOMIC 'APERTURA' AND ITS INSTITUTIONAL TRANSFORMATIONS

The beginning of the Cuban economic reform, with the opening of the economy to the outside world, was not an act of chance. Rather, it was a response to the recognition that the viability of all new economic projects in Cuba would depend on the decisive roles of two variables, the growth and diversification of exports and the search for new sources of external financing.[11]

During the first half of the 1980s, the Cuban government began to perceive the necessity of promoting new varieties of business activity in Cuba's relations with market economy countries. However, the policy of economic *apertura* was promoted to a greater extent in the 1990s, when Cuba's insertion into the world economy became a point crucial to the nation's survival.

The institutional transformations which represent the true nature of the Cuban economic apertura are of two types, organizational and normative. Organizational transformations refer to changes produced in the type of operation of economic actors, as well as to modifications undergone within the Cuban state structure. Normative transformations include modifications, in the context of the partial reform of the Cuban economy, to the legal framework and administrative norms which establish the conditions and regulate the operation of different economic factors.

Organizational Transformations

The principle organizational transformations occurring in Cuba as part of the *apertura* have been the following:

(1) *The decentralization of the management of foreign trade.* By the middle of 1993, the number of Cuban economic actors, of all types, involved in international commercial activity had risen to 287, a number considerably higher than the 70 existent at the beginning of the 1980s. There was also a noteworthy reduction in the size of firms, allowing for the existence of more dynamic and specialized management structures.

(2) *The development of commercial and financial infrastructure*, allowing for the creation of firms offering informational, financial, commercial banking, legal consulting, economic and technical and marketing services, and storage on consignment or customs deposit warehousing (as with the firm Havana in Bond S.A., from which developed the first free trade zone in Cuba).

(3) *New varieties of commercial activity*, beginning with the development of 'business engineering' in the country. By November 1993, 112 joint ventures and other forms of economic association with foreign firms had been formed, of which 83 were not in the tourism

sector. The greatest number of foreign investors were Spanish, followed by business interests from France, Italy, Canada and Mexico. Another novel element has been the growing interest by Cuban enterprises in studying the establishment of economic associations in foreign countries.

The greatest diversity of these new varieties is found in the commercial sector. For example, in the biopharmaceutical sector, research and development contracts are available in which the Cuban party offers scientific personnel and the use of installations. In the financial sphere, the Cuban government has displayed its willingness to consider flexible foreign debt renegotiations, using such mechanisms as payment in kind, payment with dividends from joint ventures (involving the participation of the same creditors) and other, more complicated forms, such as debt–equity swaps.

(4) *Self-financing in foreign exchange.* Towards the middle of 1993, some 35 schemes for self-financing in foreign exchange had been established, with encouraging results in the sugar, fishing and petroleum industries.

(5) *The creation of new economic actors.* Economic *apertura* has involved the inception and extension of a series of organizational forms within the country's economic institutions. During recent years there has been a growth and consolidation of commercial firms, principally comprised of *sociedades anónimas* (S.A.).[12] These firms are essentially of two types – the Cuban-owned firm and the joint venture between a Cuban firm and a foreign enterprise. They are substantially different from state enterprises in their autonomy, operation and labour regimes. Towards the middle of 1993, some 101 firms of both types were registered in the new Commercial Directory edited by the Chamber of Commerce of the Republic of Cuba.

In addition to this, foreign firms have been increasingly active as economic actors, significantly extending their presence in Cuba. This has been as much the result of joint ventures and other forms of economic association between Cuban and foreign firms as it has of the establishment in Cuba of 496 foreign firms from some 40 countries, of which 325 have been through the direct representation of commercial firms. In sum, at the moment, some 600 foreign economic actors are present in the Cuban economy.

(6) *The 'management revolution'*, initiated during the second half of the 1980s, reached a major scale and acquired new qualities after 1991. For firms covered by the *apertura*, the adoption of these

techniques has had a systemic quality which had been absent, or at least underemphasized, in previously undertaken experiments in management techniques. This new systemic quality is above all the result of a more general economic process in which new management techniques complement greater operative flexibility and the increased pre-eminence of commercial relations in inter-firm links.

(7) *The growing presence of marketing and competition in the Cuban economy.* On one hand, since the second half of the 1980s, there has been an increase in the organization of courses and seminars on marketing – including the most modern techniques applied in international trade – beginning particularly with consulting by Spanish, Canadian and Mexican specialists. On the other hand, participation, in the tourism sector, with foreign capital by various Cuban organizations and economic associations, has led to competition between different economic actors, a phenomenon practically non-existent in Cuba during the last three decades.

(8) *New functions and operating style among Cuban state institutions.* Up to December 1993, there had been no substantial reorganization of the institutions of the central apparatus of the Cuban government. However, in practice, various institutions had opted for a modification of functions and operating style to allow for the assimilation of the growing role of an economic actor practically unknown in Cuba until the end of the 1980s – foreign investment – which, under the new conditions dominant in the country, has become one of the most dynamic factors in the economy. Examples of these transformations are the new functions assumed since 1991 by the *Comité Estatal de Colaboración Económica* (CECE – State Committee on Economic Collaboration) in the area of foreign investment, the creation within this same organization of a new structure known as the 'Central Negotiating Group', and the formation of new agencies, also known as 'negotiating groups', within the organizational structures of the majority of ministerial branches.

(9) *The reform of wholesale prices*, initiated in July 1992, introducing the principle of real external prices at which the country would import and export merchandise. In this manner, the formation of internal wholesale prices would be based on current external prices. However, the present reform still has not responded to a central problem – that of the determination of an economically based form of internal exchange.

(10) *The growing role of non-governmental organizations (NGOs)* in the workings of the Cuban economy and society. In 1993, the viability

of the execution of various joint projects between Cuban and foreign NGOs became evident. These projects were outlined as a way of channelling small foreign enterprises into solving specific problems of a socioeconomic nature. They were initially intended to be humanitarian and non-profit activities, although in the future they could also involve commercial activity. Other Cuban NGOs also play a growing role in the country, such as the Chamber of Commerce of the Republic of Cuba which represents more than 200 firms, trading organizations, banks and other commercial entities linked to foreign trade.

Probably the most important lesson which could be extracted from the changes noted above is that they are not sufficient to promote a general economic reform, although they could serve as an 'informal' model for other organizational alterations. Fundamentally, until December 1993, the majority of organizational changes undertaken were related to external aspects of the Cuban economy, and there still remained in this area important problems to be resolved with respect to the connection of external markets to the internal economy. However, in September 1993, an organizational change (which will be discussed briefly at a later point) was adopted in the area of agriculture that could be considered as the first organizational transformation of importance for a future process of economic reform in Cuba. Inasmuch as this change has been linked to the production of exportable goods – primarily sugar – it is partially a transformation associated with *apertura*, although the true form of the measure identifies it definitively as an action of internal economic policy.

Normative Transformations

The principle normative transformations witnessed in Cuba until the middle of 1993 were the following:

(1) The constitutional reform of July 1992.
(2) Decree Law no. 50 of February 1982. (The principal legislation on foreign investment in Cuba.)
(3) The reactivation of the Commercial Code. (This establishes a juridical framework for the operation of commercial firms.)
(4) Resolution no. 151/92 of the National Bank of Cuba.
(5) Decree Law no. 124 of the State Council, of 15 October 1990, which established the Customs Duty of the Republic of Cuba.

(6) Decree no. 145/88: 'The Regulation of the National Registry of Foreign Representations', and Resolutions regarding the same issue numbered 211/89 and 102/92, all from the Ministry of Foreign Trade.
(7) Resolution no. 61 (3 April 1990) of the Ministry of Foreign Trade, and Resolution no. DEP 03-92 of the Customs General of the Republic, authorizing respectively the establishment of merchandise warehouses on consignment and warehouses under a regime of customs deposit, and the Berroa Customs Deposit Zone.
(8) Other complementary regulations (regarding finances, accounting, prices, fiscal rules, customs, trade, arbitrage, insurance, labour and special zones).[13]

With the exception of the important Decree Law no. 50 of 1982, which authorized the establishment of joint firms and other forms of association with foreign capital, the most significant normative transformations associated with the *apertura* have taken place since 1990.

Decree Law no. 50 has been a key instrument in the present economic *apertura*. Put into practice, it has demonstrated itself to constitute an adequate and flexible legal framework for the creation of economic associations between Cubans and foreign actors. Stability has been one of the most important features of the legal apparatus created in Cuba for the promotion of foreign investment, a factor which has created certainty and confidence among foreign partners.

Other than Decree Law no. 50, prior to 1990, the framework for the process of the authorization and registration of foreign commercial representations had been laid out in Decree no. 145/88, 'the Regulation of the National Registry of Foreign Representations', and Resolution no. 211/89 of the Ministry of Foreign Trade (MINCEX), both of which deal with the problem of principles for the authorization of foreign representations. Following this, the role of authorized licences for such representations was reinforced through MINCEX Resolution no. 102/92.[14]

However, beginning in 1990, there has been more activity in the legislative area related to the economic *apertura*. This has included the promulgation of new laws, complementary regulations and, above all, legal practice favouring the open and flexible juridical interpretation of the existing laws.

Also since 1990, various regulations have been issued concerning consignment and the establishment of a customs warehouse regime, as well as resolutions by the State Finance Committee regulating tax policy as applicable to customs warehouses. Furthermore, Resolution no. DEP 03-92 of the Customs General of the Republic authorized the establishment of the Berroa Customs Deposit Zone. The promulgation on 15 October 1990 of the Customs Duty of the Republic of Cuba represented an important moment in normative modifications.

However, the normative modifications of greatest impact were produced in the context of the constitutional reform realized in July 1992, the first reform of this type since a new Cuban constitution was adopted in 1976. Essentially, these modifications introduced new concepts in the area of property and its transfer, the role of the state in planning and economic management, and the foreign trade regime.

For example, Article 14 of the new constitution limits the extension of socialist property and opens up the legal possibility of private participation in various economic activities. Additionally, the 'irreversible' character that the previous constitution conferred on socialist property was eliminated. Furthermore, in Article 15, the Council of Ministers and its Executive Committee were authorized to approve the partial or total transfer of state economic objectives to certain individuals legally empowered to direct national development.

The new formulation of Article 15 also allows for the expansion of existing provisions for foreign investment. Thus there now exists a concrete possibility of full property transfer, as well as the transfer of other rights which, up to this moment, have been prohibited by law. Above all, these deal with the real costs and guarantees of undertaking obligations. Additionally, in Article 23 the new constitution offers full guarantees on foreign investment.

Although the new constitutional text reaffirms the role of state planning in the development of the country, it also establishes the concession of greater independence and flexibility for the operation of firms and the administration of their goods and capital stock. In fact, it could be said that the constitutional reform of 1992 set the basis for the initiation of a new phase of normative institutional transformations characterized in the economic field by an increasing orientation towards market regulation.[15]

Modifications of the normative type, linked to economic *apertura*, have also been established in the financial sphere. For example, the 1992 Resolution no. 151 of the National Bank of Cuba establishes the norms for collections and payments by organizations authorized to operate in legally convertible currency. Indeed, the same resolution defines the segment of Cuban economic actors which is allowed to operate in foreign currency.

As noted previously, 1992 represented a key moment in normative institutional transformations, with the inauguration of a new phase of such transformations along with the constitutional reform. However, the relatively limited character of these transformations should remain clear, as they were produced within a juridical context whose general orientation did not favour the development of the market, particularly at the internal level. Furthermore, it is significant that through the two most important normative transformations adopted in 1992 – the constitutional reform and Resolution no. 151/92 of the National Bank of Cuba – it became evident that, as opposed to the legal disposition previously attached to the economic *apertura*, these juridical modifications were not be limited to favouring solely an external *apertura*, but also have both present and potential consequences in the development of an internal market.

In 1993, other juridical transformations were implemented which more clearly indicated the movement of changes previously limited to the external apertura towards the area of the internal economy. In this way, in 1993, the market orientation of new laws and other legal arrangements began to extend beyond the area of the external market (foreign trade, tourism and foreign investment), moving more evidently towards the cautious expansion of an internal market marked by the presence of new elements.

Decree Law no. 140 of August 1993 and its complementary regulations, issued by the National Bank of Cuba, established the decriminalization of the possession of foreign funds and regulated their use by Cuban citizens. Decree Law no. 141 of September, 1993 and Joint Resolution no. 1 of the State Work and Social Security Committee and the State Finance Committee have also been important measures, establishing a new legal framework and general regulations for work performed independently. In essence, the number of activities authorized to be performed independently has been expanded, and more precise taxation regulations have been established.

Decree Laws nos 140 and 141 of 1993 represent 'explicit institutional instruments' for the legalization and regulation of internal markets that, to a great extent, already existed illegally. However, the possibility of future expansion and increased flexibility of activities regulated by these legislations remains under consideration.

Throughout 1993, what could be considered as the beginnings of the transition towards the general reform of the Cuban economy began to appear with greater clarity. A key moment in this process was the accord adopted by the Political Bureau of the Communist Party of Cuba 'to carry out important innovations in state agriculture'. In essence, this involved a measure which includes both types of institutional transformation – organizational and normative – and which potentially favours the creation of markets through the development of cooperative and, on a small scale, private forms of production. The initial forms adopted for the new agricultural transformation have limited the role of the market in it, but an eventual extension of its market orientation should not be discarded, as the very development of the programme will demand the adoption of new methods for the commercial circulation of products.

Beginning in the second half of 1993, institutional transformations, especially those of the normative type, clearly indicated that the *apertura* was beginning to transform itself into an increasingly extensive economic reform. This process of economic reform is still partial and incipient, but more all-encompassing than the opening of the Cuban economy to outside forces which preceded it.

FINAL NOTES

Economic *apertura* is not a tactical or temporary response, but one which is strategic and realistic on the part of Cuba in order to adapt itself permanently to the new political and economic international scenario.

Economic *apertura* represents a central component in Cuban plans for economic recuperation beginning with the adoption of an export strategy, and in this way the Cuban economic *apertura* shares a fundamental characteristic of all export strategies – market orientation. In the Cuban case, economic *apertura* has meant orienting towards the market the management of firms involved in the *apertura*. The determination of costs and prices in conditions of international competition, the necessity of being cost-effective and the creation of dynamic comparative advantages are factors of the market which are today present as never before during the last 35 years in a growing number of firms and institutions in the Cuban economy, although there remain problems to be resolved in this area. This has not meant a substantial reduction in Cuba of the role of the state in the economy of the country. However, what has been produced in reality has been a modification of the relative roles and weights distributed between the market and state management, where the former has become a dynamic factor, while forms of state involvement have adapted to this new circumstance. In the areas covered by the economic *apertura*, the state continues to be an important factor, although its activity corresponds more to a 'regulatory state' structure, than to one of a traditional 'managing state'.

The flexibility and dynamism of the organizations embraced by the *apertura* have allowed for the design and application of an 'industrial policy' directed towards reactivating other sectors of the Cuban economy, taking advantage of demand created by the export sector of the economy. This process, still in its initial phases and with many problems to be solved, clearly reveals that the Cuban government has tried not to adopt a conventional 'export strategy', but rather has proposed the combination of the promotion of exports with policies directed towards the reactivation of national industry. Particularly important have been the 'inwardly directed' productive links connected to the tourism industry, although this is a process which is still confronted by problems of learning and organization which reduce the efficiency of the adapted 'industrial policy'. The expansion and perfection of this 'industrial policy' would represent a potential extension of the reform towards other areas of the economy, and is probably one of the principal reserves upon which the government counts in order to reactivate the country's economy, above all as it would require modifications in the organization and operation of the internal economy.

The necessity for a general, market-oriented economic reform of the Cuban economy seems to be supported by the country's inherent need for economic development under the new conditions in which it finds itself. That is to say, general economic *apertura* must not be understood as the extension of the opening of the Cuban economy to international factors. In fact, they are two different, although interrelated, processes.

The need for an economic reform has a systemic character which embraces both internal and external factors. These external factors, projected in the form of economic *apertura*, have played a role of relative importance in the possible initiation of a process of change which could result in a general economic reform. Paraphrasing one of the classics of political economy, necessity is the mother of the reform of the Cuban economy, although economic *apertura* has acted as its father.

The specific manner in which the most recent economic policy in Cuba has evolved seems to indicate the key role that economic *apertura* has played in the launching and development of a gradual process of institutional modifications which, in its own advancement, has moved beyond the initial emphasis on the external and projected itself towards the internal. Part of the explanation for this is rooted in the growing perception that has emerged concerning the necessity, possibility and convenience of using *apertura* to stimulate the internal economy. However, perhaps most important has been the role that *apertura* has played as an 'informal model' for the rest of economic policy, and as such the institutional transformations adopted have had a general impact on all of the national economy.

The fact that, by the end of 1993, the term 'economic reform' was not fully incorporated into official discussion of economic policy does not mean that measures which could have been compatible with a reform were not already, at that time, an increasingly important – but not the only – component of Cuban economic policy. In any case, the non-use of the term reflected the complexity of a process with vast political and ideological ramifications. This is not to say only that politics and ideology are affected by economic reform, but that economic reform itself requires specific political and ideological premises which can only be established over a specific period of time.

In the case of Cuba, it remains clear that the country's increasing difficulty, under its new conditions with respect to the global economy, in generating an economic surplus has been converted into a critical factor for the viability of the economic, political and social system existent since the beginning of the 1970s. In the final analysis, this is a challenge to the basis of the political organization which has been dominant for more than 30 years.

In this way, general economic reform represents the possibility of initiating the renovation of the economic basis of the political project existent in Cuba. However, this vision of economic reform does not appear to have predominated during the initial moments of the formulation of a response to the crisis. The initial impulse appears to have been the concentration of economic policy action in two directions: economic adjustment and sectoral strategy. Time has demonstrated that the decision was correct, but insufficient. In 1993, a certain level of economic adjustment had been reached – basically imposed by the action of external factors – accompanied by measures for economic survival. However, there continued to exist enormous imbalances which demanded the adoption of new and more radical measures of adjustment.[16] On the other hand, sectoral strategies had not produced consistent results.

In reality, during the period 1990–93, the only significant effort made at economic reform was in the export sector, corresponding largely with the fact that, in an open economy like that of Cuba, difficulties in generating economic surplus tended to be identified almost exclusively with shortages of foreign exchange. Note that the initial measures of economic *apertura* assumed the possibility of authorizing only the 'isolated' treatment of the export sector. Efforts at creating an 'industrial policy' to connect this sector with other areas of the economy came later, towards the middle of 1993, and were relatively limited.

However, in 1993 it became evident that economic policy needed to advance towards a new and more profound phase of structural transformation. In the same way that this perception has gained strength, institutional design in the context of economic policy has also become more important. In this manner, as has already been noted, the process of economic *apertura* – the principal recent experience of institutional transformation in Cuba – tends to favour the idea of a general economic reform.

The very experience of economic *apertura* has also contributed to creating more favourable political bases for a general economic reform, although alone they remain insufficient. These bases are of two types: first, the necessary confidence that must be maintained by policy makers in the existent capacity of the country to undertake a controllable process of institutional reforms; and second, the idea that the concentration of political power is compatible with market-oriented economic reform.

What took place within the Cuban export sector from 1990 to 1993 has demonstrated that economic reform (in this case partial) has not been limited to economic administration, but rather has been fundamentally a process of institution-building which the government has promoted and controlled. This perception is important because, although state reform is commonly perceived as a process leading towards a more efficient public administration, in reality the most important consequence is the strengthening of the state – or, to be more precise, an increase in the ability of the state to exercise its most basic political functions.

On the other hand, the experience with economic *apertura* has made it evident that the implementation of complex institutional transformations in short periods has been favoured by the concentration of power in the hands of the executive. This condition has contributed powerfully to making possible the adoption of a series of basic changes, equivalent to the task of state formation, an activity which demands extraordinary doses of power. In this way, Cuban economic *apertura* has represented an example of the compatibility between the concentration of political power and the implementation of market-oriented economic policies. The most important analytical lesson of this experience is perhaps the relatively favourable position in which the state finds itself to undertake a general economic reform that, in its institutional design, will also be capable of preserving the social support bases of the political system dominant in Cuba since the early 1970s. It is worth noting that this more favourable position is sustained largely by the existence in Cuba of a framework of political legitimacy which has been non-existent or seriously eroded in other recent experiences of the reform of centrally planned economies.

Under Cuba's conditions, a general economic reform would imply a process of the design and implementation of a new indigenous economic model which, among others, would respond to the following criteria:[17]

(1) A guarantee of the social and political achievements of the last three decades that today form part of the heritage of the Cuban nation: free public education and health services at an elevated level,

social justice and the preservation of the independence and sovereignty of the nation.

(2) The development of a new economic culture between government directors, executives and workers which will place cost-efficiency and economic efficiency at the centre of economic analysis.

(3) A strict linking of salaries and other forms of revenues to the real results of economic activity.

(4) The increasing use of market mechanisms at the firm level. Framed in this context, financial and credit categories are conferred with truly active roles in the shaping of programmes of production and of the stimulation or non-stimulation of economic objects, such as, among other things, the rational use of energy resources and material inputs, and the promotion of exports.

(5) The introduction of new formulas that would make more practical the double condition of owner–producer, especially in those areas where the role of people is decisive, such as in agriculture and services.

(6) The development of a process of 'reregulation' that would permit the qualitative redefinition of the regulatory role of the state through the elaboration of a plan designed to guarantee the basic interests of the nation during a given period. This could be achieved through the perfection of an indispensable minimal normative (legal) framework which would permit the regulation of the role, operation and control of specific economic actors.

(7) The placing of the satisfaction of the quantitative demand of external and internal markets at the centre of the economic management of firms, thus altering the present situation in which the internal client is relegated to a secondary role by having to consume 'what he/she produces'. This would demand the extension of free market norms to the entire commercial system.

(8) The introduction of essential changes in fiscal and monetary policy that would permit the reduction of the fiscal deficit and creation of budget surpluses, both of which are basic to healthy domestic finances.

(9) Guaranteeing greater autonomy at the firm level in the elaboration and execution of commercial plans, reducing to a minimum bureaucratic elements which restrict entrepreneurial initiative.

(10) Promoting the creation of an ample and solid infrastructure of support services for firms (legal and economic consultants, financial firms, information networks and so on).

(11) Full self-financing (in foreign exchange and in pesos) as a basic

criterion for the very existence of economic activities, reducing to a minimum those which receive budgetary subsidies.

(12) The promotion of economic competition, whenever advisable, in order to raise the quality of production and services, and of economic yields.

(13) The perfection of pricing policy in such a way that the formation of internal prices would relate to current external prices and sound economic bases. Also the favouring of a greater decentralization of prices, so that they reflect real costs of production, and reduce to a minimum subsidies intended to cover firms' losses.

There exist two important questions with respect to the advancement of a process of economic reform in Cuba: the conceptual precision concerning the nature and extent of the necessary changes, and the definition of a political strategy that would act as an adequate subjective context for the transition towards a new economic structure.

As for the first aspect, as we have already noted, the key is not rooted in the initial availability of a perfect scheme. Rather, it is to be found in accepting the relatively radical nature of the necessary changes, and from this assumption defining the conceptual requirements that will permit the elaboration of a proposal for general economic reform.

On the other hand, the definition of a political strategy is absolutely necessary for the development of economic reform, inasmuch as the latter is a complex social process with vast political, social and ideological implications. Strategy is not only important for giving coherence to the very process of reform, but also becomes essential for adequately confronting the inevitable political consequences resulting from the transformation of the economy.

Experience has demonstrated that the success of economic reforms does not depend so much on their technical design as on the evolution of the most general context in which they unfold, above all the political context. A key factor in the preservation of an adequate political environment is the type of institutional transformation which will be produced, given that this environment determines to a high degree the quality of the state reconstruction necessary for the preservation of the social basis of political power, and demands the existence of a political strategy for reform.

Cuban economic *apertura* has demonstrated, on a partial scale, that the transition of one economic structure to another while preserving the social basis of political power is possible. There exist no significant indications in the experience of *apertura* which deny the possibility that this would also occur in a more general economic reform.

In sum, towards the middle of 1993, Cuba appeared to have begun the gradual transition towards a new economic structure, in the determination of which market-oriented economic measures were beginning to assume a growing role. What had begun as a selective *apertura* of the Cuban economy was on the way to transforming itself into a general reform of the economy, responding to a profound economic crisis which appeared to challenge the idea that it could be overcome by a series of specific measures.

Notes

1. With the exception of areas affected by the *apertura*, the rest of the Cuban economy continues to operate on the basis of the so-called *Sistema de Dirección y Planification de la Economía*, implemented in the mid-1970s and partially modified in the 1980s. For more information about the principal challenges currently facing the Cuban economy, see Julio Carranza, 'Cuba: los retos de la economía', in *Cuadernos de Nuestra América*, No. 19, July–December 1992, Centro de Estudios sobre América, Havana.
2. It is worth noting, however, the analytical efforts undertaken in this area by the *Instituto Nacional de Investigaciones Económicas* (INIE – National Institute for Economic Research). In May 1993, INIE organized a scientific workshop around the theme of the 'Emerging Economy', a term which its specialists give to that sector of the Cuban economy reformed in the context of the policy of economic apertura.
3. For a critique of the teleological focus see Hector Schamis, 'On the Relationship Between Political and Economic Reform: Lessons from the Chilean Experience', a paper prepared for *The South California Workshop on Political and Economic Liberalization*, The University of Southern California, Los Angeles, February 1993.
4. The relatively limited purposes of this chapter and the corroboration of its central hypothesis do not demand a detailed critical examination of the terms 'transition', economic liberalization' and 'political reform'. These terms, and others which will be used hereafter, have been placed in quotation marks to denote that they have been taken directly from the reviewed literature.
5. William Maloney, 'Lessons from Chile', paper prepared for *The South California Workshop on Political and Economic Liberation*, The University of Southern California, Los Angeles, 18 February 1993.
6. Some authors also define as a 'sequence problem' the order in which the distinct phases of a process of economic reform are produced. See Sebastian Edwards, *The Sequencing of Structural Adjustment and Stabilization*, Occasional Papers, No. 34, International Center for Economic Growth, San Francisco, 1992.
7. The disagreement seems to be largely explained by the fact that the practical conclusions derived from the analysis of certain experiences is incompatible

with certain ideological schemes; that is, through the idea that the concentration of political power is not favourable to market reforms.

8. In this chapter, economic reform is understood to be a particular form of relatively stable economic transition which is generally promoted 'from above', that is, by the political groups who are in power.
9. Adopting this definition of the market, at so general a level, has the advantage of alllowing for the essential explanation of one of the most enduring phenomena of the economic organization of humanity. In its solidification throughout history, the market has become a much more complex phenomenon, with precise political, social and ideological connotations. However, in its essence, it is a form of organization of the social economy.
10. See Hector Schamis, 'On the Relationship Between Political and Economic Reform'.
11. The process of the *apertura* of the Cuban economy has occurred in an area of the export sector which supplies approximately 50 per cent of foreign exchange receipts. Up to December 1993, the sugar industry had not been, to any important degree, included in the process of *apertura*, although refining and the sugar derivatives industry have been opened up to foreign capital.
12. The present Cuban Commercial Code defines four types of commercial firms: the regular collective, the limited liability firm, the *comanditaria* (limited partnership) and the *sociedad anónima* (corporation). However, at the present time in Cuba, only corporations employ personally held shares. See Nieves Pico and Amelia Mendoza, *Caracterización de las formas legales y organizativas que operan en la economía emergente*, Instituto Nacional de Investigaciones Económicas (INIE), May 1993.
13. See CONAS S.A., *Abstract of the Legislation on Investments in Cuba*, Havana, 1993.
14. The Registry licences representations for five-year terms, extendable for equal periods following application by the interested party, and based on the party maintaining the conditions and reasons which originally justified the original authorization.
15. The concept of market regulation is used in a wide form, including all types of markets, independent of the reforms of property upon which they are based.
16. See Julio Carranza, 'Cuba'.
17. These criteria are general, and do not represent in any way a proposal for reform. In fact, this chapter has attempted to avoid the prescriptive focus. As such, the enunciated criteria for reform represent basically either a list of the principles explicitly incorporated in the most recent economic policy of the country, or, without having been explicitly formulated, those which the authors perceive as having been part of this policy, albeit in an incipient manner.

4 Prospective Dollar Remittances and the Cuban Economy

Carmelo Mesa-Lago

In the summer of 1993 the Cuban government introduced a dramatic change in monetary policy by authorizing the possession and circulation of hard currency, particularly dollars. This chapter summarizes the economic situation prior to the introduction of that measure, describes the features of the new monetary policy, assesses its consequences for the Cuban government, analyses the restrictions imposed by the United States and inquires if this surprising step will help to improve the Cuban economy.[1]

THE ECONOMIC CRISIS AND ILLEGAL EXPANSION OF THE USE OF THE US DOLLAR

The Cuban economy declined between 29 per cent and 58 per cent in 1989–93 and government officials' best hope is for zero growth in 1994. In the same period imports shrank to about one-fifth and exports probably to one-third of their 1989 levels. In 1993, sugar production, the most important source of exports earnings, declined by 40 per cent and was at the lowest level for the last 30 years.[2]

Surplus money in circulation (an indirect indicator of inflation) surpassed 10 billion pesos by the end of 1993, an almost twofold jump since 1989.[3] This means that each Cuban has theoretically an average of 890 pesos which are of limited value owing to lack of consumer goods in the official economy. The official commercial exchange rate of the peso is par with the dollar but, in the black market, the rate catapulted from 8 to 80 or 100 pesos to the dollar from 1990 to 1993. Rationing quotas are the lowest under the revolution and insufficient to sustain minimal nutrition levels. The lack of food, vitamins and medicines led to malnutrition and a widespread epidemic of optic neuritis which afflicted 50 000 Cubans in 1993. It is virtually impossible to survive without resorting to the black market which is becoming more and more dollarized. One chicken bought in pesos on the black market takes the whole monthly wage of an average

Table 4.1 The deterioration of the Cuban economy, 1989–93 (in billion pesos unless specified)

Indicators	*1989*	*1993*	*Change (%)*
National product (GSP)	27.2	19.4–12.5	–29 to –54
Soviet and CMEA aid	6.0	0	–100
Domestic investment	4.5	1.4–1.0	–69 to –78
Surplus money in circulation	3.5	10.0	+186
Transactions of consumer goods in black market	2.0[b]	14.0	+600
State budget deficit	1.4	4.8	+243
Total foreign trade transactions	13.5	3.4	–75
Oil and oil-by-product imports[a]	13.4	3.2	–76
Sugar output[a]	8.1	4.2	–48
Exchange rate of peso per one dollar in black market	8	65–100	+712–+1 150
Unemployment as % of labour force	6	10–18[c]	+66–+200

Notes:
[a] Million metric tons.
[b] 1990.
[c] Displaced workers, some receiving unemployment compensation, others relocated and others jobless.

Sources: Based on official Cuban sources quoted and analysed in Carmelo Mesa-Lago, 'The Social Safety Net in the Two Cuban Transitions', in Cuban Research Institute, *Transition in Cuba: New Challenges for US Policy* (Miami: Florida International University, 1993), *Historia económica de Cuba socialista* (Madrid: Alianza Editorial, 1994); *Are Economic Reforms Propelling Cuba to the Market?* (Miami: University of Miami, North–South Center, 1994).

worker and a pair of shoes is worth five times the average wage.[4] A series of indicators showing Cuba's economic deterioration in 1989–93 is presented in Table 4.1.

Prior to the summer of 1993 dollars entered Cuba through illegal remittances, foreign students and tourists, visiting exiles, Cuban employees working abroad and in joint ventures, and foreign investors. These operations in dollars were illegal and sanctioned by severe fines and imprisonment. Cuban artists working and earning hard currency abroad had to deliver it to the government and receive pesos in exchange. A famous painter was paid 42 000 pesos (worth $700 on the black market) for $104 000 earned in an exhibit in Mexico. (He subsequently defected.) Citizens entitled to foreign inheritances were paid half in hard currency and half in pesos at the official rate. Those who received dollars from relatives in the United States were forced to relinquish them to the government which exchanged them at the rate of two pesos for one dollar, and that exchange rate was imposed on visiting exiles also. Agencies in Miami sent remittances illegally to Cuba at the rate of 25 pesos per dollar making a significant profit. These stiff regulations and practices led millions of Cubans to violate the law: those who had dollars asked tourists to buy precious consumer goods for them in the tourist shops or simply got the merchandise on the black market.[5] Bank savings slipped to the lowest level under the revolution because people withdrew their deposits to buy on the black market. In addition, many immediately changed their wage into dollars to beat the devaluation of the peso.

The black market rapidly expanded, became dollarized and was increasingly supplied by goods stolen from the state sector and foodstuffs illegally sold by private farmers. In 1992 the value of black market transactions on consumer goods was 14 billion, while the official market was 7 billion, only one-third of the total.[6]

LEGALIZATION OF HARD CURRENCY POSSESSION AND CIRCULATION

Confronting this harsh reality, the Cuban government began to relax the law. In June 1993, 10 categories of Cubans were authorized to possess dollars and permitted to purchase in special state stores. Included were workers in tourist facilities and joint ventures, as well as government employees and artists working abroad. An experimental store was opened in Varadero Beach which informally allowed Cubans with dollars to buy in it.

At the end of June 1993, Castro told the National Assembly that the dollarization process was a reality because of the economic situation and insufficient policemen to enforce the law, hence the time was ripe to change it.[7] In front of 100 Latin American leftists invited to the celebration of the 40th anniversary of the July 26th Revolutionary Movement, Castro bitterly acknowledged: 'Today life, reality . . . forces us to do what we would have never done otherwise . . . we must make concessions . . . to save the Revolution and the accomplishments of socialism.' He then announced the measures: (1) Cubans will be permitted to possess foreign currency and buy directly in special stores; (2) in the future the government will consider the issuing of a 'national convertible monetary currency' (as in China) to buy scarce goods; (3) principal domestic economic operations will continue to be done in pesos but the rest could be done in dollars; (4) Cubans may hire workers (for example, for repairs) and pay them in dollars; (5) the rationing system will stay ('perhaps our grandchildren will live without it'); (6) the number of Cuban exiles allowed to visit Cuba will be increased and their dollars will be welcome; and (7) bank accounts in dollars will become legal.[8]

A decree law of 13 August introduced the measures announced by Castro. Cuban citizens were authorized to possess dollars and other hard currencies received from abroad, exchange them for pesos and use them to buy goods and services in state dollar shops. Hard currencies could freely enter Cuba as well. Bank accounts in hard currency were authorized.[9]

Additional details on the policies were leaked to the news media. The number of visas for exiles' visits (extending from one week to one month) would increase from 4680 annually to 23 000–80 000 (according to different sources), the latter figure similar to the visas granted in the peak visiting year of 1979. Such visas would be processed in two or three days instead of the several months or even years it currently takes. Cubans who left prior to 1980 would be able to enter the island using their US passport instead of the Cuban passport which is now required. Exiles would be allowed to bring in an unlimited amount of dollars which they would not be forced to change into pesos. The hard currency could be freely given to Cuban relatives who might be invited by the visitors to stay with them in tourist hotels and eat at dollar restaurants. United Airlines announced it would charter flights to Cuba starting on 17 August and that by September there would be six weekly flights. There are also three other enterprises operating charter flights. The change in Cuban policy split the exile community in Miami.[10]

BENEFITS FOR THE CUBAN GOVERNMENT

Rough estimates of potential foreign exchange receipts for Cuba before and after the new policies that were enacted are presented in Table 4.2. The major sources of revenue by far are remittances by Cuban exiles, followed by exiles' visits to Cuba and Cubans' visits to the United States; very little comes from the small taxes charged on packages of food and medicine sent by exiles. Prior to the new measures, total annual revenue earned by Cuba may have ranged from $112 to $322 million, about 90 per cent of it from dollar remittances.

The new policies may double Cuba's total earnings. There are about one million Cubans living abroad but not all of them are engaged in dollar remittances. The large majority who send money probably do not reach the annual maximum of $1200 imposed by the US Treasury and few exceed such a maximum ($100 monthly buys a lot in Cuba). The table estimates revenue from remittances at between $160 and $600 million,

Table 4.2 Author's estimates of potential annual revenue of the Cuban government resulting from new measures, 1993–94

		Annual income (million dollars)
I	*Revenue before measures (1990–92)*	
	A Dollar remittances[a]	100–300
	B Visits to Cuba[b] (4 680 visitors spending $500–$1 200 each)	2–6
	C Visits to USA (20 000 spending $500–$800 each)	10–16
	D Packages[b] (an undisclosed tax, said to be small: see IID)	0.1–1
	E Total[b]	112–322
II	*Revenue after measures*[b]	
	A *Remittances*[c]	160–600
	200 000 exiles send $800	160
	300 000 exiles send $1 000	300
	500 000 exiles send $1 200	600
	B *Exiles' visits to Cuba*	40–120
	One visitor weekly expenditure from $500–$1 200	
	80 000 visitors	40–96
	100 000 visitors	50–120
	C *Cuban visits to USA*	10–24
	One visitor expenditure from $500–$800	
	20 000 visitors	10–16
	30 000 visitors	15–24
	D *Packages*	0.2–2
	Tax per package from $1–$4	
	200 000 packages	0.2–0.8
	300 000 packages	0.3–1.2
	500 000 packages	0.5–2.0
	E Total[d]	210–746

Notes:

[a] Rough estimates given by others.

[b] Author's estimates.

[c] Remittances from comparable countries: El Salvador and Dominican Republic (one million abroad): $700 to $1000 million annually.

[d] Other estimates range from $500 million (Sergio Roca) to $600 million (Andrew Zimbalist).

Sources: Pedro Alfonso, 'Castro sugiere legalizar dólares,' *Nuevo Herald*, 3 July 1993, 1A, 6A; Ana Santiago, 'Dolarización de Cuba,' *Nuevo Herald*, 16 July 1993, p.6A and 'Exiles' Trips to Island Likely to be Made Easier', *Miami Herald*, 28 July 1993, pp.1A, 10A; Carmelo Mesa-Lago, *Are Economic Reforms. Propelling Cuba to the Market?*

depending on whether 200 000 or 500 000 exiles send from $800 to $1200 each; a figure of $300 about million is probably the most realistic.

Remittances sent by other Latin Americans residing in the United States, whose numbers are similar to those of Cuban exiles (for example, El Salvador and the Dominican Republic each with about a million living abroad), fluctuate from $700 to $1000 million annually. But these groups are not subject to US restrictions in their remittances as the Cubans are, and the latter are under political pressure by the most radical anti-Castro groups to refrain from sending remittances as they are depicted as contributing to keep the regime in power.

A recent study analyses other factors that tend to reduce the volume of remittances by Cuban exiles: (1) the long time such exiles have lived in the United States, which has led to erosion of family ties; (2) the lower income of recent exiles who have stronger ties with Cuba but face difficult economic conditions in South Florida; and (3) the fact that Cuban exiles do not usually invest in the island as their counterparts do.[11]

In March 1994 an average of about 1600 exiles a week were visiting Cuba, spending a minimum of $500 each, limited to airfare, passport, visa and gifts for the family. The most expensive package tour (including hotel and meals) costs $1200. The annual projection of these figures (80 000 visitors) results in a revenue between $40 and $96 million. If we use the optimistic scenario of 100 000 visitors (in 1994) the revenue would be $50 to $100 million.

Earnings from Cubans visiting relatives in the United States oscillate from $10 to $24 million, based on 20 000 and 30 000 visitors, respectively, expending $500 to $800 each; the second figure is probably an overestimate. Finally, revenue from taxes charged to packages would be very small, not more than $2 million in the most optimistic scenario.

The estimated total revenue from the four sources in 1994 ranges from $210 and $746 million, a twofold increase over the pre-reform revenue (Table 4.2), but the higher figure is unrealistic. Cuba's own total estimate is $281 million (Table 4.3), quite close to the first estimate in Table 4.2. Cuban figures probably underestimate remittances and overestimate revenue from other sources. The dollar authorization policy will provide a desperately needed dollar injection to the moribund Cuban economy, but it will certainly not cure the malaise as $7 to $13 billion will be needed to recover the economic level existing in the late 1980s prior to the crisis.

Other additional advantages of the new policies would include incentives to the labour force, reduction of the importance of the black market and a political split of the exile community.

Table 4.3 Cuban estimates of potential annual revenue of the Cuban government after new measures, 1993–94

			Annual income (Million dollars)
A	*Remittances*		
	50 000 exiles send $800		40[a]
B	*Exiles' visits to Cuba*		207
	Expenditure per visitor		
	Passport	$70	
	Airfare	$300	
	Hotel (one week, obligatory)	$700	
	Purchases in Cuba	$1 000	
	100 000 visitors × $2 070		207[b]
C	*Cuban visits to USA*		24
	Expenditure per visitor		
	Invitation request	$136	
	Airfare	$300	
	Extensions of stay	$270	
	Money brought back	$500	
	20 000 visitors × $1 206		24[c]
D	*Packages*		
	200 000 packages, 10 lb each, at $5 per lb		10[d]
E	Total		281[e]

Notes:
[a] Figure grossly underestimated as a considerably higher number of exiles send remittances.
[b] Figure probably overestimated as visitors bring gifts in merchandise bought in USA, and the number of visitors projected for 1994 is 80 000.
[c] Figure probably overestimated as Cubans bring back gifts from relatives in the form of merchandise, and cash might be hidden.
[d] Figure probably overestimated.
[e] Out of this figure, $150 million, it is estimated, will be spent in state dollar shops.

Source: Instituto de Investigaciones Económicas (INIE), 'Reflexiones sobre la despenalización de la tenencia de divisas en Cuba', *Cuba en el Mes* (Havana), dossier 3, 1993, pp.40–47.

NEGATIVE CONSEQUENCES OF THE NEW POLICIES

The benefits described above would be offset by a series of problems and disadvantages. The government must import consumer goods, organize a network of ad hoc stores and stock them with merchandise which should be systematically replenished. If prices of goods are set too high, the special stores will not be competitive with the black market. Therefore government profits could not be too high. In an attempt to increase profits, but ignoring market forces, the government recently increased prices of goods in state dollar stores by 50 per cent. That action made black market prices more competitive and selling in the state stores declined sharply.[12] Furthermore, black marketeers are offering additional conveniences such as delivering goods at home.

An immediate acceleration in the devaluation of the peso has occurred. In the short run, while the inflow of exiles' dollars is still small, there may be an increase in demand for dollars on the black market (from those who do not yet have access to that currency) in order to buy goods in the special stores. (This actually happened in August 1993 when the exchange rate of the dollar on the black market jumped from 65 to 100 pesos.) In the medium run, there should be a reduction in the demand for black-market dollars from the population who receive them from relatives and spend such currency in the special stores. Still a very large proportion of the population (probably a majority), who do not have relatives abroad, will have to obtain dollars on the black market at a worse rate of exchange. The demand for dollars of this group will remain the same or even increase because of its access to special stores. In the long run the unofficial exchange rate of the peso may tend towards greater stability providing that the government meets the aforementioned conditions, a difficult task indeed.

Privileges and inequalities may also expand as the most loyal revolutionaries may have fewer relatives abroad, hence little access to dollars and goods in special stores. The opposite should be true of government opponents. Black Cubans would be most disadvantaged because only 3 per cent of the exiles are non-white, while the majority of the island population is black or mulatto. The new policy, therefore, will penalize supporters and reward opponents, a repetition of what happened with the massive exiles' visits in 1979–80.

Inequalities may also occur among different occupations. Workers in tourism and foreign ventures as well as black marketeers have access to dollars, but those employed in the state peso sector do not. Therefore bartenders, waitresses, chauffeurs and illegal operators of restaurants are living much better than university professors, professionals, military men and technicians. The second group has become demoralized and is searching for jobs that have access to dollars.[13]

Castro has acknowledged this inequality problem in various speeches in the second half of 1993 and ended up recognizing that egalitarianism was an error of the revolution that had to be rectified.[14] Trying to compensate for the blatant inequalities, the government opened a store in Havana in which exemplary workers can buy some of the goods in pesos sold in dollar stores.[15] More recently, workers in strategic industries (such as energy) are being paid a fraction of their salary in dollars. But Cuba's top economist has warned that such types of incentives cannot be extended to all of the labour force owing to lack of resources.[16]

Another disadvantage is that an increasing segment of the population is becoming self-sufficient and economically independent from the government. As the most basic consumer needs of this segment of the population are satisfied, it may invest its dollars in other ventures and hire workers, thereby expanding the independent labour sphere. Furthermore, this group could put pressure on the government for more liberalization measures. A significant shift of the labour force away from the state sector and towards the informal–private sector will probably occur in the medium term as workers pursue dollars to buy goods in the special stores. Therefore state production and productivity may decline.

Last but not least, a large inflow of Cuban Americans could also contribute to social and political tensions as those Cubans might provide dollars to dissident and human rights organizations. The government has probably foreseen some of these problems and is taking some precautionary measures. The newspaper *Granma* warned that the new policies will be applied gradually because they require changes in legislation, development of a commercial network and careful price revision. In May 1994 the National Assembly empowered Castro to mandate the exchange of dollars into a 'convertible peso'; if that measure is introduced, the legal circulation of the dollar will end, thus creating disincentives for dollar remittances.

ADDITIONAL COMPLICATIONS

The problems described above are compounded by US restraining actions. Current federal regulations allow remittances of $300 per quarter by Cuban-Americans to close relatives living in the island. Exiles visiting Cuban relatives are authorized to spend a maximum of $700 weekly, but the cheapest tourist hotel in Havana costs almost $600 a week, leaving only $100 for transport and gifts to the family, and some of the package tours cost as much as $1200. Violators of the law face fines of up to $250 000 and/or imprisonment.[17] These regulations, nevertheless, are difficult to enforce: dollars above the maximum can be illegally carried to Cuba by visiting exiles or by friends, sent by mail or through a third country. Furthermore, US control of actual expenditures in Cuba is virtually impossible.

The US Department of Transportation first authorized the expanded trips of Cuban exiles. But early in August 1993, the Assistant Secretary of State for Interamerican Affairs told the House Subcommittee on Western Hemispheric Affairs (chaired by Robert Torricelli, author of the 1992 bill that tightened the Cuban embargo) that authorization for the flights to Cuba had been indefinitely rescinded. In September, nevertheless, the flights were approved.

Still at issue is whether the travellers will spend more than is allowed. The US government insists that lodging must not be obligatory but optional and, if Cuba approves only those travellers who take a full package (that is, discriminates against those who only want the air fare) the authorization will be rescinded again. But travelling to Cuba without lodging and meals is difficult owing to the lack of electricity and water at relatives' homes (food can be bought in dollars). Both the Cuban government and US tourist agencies are interested in selling full packages to maximize revenue and commissions. In November, however, one of the travel agencies reported that the Cuban government had approved 50 visas (out of 200 applications) from exiles that wanted to travel without full packages. The cost of such trips is less than $400 and includes flight, visa and airport taxes. The Assistant Secretary of State declared in the same month that so far there has been compliance with the travel regulations but additional flights were being carefully reviewed and approved on a monthly basis.[18]

Six weekly flights and as many as 40 000 visitors annually were initially predicted but, one month after the flights started, there were only three weekly flights and half of their seats were empty. Reasons for this poor initial response were: (1) political pressure and public campaigns in Miami asking Cuban Americans not to travel to the island because their trips would help Castro to keep his power; (2) confusion over whether travellers could go without a package arrangement or only with it; and (3) a wait-and-see attitude of the majority of exiles who hoped that the poor outcome so far would force Castro to offer cheaper tour packages and lift the remaining travel restrictions.

In January 1994 the Cuban government made travel conditions for exiles more flexible; visitors can now spend from one to 21 days on the island, and if a hotel is booked the meals are optional. The exiles' reaction was fast and positive: in March there were 11 full weekly flights carrying 1600 Cuban-Americans, and a total of 80 000 visitors were projected for the year 1994.

DOLLAR SALVATION OR DAMNATION

The new policies introduced in the summer of 1993 and analysed in this chapter may generate an additional $100 to $400 million annually over the dollar revenue earned by Cuba before the reform. That sum equals about 1.6 per cent to 5.3 per cent of Cuba's foreign exchange earnings reduction from 1989 to 1993. Even if the best scenario materializes, it is obvious that the dollar-pursuit measures will not by themselves turn the Cuban economy around.

The US government is monitoring Cuban actions, trying to ensure the enforcement of current US legislation (the embargo, the Torricelli bill) such as restrictions on dollar remittances and money spent in exiles' visits to Cuba, but the power to enforce those restrictions is limited in practice. Initially, Cuban revenue was also limited by the exiles' lukewarm attitudes, particularly related to visits to the island, but that situation changed in 1994 and the number of visitors increased significantly.

On the other hand, such measures have unleashed negative consequences for the Cuban government, such as (1) expanding inequalities among groups of the population: government supporters and Afro-Cubans (when they do not have access to dollars) are disadvantaged vis-à-vis regime opponents and whites, resulting in demoralization among the former; (2) acceleration in the dollarization of the economy and devaluation of the peso, at least in the short and medium term; (3) a shifting of the labour force from the state peso sector to the dollar sector, both legal and illegal (black market, non-authorized occupations), which in turn has led to an increasing segment of the labour force being economically independent of the government; and (4) an expansion of visits of exiles whose adverse demonstration effect upon desperate Cubans could have worse consequences than the visitors' wave of 1979–80 which led to a massive exodus of Cubans through Mariel.

The policies discussed in this chapter should not be judged in isolation as other market-oriented reform measures were introduced in Cuba in the second half of 1993, such as authorization of self-employment work and transformation of state farms into cooperatives. Additional reforms were introduced or have been announced in 1994, for instance fiscal reform, price increases, a new tax system and the issuing of a convertible Cuban peso.[19] The dollar pursuit measures, nevertheless, have been so far the most spectacular within the set of enacted reforms, both economically and politically, and have contributed to Cuba's transition to the market.

Notes

1. For previous treatment of this topic, see C. Mesa-Lago, 'Sink or Swim', *Hemisfile*, 4:5, September–October 1993, pp.6–7; 'Cuba Under the Dollar Sign', *ASCE Newsletter*, December 1993, pp.32–5.
2. C. Mesa-Lago, *Are Economic Reforms Propelling Cuba to the Market*?, University of Miami, North-South Center, Miami, 1994.
3. 'Interview with Carlos Lage', *Granma International*, 10 November 1993, p.9; Mesa-Lago, *Are Economic Reforms Propelling Cuba to the Market*?
4. Mesa-Lago, *Are Economic Reforms Propelling Cuba to the Market*?
5. Fidel Castro acknowledged some of these problems in his 'Discurso en la clausura del 40 aniversario del asalto al Cuartel Moncada', *Granma*, 28 July 1993, pp.3–7.
6. Julio Carranza Valdés, 'Cuba: los retos de la economía', *Cuadernos de Nuestra América*, 19 (1993) p.153.
7 F. Castro, speech to the National Assembly on 29 June 1993, cited by Pablo Alfonso, 'Castro sugiere legalizar dólaries', *El Nuevo Herald*, 3 July 1993, pp.1A, 6A.
8. Castro, 'Discurso', pp.4–5.
9. 'Decreto Ley N° 140' and 'Información and Banco Nacional' *Granma*, 14 August 1993, p.2. Cuba's new monetary policy generated a flood of newspaper articles: Mimi Whitefield, 'Soaking Up Dollars', *The Miami Herald*, 4 July 1993, pp.Kl, K3; Arturo Villar, 'The Dollarization of the Cuban Economy', *Wall Street Journal*, 9 July,1993, p.9A; Andres Oppenheimer, 'Cuba's Stopgap Steps May Open Capitalist Floodgates', *The Miami Herald*, 28 July 1993, pp.1A, 10A; Pablo Alfonso, 'Cuba por dentro', *El Nuevo Herald*, 29 and 30 July 1993, p.3A; Teo A. Babun, 'Havana Takes a Big Risk in Legalizing the Dollar', *The Miami Herald*, 1 August 1993, p.4C; Jane Bussey, 'Castro Opens Cuba's Door to Capitalism a Crack', *The Miami Herald*, 1 August 1993, pp.1K, 3K.
10. Ana Santiago, 'Exiles' Trips to Island Likely to be Made Easier', *The Miami Herald*, 28 July 1993, pp.1A, 10A; 'Nuevos viajes a Cuba dividen a exiliados', *El Nuevo Herald*, 29 July 1993, pp.1A, 16A.
11. Sergio Díaz-Briquets, 'Dollarization: Castro's Latest Economic Miracle?', *Hemisphere*, 5:3, Summer/Fall 1993, pp.8–9.
12. 'Cuba Raises Prices for Dollar Items', *The Miami Herald*, 10 August 1993, pp.1A, 6A.
13. Soledad Cruz, *Juventud Rebelde*, 20 June 1993, p.10.
14. F. Castro, 'Discurso', p.7 and 'Speech at the 5th UNEAC Congress', *Granma International*, 8 December 1993, p.4.
15. Pablo Alfonso, 'Abren tiendas para obreros destacados', *El Nuevo Herald*, 29 September 1993, p.3A.
16. 'Interview with Carlos Lage', p.9.
17. Ana Santiago, 'Exiliados que viajen podrían violar embargo', *El Nuevo Herald*, 30 July 1993, pp.1A, 12A.
18. 'The Cuban Democracy Act: One Year Later', *Free Market Cuba: Business Journal*, 2:2, Fall/Winter 1993, p.5.
19. For an analysis of these measures, see Mesa-Lago *Are Economic Reforms Propelling Cuba to the Market*?

Part II

Cuba's International Relations: Reconsideration and Redesign

5 Cuba's Current Integration into the International and Hemispheric Systems

Julie M. Feinsilver

Although the prevalent image of Cuba is that of a country isolated from, or on the margins of, the hemispheric and international systems, this position fails to capture significant aspects of Cuba's current integration into those systems. While recognizing that Cuba is, indeed, isolated from the most important institutions, the multilateral development banks, Cuba does, nonetheless, have extensive bilateral diplomatic, economic, scientific and cultural relations with most of the countries in the Western hemisphere, and has some form of relations with most of the world. This chapter seeks to address both the image and the broader reality of Cuba's current position, and to emphasize Cuba's integration, but also attempts to consider its isolation.

Suspension from the OAS in 1962 clearly led to Cuba's isolation in the Western hemisphere, but throughout the revolutionary period Cuba not only maintained but also increased its participation in numerous other international organizations and professional and scientific associations. Cuba continued to be an active member of the United Nations and its numerous subsidiary agencies as well as other international organizations, among which are the Caribbean Council of Churches (CCC), the United Nations Economic Commission for Latin America and the Caribbean (ECLAC), the Food and Agriculture Organization (FAO), the Group of 77 (G-77), the International Atomic Energy Agency (IAEA), the Intergovernmental Oceanographic Commission (IOC), International Bank for Economic Co-operation (IBEC), the International Civil Aviation Organization (ICAO), the International Fund for Agricultural Development (IFAD), the International Labour Organization (ILO), the International Maritime Organization (IMO), the International Criminal Police Organization (INTERPOL), the International Sugar Organization (ISO), the International Telecommunications Union (ITU), the Nonaligned Movement (NAM), the Panama Canal Authority (PCA), the United Nations Conference on Trade and Development (UNCTAD), the United Nations Educational, Scientific and Cultural Organization (UNESCO), the United Nations Children's Fund (UNICEF),

United Nations Industrial Development Organization (UNIDO), the Universal Postal Union (UPU), the World Confederation of Labor (WCL), the World Federation of Trade Unions (WFTU), the World Health Organization (WHO), the World Intellectual Property Organization (WIPO), the World Meterological Organization (WMO) and the World Tourism Organization (WTO).[1]

Despite US-orchestrated attempts to isolate the Cuban government, Cuba has been active in some important organizations such as the United Nations Security Council, to which it was elected for the 1990–92 term, and the United Nations Human Rights Commission, where it was chosen for the vice-presidency in 1989. Among the other international organizations in which Cuba has been elected to leadership positions in the past two decades are the following: the Non-Aligned Nations Movement, the United Nations Council for Social, Humanitarian and Cultural Affairs, the International Atomic Energy Agency, the United Nations General Assembly, the Council of the Latin American Economic System, UNESCO and the United Nations committees on Budget and Finance and Science and Technology. Medical organizations in which Cuba has held leadership roles include the Executive Committees of the World Health Organization and the Pan American Health Organization, the Latin American Pediatric Association, and the Latin American Genetics Association.[2]

In 1992 the Latin American Parliament (Parlatino) created a Commission for Health, Labor and Social Security to which Cuba was elected as the chairperson. Accordingly, the first meeting of 80 parliamentarians was then held in Havana that year.[3] In February 1993 Cuba was elected to serve a two-year term on the United Nations Economic and Social Council's Commission on Sustainable Development.[4]

The Cuban government has been able to project its relative influence in the international arena because of the effective participation of its representatives in the organizations to which Cuba belongs. Cuba has an extremely professional, well-trained diplomatic corps that sends well-prepared delegates to meetings of international organizations. An excellent example is the very effective international lawyer, Miguel Alfonso, who was elected to the vice-presidency of the United Nations Human Rights Commission despite US campaigns against Cuba in that forum.

Furthermore, the Cuban government sends very capable and scientifically qualified representatives to specialized technical meetings. These representatives take an active part in discussions but often lack the institutional resources to participate fully in all of the projects.[5] At the Pan American Health Organization (PAHO) ministerial meetings, for example, only the Cubans along with the US and Canadian delegations actually read and study all of the voluminous documents presented, prepare position statements on issues of particular interest to them based on records of all of their previous statements, and participate actively in deliberations on a regular basis.[6]

There are a number of regional organizations to which Cuba belongs either as a full member, such as the Latin American Economic System (SELA), the Latin American Parliament (Parlatino), the Coordination of Latin American Governments in the UN System (GRULA), the Inter-American Institute for Global Change Research (IAI), the Latin American Confederation of Tourism Press (CLAPTUR), the Caribbean Tourist Organization (CTO), the Group of Latin American and Caribbean Sugar Exporting Countries (GLACSEC) and the Latin American Energy Organization (OLADE), or as an observer, such as the Latin American Integration Association (ALADI) and the Andean Pact.[7] Moreover, Castro has participated in the Ibero-American Presidents' Summit meetings and in recent years has taken to attending presidential inaugurations in the hemisphere.

Not surprisingly, the Cuban government has promoted the strengthening of the Latin American Economic System, of which it was a founding member in 1975, to circumvent the OAS and the Group of Eight, two organizations from which Cuba is excluded because it is non-democratic.

Cuba's continued membership in some international organizations, however, is irrelevant at this time because of economic conditionality. For example, Cuba remains a member of the General Agreement on Tariffs and Trade (GATT) and attends meetings, but until Cuba makes a transition to a market economy it will have no real role in GATT and GATT will have no relevance for Cuba. Moreover, GATT governs exchanges for money rather than barter trade, and it is not clear whether Cuba will have the money for trade or whether GATT will ever accede to barter trade.[8]

Political rather than economic conditionality previously excluded Cuba from the Caribbean Community (CARICOM), but Cuba signed an accord with CARICOM on 7 July 1993 to create a joint commission to explore technical cooperation in agriculture, biotechnology and tourism.[9] This agreement, which had been in the making for a year, met with considerable pressure from Rep. Torricelli and the Cuban-American Congressional delegation who sent a letter to the CARICOM heads of state threatening to reconsider support for NAFTA (North American Free Trade Agreement) parity for CARICOM, a point dealt with in Chapter 8. In a meeting with five CARICOM heads of state on 30 August 1993, President Clinton said that 'the US will not punish CARICOM for increasing its ties with Cuba' and the Caribbean leaders indicated that they would not do anything in their relationship with Cuba that would be inimical to US interests.[10]

The CARICOM–Cuba Joint Commission was actually established in mid-December 1993 with the mission of identifying not only opportunities for cooperation, but also ways and means and timetables for action. The West Indian Commission, which had submitted its recommendation for this course of action in 1992, also advocated the establishment of an Association of Caribbean States (ACS) which would, of course, include Cuba. Both the joint commission and the ACS initiatives were heartily endorsed by Yesu Persaud, president of the Caribbean Association of Industry and Commerce (CAIC), whose fellow-businessmen are already investing in Cuba and seeking methods of economic integration with Cuba. Edwin Carrington, the Secretary-General of CARICOM, has said that the creation of a joint commission is a step in the direction of establishing the ACS and 'the boldest and most important initiative on the part of our region in recent times'.[11] Clearly, defying the Cuban-American lobby in the US Congress was very bold indeed, but in some ways not surprising. Caribbean governments were, after all, the first in the hemisphere to re-establish diplomatic relations with Cuba in 1972, leading the way to the lifting of all OAS sanctions against Cuba in 1975.[12]

Political conditionality is the main impediment to Cuba's full reintegration into hemispheric organizations. Although Cuba was a founding member of the Organization of American States, the current government of Cuba was suspended from active participation in 1962, yet the state of Cuba remains a member. Upon internal political change, that is democratization, Cuba will be eligible for reinstatement and resumption of active participation with a two-thirds majority vote by the 34 active Permanent Council members (the foreign affairs ministers).[13] Because Resolution 1080 of 1991 amended the OAS Charter to make the preservation of democracy the organization's number one goal, Cuba would have to hold free, multi-party elections prior to submission of an official letter requesting re-entry. The Permanent Council would then designate a working group to study Cuba's new constitution and its laws to ascertain whether the legal structure for the development and protection of democracy was in place. The working group would also investigate human rights issues. If political prisoners were still being held, they would either have to be released or guaranteed due process. Because the working group's research would most likely require travel to Cuba, its work could take considerable time unless the Permanent Council were to set a deadline for a recommendation from the working group to speed up the process, something it would do if there were a threat of starvation or political violence.[14] On the other hand, the process of re-entry into the OAS may take only five minutes if a majority of the Permanent Council so decides.[15]

Suspension from the OAS means that Cuba is also suspended from the OAS's sub-regional organizations, such as the Inter-American Institute for Cooperation in Agriculture (IICA), the Inter-American Defense Board and, most importantly, the Inter-American Development Bank (IDB). Reinstatement as an active member of the OAS does not, however, necessarily make Cuba a member of the sub-regional organizations. For example, Cuba has never been a member of the Inter-American Development Bank although a subscription fee was assigned to it in 1959 when the bank was established. An OAS seal of approval would, of course, be a necessary but not sufficient precondition for entry. The IDB has no formal rules of political conditionality; its policy is flexible and applied differently to different countries. Not having been a member, Cuba has no prior debt with the IDB, and thus is not faced with the problem of having to pay arrears before receiving any fresh loans, as was the case with Nicaragua and Panama.[16]

Cuba would, however, most likely try to negotiate a new entry subscription to the bank's capital stock and contribution quota for the Fund for Special Operations as the ones assigned to it in 1959 reflected Cuba's relative economic position vis-à-vis the rest of the member countries at that time. Cuba's relative economic strength has, of course, changed considerably since then. Cuba's subscription to capital stock and its quota to the Fund in 1959 were greater than those of all other countries except the United States, Argentina, Brazil, Mexico and Venezuela.[17] Given the weakness of the Cuban economy today and the government's lack of hard currency reserves, it will be exceedingly difficult for Cuba to meet any but the lowest subscription fees.

Cuba will face this problem with the other international financial institutions as well. In fact, even non-financial institutions have quotas to be paid by the members and these are generally based on per capita income. Because the Cuban peso is a non-convertible currency and thus has an artificially high exchange rate vis-à-vis the US dollar, Cuba's per capita income is considerably higher than it would otherwise be. This means that the quotas and subscription fees assigned to Cuba by the OAS and international lending institutions are exceedingly high. Recognizing this, the Cuban government has been attempting to get PAHO, for example, to reduce its quota, but the quota is determined by the OAS. This decision is not based on politics, but on the official data provided by the member governments. If the Cuban government used the same statistical methodology as market economies, its quota would be lower, as would its per capita income, a symbolically important figure.[18]

Membership of the IDB is open to members of the OAS, among others, 'at such times and in accordance with such terms as the Bank may determine'.[19] Membership in the International Monetary Fund (IMF) is a prerequisite for countries to join.[20] As a member of the IDB, Cuba would most likely be classified in a category which would make it eligible for very concessionary loans for Special Operations.[21]

Cuba was a member of the IMF until it withdrew in 1964 after failing to meet its obligations both in reporting financial data and in repaying its debt. Debt settlement was finally made in 1969, but Cuba has not rejoined. The IMF's rules for rejoining are the same as those for new membership and do not require the creation of a market economy; but they do require lifting exchange rate restrictions and adherence to the purposes of the IMF. The Executive Board, however, will only submit an application to the Board of Governors if there is evidence that the country can meet the membership obligations. A fact-finding mission is dispatched to study the country's financial and economic systems and determine a quota for membership. If the country agrees to the quota and the Fund's rules, it may be admitted to membership by a simple majority vote of the Board of Governors, but at least two-thirds of them must vote.[22]

As is well known, economic conditionality imposed by the IMF requires the acceptance of structural adjustment programmes that are politically unpopular and often lead to social unrest. Whether self-imposed or IMF-imposed, decreasing government subsidies and government employment, relinquishing price controls and controlling inflation are politically difficult to carry out. If, however, a country fails to do so, IMF loans may be withheld or delayed, as is the case today with the US$ 1.5 billion aid package for Russia.[23] Cuba's austerity programme, combined with recent economic liberalization policies, do not yet approach the IMF's structural adjustment requirements, but are a step in the right direction.

Spain's former economics minister, Carlos Solchaga, led a commission to Cuba which made economic recommendations similar to some of the reforms announced in the summer of 1993 but under consideration for some time before then. Although Solchaga is now an advisor to the Director-General of the IMF, Michel Camdessus, and thus in a position to facilitate communication between Cuba and the Fund, he had nothing to do with the Cuban National Bank's recent invitation to two IMF officials. The executive director of the IMF for Austria, Belarus, Belgium, the Czech Republic, Hungary, Kazakhstan, Luxemburg, the Slovak Republic and Turkey, Jacques de Groote, and his assistant, Frank Moss, went to Cuba on a 'totally personal basis' in November 1993 to discuss the experiences in transition of the countries for which they are responsible. The two held unofficial meetings (from the IMF's perspective) with the Cuban government's economic team (their interlocutors were primarily reform-minded economists who wanted to learn from these experiences) and upon their return gave an informal debriefing at the Fund.[24]

Talks with Cuban reformist economists were encouraging to de Groote and Moss, and gave them the impression that some positive changes were being made.[25] Good intentions and reformists desires aside, however, the National Assembly of People's Power semi-annual meeting the following month (December 1993) reversed some of the previously announced liberalization measures. It seems that the dilemma of trying to keep the political lid on while making economic change has led to timid and tentative measures, as well as to tinkering with and rethinking of economic policy in the light of the changing relative weight of hardline and reformist political factions.

Moss opined that the Cuban government is in a good position to make the transition to a market economy now while it is still politically stable; otherwise, political disarray would make economic reform extremely difficult, as is the case in Russia. He suggested that, if Cuba were to continue expanding its market measures, then pressure to admit Cuba to the international (financial) system would increase and that probably even the United States would accede, as it has done with Vietnam.[26] This is optimistic in the light of Assistant Secretary of State for Inter-American Affairs Alexander Watson's 25 January 1994 statement to the press that 'it would be premature to consider admitting Cuba back into full membership of the OAS . . . until Cuba really makes some fundamental steps towards true democracy and protection of human rights inside that country'.[27] Many countries, both in the Western hemisphere and elsewhere, however, favour readmitting Cuba into the institutions from which it is excluded, and recent UN General Assembly votes have overwhelmingly favoured lifting the US embargo against Cuba.[28]

Much has been made of this 'IMF' trip to Cuba, as if Cuba were poised for entry into the Fund, but this is not the case. The government of Cuba has made no official request for membership and the US controls 18 per cent of the vote, thereby precluding the necessary 85 per cent majority required for admission to the Fund.[29] Perhaps the most meaningful result of the de Groote–Moss trip, according to economist George P. Montalván, is that, after they told Cuban National Bank officials that from the IMF perspective an initial step the Cuban National Bank would have to take is to produce an objective report on the economic situation and on economic policies using 'standard statistical methodology', Bank officials agreed to do so for 1994. Montalván argues that, apart from all of the other preconditions, integration into the international financial system is impossible without reporting economic indicators in 'standard' form.[30] In all fairness, reformist Cuban economists (some of whom are now in power) have talked about changing their statistical methods in this way for the past few years, and long before de Groote and Moss arrived on the scene. Nonetheless, the Cuban economists' commitment to change is significant. The methodological change would most certainly lead to a paper decrease in Cuba's per capita income and thus decrease the quotas and subscription fees Cuba is or would be assessed by international institutions.

Membership of the World Bank is restricted to the members of the IMF, and the Bank's subscription quota is based on that of the Fund.[31] Cuba, therefore, remains excluded from all of the institutions of the World Bank Group, which include not only the two public-sector development loan facilities, the International Bank for Reconstruction and Development (IBRD) and the International Development Association (IDA), but also the three units that provide various types of aid to attract private sector investment: the International Finance Corporation (IFC), which provides loans, the Multilateral Investment Guarantee Agency (MIGA), which gives technical advice and supplies political risk insurance, and the International Center for Settlement of Investment Disputes (ICSID) and advisory group.[32] Some argue that the international economic information and technical assistance that these financial institutions could offer Cuba in making the transition to a market economy, privatizing industry and agriculture, devising tax plans, monetary reforms, regulatory mechanisms, a stock market, a legal framework for market regulation and so on are probably more important than any financial aid that might be dispersed.[33]

If Cuba were to join the banks, the country would receive not only long-term low-interest loans on a highly concessionary basis and technical expertise and information on other economies and economic practices, but also an IMF seal of approval. While this is not a prerequisite for private commercial bank loans, IMF approval is highly advantageous and more likely to lead to fresh credits than not. The lessons learned from transitions from socialism to capitalism in the former Soviet bloc and the expertise gained therefrom could be readily shared with Cuba if Cuba were a member of the IMF and World Bank. On the other hand, a disadvantage of joining the banks is their right to interfere or intervene in domestic economic policy, something that for obvious reasons Castro has been loath to permit.

Suspension from the OAS affected Cuba's participation in all OAS subregional organizations except the Pan American Health Organization (PAHO) which has a special relationship with the OAS because of both the timing and conditions of its founding as well as its role as the regional office of the World Health Organization (WHO). PAHO predates the OAS by over 40 years. Had PAHO not been the regional office of the World Health Organization, a United Nations organization, Cuba would have been suspended from PAHO in 1962 when it was suspended from the OAS.[34]

Cuba's successive governments have been very active members since PAHO's inception. The current Cuban government was on the Executive Committee of PAHO (1990–93 and 1982–), the AIDS working group of the Executive Committee with both the United States and Mexico, and in 1993 became a member of the Health Research Advisory Committee.[35] Moreover, Cuba has been a major catalyst for the integration of Latin American medical and scientific organizations, sponsoring both their development and international conferences through which many Latin American scientists have come together, often for the first time.[36]

Recognizing (1) that Cuba is an integral part of the hemispheric community, and (2) that the best way to foster change in Cuba is to reintegrate Cuba fully into the community of nations, the Rio Group, since 1987, has repeatedly called for Cuba's reinsertion into the OAS. Political conditionality makes this most unlikely without radical change in the structure of Cuba's political system.[37] In the interim, Cuba enjoys greater links with its neighbours on a variety of levels than at any time in the past few decades. Private-sector interest in the potential Cuban market and in Cuba's human and physical resources may pressure other governments to reassess their relations with Cuba, following the lead of CARICOM – not to mention the long-standing examples of Canada and Europe.

Notes

1. Central Intelligence Agency, *World Factbook, 1992* (Washington, DC: CIA, 1992) p.86.
2. Julie M. Feinsilver, *Healing the Masses: Cuban Health Politics at Home and Abroad* (Berkeley: University of California Press, 1993) p.201.
3. Interview with Dr César Vieira, Coordinator of Health Policies, Pan American Health Organization, Washington, DC, 17 September 1993.
4. 'Semi-Annual Review: January–June 1993 Prepared by WHO/UN', World Health Organization (WHO) Internal document, 26 July 1993, p.6 and Annex 3.
5. Interview with Bill Erb, State Department Office of Ocean Affairs, US representative to various organizations including the Intergovernmental Oceanographic Commission, 10 and 12 September 1993; and with various

international organization officials who asked to remain anonymous (1993).

6. Anonymous source 10 September 1993.
7. John Walton Cotman, 'Cuba and the CARICOM States: The Last Decade', in Kaplowitz (ed.), *Cuba's Ties*, p.148; Implementational Committee of the Inter-American Institute for Global Change Research (IAI), *ICIAI News-Letter*, Issue 2, April 1993, p.4; and Boris Yopo H., 'Latin American Perspectives on the Cuban Transition', *Cuba Briefing Paper Series* (Georgetown University Center for Latin American Studies) Number 3, July 1993, p.3.
8. Interview with Jorge Pérez-López, Bureau of Labor Statistics, US Department of Labor, Washington, DC, 13 August 1993.
9. 'CARICOM Approves Cuba Cooperation, Clinton Implements Toricelli [*sic*]', *Inter-American Trade Monitor*, 8 July 1993 (e-mail).
10. *Inter-American Trade Monitor*, 30 August 1993 (e-mail); *The Gleaner* (Jamaica), 8 September 1993.
11. 'CARICOM-Cuba commission launched', *Caribbean & Central America Report*, 27 January 1994, RC-94-01, p.4.
12. Peter G. Bourne, *Fidel: A Biography of Fidel Castro* (New York: Dodd, Mead & Company, 1986) p.282.
13. Interview with Enrique Lagos, Chief, International Law Section, Washington, DC, OAS, 10 September 1993.
14. Interview with Nancy Irigoyen, Department of Public Information, Organization of American States, Washington, DC, 8 September 1993.
15. Interview with Enrique Lagos, PAS, Washington, DC, 10 September 1993.
16. Interview with Rolando Castañeda, Senior Operations Officer, Inter-American Development Bank, Washington, DC, 9 August 1993.
17. Inter-American Development Bank, *Agreement Establishing the Inter-American Development Bank* (Washington, DC: IDB, reprint January 1988) pp.26, 28.
18. Interview with anonymous source (legal expert), 31 January 1994.
19. Ibid., p.1.
20. Ibid., p.2.
21. Joaquín P. Pujol, 'Possible Role of International Financial Institutions in the Reconstruction of Cuba during the period of Transition', typescript, n.d. (1993?) p.2 (section on IDB). This is a detailed study of all of the major financial institutions that delineates their structure, resources, functions, membership rules, member quotas and benefits provided.
22. Joaquín P. Pujol, 'Membership Requirements in the IMF: Possible Implications for Cuba', in *Cuba in Transition, Vol. 1, Papers and Proceedings of the First Annual Meeting of the Association for the Study of the Cuban Economy* (Miami: Florida International University, 1991) pp.98–9.
23. *New York Times*, 20 September 1993, p.A3.
24. Interview with Frank Moss, IMF, 31 January 1993.
25. Ibid.
26. Ibid. The United States began to allow IMF financial assistance to Vietnam in 1993 and in February 1994 President Clinton decided to lift the embargo.
27. 'Alexander Watson Speaks on Cuba's Readmission to OAS', *CubaInfo*, 6:2, 28 January 1994, p.1.
28. The UN General Assembly in 1992 and 1993, the Ibero-American Summit

of Heads of State in July 1993, the European Parliament in 1993 and the Vienna Human Rights Conference in 1993 all passed resolutions against the US embargo of Cuba.

29. Interview with Frank Moss, IMF, 31 January 1994.
30. Interview with George Plinio Montalván, 1 February 1994.
31. Ibid., p.93.
32. Pujol, 'Possible Role of International Financial Institutions', p.1 (World Bank section).
33. Rolando H. Castañeda and George P. Montalván, 'In Search of a Way Out for Cuba: Reconciliation, Stabilization and Structural Reform', Paper presented at the 1993 Annual Meeting of the Eastern Economic Association, Washington, DC, 19 March 1993, pp.38, 40; interview with the authors, 9 August 1993; and Joaquín P. Pujol, 'Membership Requirements in the IMF: Possible Implications for Cuba', *Vol. 1, Cuba in Transition: Papers and Proceedings of the First Annual Meeting of the Association for the Study of the Cuban Economy (ASCE), August 15–17, 1991* (Miami: Latin American and Caribbean Center, Florida International University, 1991) p.101.
34. Interview with Enrique Lagos, OAS, 10 September 1993.
35. Organización Panamericana de la Salud, *Informe final. 111a Reunión* (CE111/FR (Esp.). 1 julio de 1993, p.6; and participant observation of Cuban participation on the Health Research Advisory Committee, Washington, DC, 2–5 August 1993.
36. Feinsilver, *Healing the Masses*, pp.179–81; interview with Dr. José Romero Teruel, Director, Division of Health and Development, Pan American Health Organization, Washington, DC, 14 September 1993.
37. Boris Yopo H., 'Latin American Perspectives on the Cuban Transition', *Cuba Briefing Paper Series* Georgetown University Centre for Latin American Studies, Number 3, July 1993.

6 Cuba's Foreign Policy in the 'Special Period'*

Luis Suárez Salazar

INTRODUCTION

In this chapter, I will refer broadly and in a schematic manner to the internal economic, political and ideological processes which, together with the dynamic of the international situation, have conditioned the projection abroad of the Cuban Revolution. Hence, the chapter title, with which I hope to emphasize the inseparable, but not mechanical or linear, relationship that exists between developments within the Cuban domestic situation (for three years officially referred to as the *special period in times of peace*) and events in Cuba's foreign policy.

A BRIEF CONTEXTUALIZATION

In 1992, Cuban society began to suffer the effects at all levels of what President Fidel Castro referred to as the first year of the special period.[1] Among other variables, the following characterize the internal aspects of this moment in history: (1) great difficulties in sustaining the population's individual and social consumption; (2) the critical situation in the supply of fuel and other products, as well as agricultural and industrial inputs; (3) the accompanying decline, for the third consecutive year, in all macroeconomic indicators; (4) the growth of incipient discontent (not necessarily anti-systemic) among the populace; (5) the activation of a minuscule, ununified and personalized counterrevolutionary 'dissidence', stimulated by the United States; and (6) as paradoxical as it may seem to some analysts of the Cuban situation, the continuation of support from the majority of the populace for actions undertaken by the political leadership of the

---

* This chapter further develops and presents an article written under the same title (still unpublished) submitted in early 1993 to *Anuario de Políticas Exteriores Latinoamericanas* (Latin American Foreign Policy Annual), which has been publishing the PROSPEL programme in Santiago, Chile. It would not have been possible without the assistance of Elsa Barreras, head of the Scientific Information Section of the CEA, which annually produces *Cronología Básica de Cuba* (Basic Chronology of Cuba).

country in order to overcome the situation and, as quickly as possible, once again find the road to the self-sustaining development and independence of the island.

The preparation for and carrying out of the municipal and general elections of, respectively, December 1992 and February 1993 (along with other events, like the massive celebration of May Day in 1993) are testimony to this latter factor. These elections were held within the new legal–political framework created by the reform of the constitution and electoral law, passed in July and October 1992, respectively, by the *Asamblea Nacional del Poder Popular*. The high level of popular participation in these processes demonstrated the legitimacy of the one-party political system which currently exists in Cuba. The election of multiple representatives from the ranks of the Communist Party of Cuba and the Union of Young Communists, as well as the absolutely minimal level of null or blank votes, are evidence that, among the majority of politically active Cubans, there exists a clear understanding of the predominantly exogenous reasons which have determined the complex situation through which Cuban society is currently living.[2]

I do not wish to play down the effect, among the many contradictions that characterize the Cuban situation, that the inability of the country to transcend the physical and structural limits of its economy and international relations has had, as well as its well-known errors and inefficiencies (not always overcome in recent years[3]). However, it is undeniable that what has played a prevailing role in the causality of the condition in which the nation finds itself is the hardening of the international context that, in recent years, has surrounded the economic, social, political and ideological/cultural development of the largest of the Antilles.

In the period under analysis, the disappearance of the Soviet Union and the reversion of socialism, and ambience of instability established in the greater part of the former Soviet republics (in particular, the Russian federation) have had a particular impact on the Cuban situation. This has created a crisis, as yet not overcome, within Cuban strategic/military, political/diplomatic, commercial, scientific/technical and economic relations. Empirical evidence of the significance that the disintegration of the USSR has had for Cuban society is seen in the following factors: the atmosphere of incompleteness that has surrounded the economic relations of the former Soviet republics with the island; the paralysis of 80 joint-investment projects, including the Juraguá Nuclear Power Center; the loss of an extensive complementary market for Cuban foreign trade (obliging the country to seek a rapid geographic relocation of its exports and imports); the deterioration of the terms of trade in reciprocal commerce, with the consequent fall in Cuban import capacity; the removal of the Soviet military brigade that had been on the island since 1962; and the support or abstention of Russia and/or other republics of the unstable Confederation of Independent States (CIS) for some of the anti-Cuban policy actions of the United States.[4] Despite their importance, the recent commercial agreements between Russia and Cuba do not mean a qualitative change in the type of relationship described above.

In a certain way, deriving from the above processes, there was, simultaneously, an undeniable hardening on the part of the Bush administration of the economic and political blockade imposed on Cuba, along with the strengthening of American actions aimed at 'democratically subverting' the Cuban political model. Presidential approval, in October 1992, of the so-called Cuban Democracy Act (internationally known as the Torricelli Bill) consolidated and renewed the arsenal of actions developed by American circles of power over more than three decades, in order to smother the Cuban people.[5] Particularly demonstrative of this intention are the penalties dictated within the Act against subsidiaries of American firms, established in third countries, that trade with Cuba, especially in food and medicines lacking in the Cuban market. It is also seen in the threats extended by the United States against foreign governments (and other economic actors) that maintain relations with the island.

The passing of this law was preceded by American official indifference towards the planning and realization of terrorist actions against Cuba by radical Cuban counterrevolutionary groups within the United States,[6] by the ratification of budgets for the operation of the so-called Radio and TV Martí, by the increase in congressional funds explicitly directed to the internal subversion of the Cuban government, by continuing pressure against Cuba within the framework of the UN Human Rights Commission, by difficulties created by the American government in telephone communication between Cuba and the United States, and by the continuation of threatening military manoeuvres in the Caribbean and within Guantánamo Naval Base itself. With reference to this final point, former Head of the Joint Chiefs of Staff Colin Powell has reaffirmed that the goal of official US action is to overthrow the Cuban government within as short a time as possible.[7]

Despite undeniable positive changes in the rhetoric concerning Cuba, and some action in the practical field (disincentives to terrorism, approval of visits by American doctors to Cuba, the search for means of normalizing telephone communications and new talks on immigration) the administration of William Clinton still has not substantially modified the legal–political framework laid down by his predecessors.

To the aforementioned adverse factors are also added the endurance of existing asymmetries in the development of North–South economic relations. Demonstrative of this reality are the vicissitudes of the GATT Uruguay Round, the strengthening of the European Economic Community's protectionist agricultural policy and the treatment that continues to be given to the external debt problem of the less developed world, together with the limitations which are constantly imposed on official development assistance programmes, now that they are also under siege from demands resulting from the reversion to capitalism of Eastern and Central Europe, German unification and the equalization of economic conditions in Greece, Spain and Portugal in order to fully integrate them into the European Union (EU). In the case of Cuba, this is expressed in the constant fall of the prices of its principal export products (sugar, nickel, citrus fruits and so on), in the deterioration of its trading relations and in the lack of political will on the part of its creditors (particularly from Western Europe, but also from Japan) to seek out mutually advantageous solutions to the renegotiation of Cuban external debt (calculated at approximately US$ 6.5 billion in 1991). This is also seen in the unilateral cancellation of some development aid projects implemented on the island. All of this has greatly limited the entrance of fresh resources into the country, which might have relieved the critical situation existent in its balance of payments. The flow of foreign direct investment into the island, although important, is still not enough to modify the situation.

In the political realm, the short-term deepening of the tendency, characterizing the workings of the current world system, towards a unipolar strategic–military (and North-centric political–economic) ordering under American hegemony, acts against Cuba. Above all, this is because, despite its importance, the growing resistance to the evil known as the 'New World Order' is not sufficient to generate an appropriate security and sovereignty space for all the world's nations, and particularly for those less-developed countries that, like Cuba, decide to construct alternative models to that advocated by the central capitalist powers. The intention of the hegemonic powers of the global system of imposing a regime of limited sovereignty on the greater part of the world's nations is confirmed by, among other facts, the difficulties imposed by the United States on the political solution of the Korean Peninsula conflicts, the indifferent attitudes of the central powers towards violations by Israel and South Africa of agreements and resolutions of the UN Security Council, the contrasting strictness in the application of similar resolutions against Libya and Iraq, and the support given to the 'humanitarian military intervention' in Somalia. These interventionist intentions have also revealed themselves in the modification of the constitution and structures of the UN promoted by new Secretary-General, Boutros-Ghali, and – at the Inter-American level – in the modifications successfully pushed through by the United States and certain of its regional allies to allow the OAS, under the pretext of the defence of democracy, to transcend the principles of non-intervention which, despite practical violations (mainly unilateral on the part of the regional hegemon), had governed the operation of this Pan-American organization. This, in the case of Cuba, imposes vast social and economic costs due to expenditures for the defence of the country's sovereignty.

In the period under consideration, the perception of the internal and international realities outlined above have determined, in our analysis, that the Cuban political and state leadership will continue (as in preceding years) to promote a combination of policies with the goals of (1) preserving, through popular organization and mobilization (the so-called *guerra de todo el pueblo* – All People's War), the island's security and self-determination; (2) working to guarantee the equal distribution of the social effects of the crisis, and of the adjustment that is currently being attempted; (3) raising the levels of electricity and food assured by the government; and (4) implementing new options (such as associations with foreign private capital) directed at complementing state efforts to reactivate the national economy and create new bases of domestic accumulation for the reinsertion of the Cuban economy into the capitalist world market. New investments made in the tourism sector, in the production and commercialization of biotechnology products for the pharmaceutical industry and for agriculture, and in high-technology medical teams, form a part of Cuban efforts directed at generating new economic complementarities which might link the country to dynamic sectors of the international economy.

Complementary to realizing these efforts through guaranteeing a resuscitated and self-sustaining Cuban economy in the medium run, new steps have been consolidated, directed at deepening the democratic workings of the country's political system. To the aforementioned changes to the constitution and electoral law have been added – in keeping with the resolutions of the IV Congress – the processing of a wide reform within the statutes of the Communist Party of Cuba and new experiments with respect to the participation of workers in the process of the planning and control of productive management, as well as to the teaching of labour law. In the same way, decentralizing measures have been taken in the management of the finances and foreign trade of the more than 500 Cuban state firms, and in the operation of municipal governments. The extension, at the national level, of the *Consejos Populares* (Popular Councils) has created a new, decentralizing authority in the popular control of the activities of local authorities. The law regulating independent work and modifications passed in the area of agricultural property are aimed at the decentralized processing of some economic decisions.

NECESSARY REDEFINITIONS

All of the superficial and schematically proclaimed actions within the internal sector have interacted with a clear process of the redefinition of the objects, priorities, methods and institutional actors that participate in the design and implementation of Cuban foreign policy. The changes introduced increasingly recognize (although not always sufficiently[8]) the profound transformations of all types which have been produced in the international situation. They also recognize the sharpening of contradictions that have always existed between the strategic objectives of the Cuban projection abroad and the limited material power of the nation to achieve these by itself. This is all the more true under the conditions of the 'special period' to which we have referred.

Without wishing to be exhaustive, I would identify the following changes in the design and projection of Cuban foreign policy:

(1) For Cuba, in its present internal and international circumstances, the *principal objective* of its foreign policy has grown to be (more than ever before, since the first years of the 1960s) the defence of its threatened national sovereignty and the search by all possible ways and means to preserve the principal achievements of the socialist system being constructed in Cuba, as well as building a renewed security area within the world system.

(2) In this context, the defeat or radical modification of the economic blockade imposed by the United States, and the isolation of the more aggressive postures enduring within American circles of power, have become *one of the principal priorities* of Cuban foreign policy. The moderate sector within the United States could play a part in this goal, although the Cuban government has publicly assessed some negative movements made in relation to Cuba by President Clinton.

(3) Interacting with the previous priority is the obvious need for the island to stabilize and geographically relocate all of the integrationist, commercial, financial, scientific–technical and cooperative/development links that it once had with the socialist community, in particular with the now-defunct Soviet Union and Democratic

Republic of Germany. *Economic diplomacy* will have to contribute to guaranteeing, in the short run, the survival and reactivation of the economy and, in the medium run, a widespread resuscitation of Cuban economic development.

(4) Among these goals, the development of the island's relations with countries of socialist orientation is important. From some of these (such as China, Vietnam and Korea), Cuba seeks both room for the growth of economic exchange and reserves for maintaining the operation of the country's military defensive system. However, within the discourse and practice of Cuban foreign policy, the accent that formerly was placed on the strengthening of the so-called socialist community has disappeared. This is not only because its virtual non-existence has left such statements hanging in the vacuum, but is also due to the Cuban understanding that the historic confrontation between capitalism and socialism, without disappearing, no longer has the same importance as before.

(5) Consequently, for Cuba, there is a new relevance in the development of relations with various state and non-state actors of what is still called the First World, as well as with what was formerly known as the Second World. This will be particularly important with those that maintain an attitude of respect for the political system of the island and are perceived as obstacles to the more aggressive plans against it that continue incubating within American circles of power. Given the disappearance of the USSR and the inconsistencies of the foreign policy of the People's Republic of China, the encouragement of the various divisions and contradictions existing between the United States and the governments of other Western countries will have to contribute to the creation of new *factors of stability* favourable to Cuba, between the powers which today dominate the global system. Put another way, traditional, but relatively marginal (above all in the economic sector), differentiated political relations[9] that the Cuban government has maintained with the principal of central capitalism are now to be called upon to contribute decisively to Cuba's goal of *confronting the clear international tendency towards unipolarity dominated by the United States* which prevails in the workings of the international system. From the same perspective, Cuba could also obtain benefits from the multipolarity (at least economic, but also political-military) that it would simultaneously be creating.

(6) The above has not been, nor will be, an obstacle for Cuba in maintaining and renewing its multiple relations and common interests

with the developing countries of Asia, Africa and especially Latin America. Nor should it prevent Cuba from reinforcing actions within international organizations (like the Nonaligned Movement and the Group of 77) expressing the interests of the dominated Third World. This could be achieved, above all, through Cuba's understanding of the growing importance of North–South contradictions in the workings of the world system. The continued articulation, in the theory and practice of Cuban foreign policy, of its support for all of the national and international economic, social and political grievances of the countries of the *South* forms a significant part of present Cuban efforts to confront the *North-centric tendencies* which prevail in the world system. These links with other less-developed nations must also contribute to the essential development of previously unknown forms of *South–South cooperation.* With all due respect to present Cuban humanitarian cooperation with relatively less-developed countries, South–South cooperation in the future will have to be based more on triangular agreements with international organizations and on mutually beneficial bilateral agreements than on unilaterally expressed solidarity on the part of Cuba.

(7) Within the previous context, the development of economic, political, cultural and scientific–technical relations with Latin America and the Caribbean has acquired particular importance for Cuba. It is obvious that, despite their past or present weaknesses, the governments of the continent play a dynamic role in Cuba's historic conflict and present relationship with the United States. Despite some isolated cases (like that of Argentina), this is also due to the fact that present Latin American and Caribbean conduct defies American plans, not only to isolate the Cuban government, but also to use the region's governments as a source of indirect pressure on Cuba to modify its political and social system in a way that would be favourable to US interests. Within the subcontinent, respect for Cuban self-determination remains predominant, in spite of critical judgements and counterproductive actions. This creates a wide range of possibilities for Cuban relations with Latin America and the Caribbean, as recognized recently by the Cuban government with the conferring of constitutional status on its goals of harmonizing, integrating and collaborating with the countries of the region.[10]

(8) In recent years, but particularly in the period under study, the realization of this goal of harmonization with less-developed countries has been reinforcing the growing importance that Cuban foreign policy offers – through its methods – to international forums

(particularly in the UN system) in confronting the unipolar and North-centric tendencies that characterize the global system. Although Cuba has always worked constructively within the UN, it was not until very recently that, as the result of new circumstances, by its own and foreign will, it converted this organization (including the Security Council) into a forum for confronting the anti-Cuban policy of the United States. In the UN, as in other multilateral spheres (like the Earth Summit, the Conference of Ibero-American Heads of State and Governments, and the World Conference on Human Rights), Cuba has also promoted other dimensions of its international policy. This has included in particular those likely to be decided in its favour, given present tendencies in North–South relations. That aspect of Cuban foreign policy that we could describe as *the development of multilateralism against the unipolarism and North-centrism of the international system* should be emphasized in the near future of Cuba's international relations.

(9) In order for Cuba's support of multilateralism against unipolarity and North-centrism to advance efficiently, the expansion of the democratic workings of the United Nations system, particularly its General Assembly and Security Council, is required. For this reason, it is useful to affirm that the struggle for the democratization of the UN (although for a long time present in the theory and practice of Cuban foreign policy) has now acquired a new level of priority. The measures for modifying the composition of the Security Council, annulling or regulating the power of veto of some of its members, making transparent its workings and imposing limits on its resolutions and actions, together with strengthening the role of the General Assembly, form and will form increasingly a part of the statements and practice of Cuban diplomacy.[11]

(10) However, within Cuban international policy, the growing priority of the deployment of all of its inter-state relations does not ignore the importance that the country's political and state leadership has historically conferred on the development of a wide range of connections with multiple and diverse non-state actors from the various countries of the world. The enrichment of these connections with parties and political movements of different ideological tendencies and, in particular, with those of the plural and diverse left of the world and the region has increased links to non-governmental organizations, and with various groups of different beliefs who display sympathy for, and solidarity with Cuba. This has been done through the development of the relations of group actors from Cuban society

(union, women's and youth groups) with their counterparts from abroad. This has been favoured by a policy of openness on religious issues established as much by the Communist Party of Cuba as by the modifications that were recently introduced in the constitution of the Republic.[12] This is occurring in the same way that the changes produced in the constitution, in laws and in the design of foreign policy (in particular the search for different types of associations with foreign private capital) have opened new and growing connections with non-governmental economic actors.[13] On the other hand, it also recognizes the growing importance acquired by private capital, which has been more or less transnationalized in current developments in the international economy. Moreover, this has tended to create special interest groups favourable to Cuba within those nations whose governments maintain negative or hostile policies towards the Cuban revolutionary phenomenon, including within the United States itself.[14]

(11) The combined action of the aforementioned elements has meant that the search for and realization of various actions of solidarity with Cuba have been converted into one of the most dynamic aspects of the current projection abroad of the Cuban Revolution. There is no doubt that the development of reciprocal solidarity has always formed a part of the island's international interactions. However, international solidarity has taken on a new quality, even contributing to the resolution of the concrete economic and social problems suffered by the island as a consequence of the American blockade and/or the abrupt reduction of its import capacity. Beyond its greater or lesser material importance (which it also has), solidarity has been generating a wide moral–political space that acts in favour of the defence of Cuban national sovereignty and imposes limits on more actions against the revolution, even acting within American society. This solidarity also counteracts the tendency towards the international ideological isolation placed on the island's leadership by the collapse of European socialism.

(12) Among the majority of official and unofficial actors involved in the design and implementation of Cuban foreign policy, it is recognized that international solidarity is a 'two-way street'. Thus, in the theory and practice of the Cuban projection abroad, there remains a clear anti-imperialist and international solidarity commitment towards the peoples of the world who struggle to produce transformations of different types in their corresponding societies and/or in the international setting. But the projection of internationalist and anti-

> imperialist solidarity does not and cannot have today the same priority that it formerly had in the design and implementation of the foreign policy of the revolution. Such a switch, without doubt, recognizes the changes that have been produced in the international and Latin American situations, but also expresses the self-consciousness of the Cuban political leadership concerning the fact that the limited material power currently possessed by the island imposes changes on the specific methods and forms of executing its vocation of solidarity and anti-imperialism. It also seeks to resolve in practice the objective contradictions that certain forms and methods of Cuban solidarity (like its military commitments) generate with different international governmental and non-governmental actors needed by Cuba in order to complete the objectives and principal priorities of its foreign policy. These changes also remove elements of domestic and international legitimacy from those in the United States who would continue promoting aggressive actions such as the blockade or 'humanitarian' military intervention in Cuban domestic affairs. They lay bare the inherent meddling nature that has historically acted as a principal motivation for the anti-Cuban policy of the United States.

All of this dynamic for change in Cuban foreign policy has had an impact on the institutional actors that participate in the elaboration and implementation of it. The year 1992 and the first part of 1993 were, without a doubt, the period of the greatest ever simultaneous change in the political and governmental organizations and institutions that participate in the development of Cuban international relations. For various reasons (too extensive to analyse here) certain figures, that have historically been involved in the choosing and implementation of this policy, have been relieved of their positions. Beyond individual reasons, or those of a domestic political nature, the fact points to a diversification and renovation of the roles of the institutional actors participating in the realization of the international objectives of the revolution.

As such – although it is worth affirming that, in the completion of the strategic objectives of Cuban foreign policy, all of the institutional actors traditionally affecting it continue to take part – the process of a revaluation of these roles is appreciated, in keeping with current objectives and priorities. While preserving the managing role of the Communist Party of Cuba in the workings of all of society, and specifically in the development of inter-party political relations, the various institutional actors linked to the development of state policies have acquired a new relevance. Together with the strengthened role played by the Ministry of Foreign Affairs, a wide space has also been opened for the participation of institutional actors linked to the execution of international economic relations. These have had to confront the aforementioned stabilization and geographic relocation of all of the island's economic relations, but also play an important role in the formation of different types of associations with foreign capital. These associations, as already indicated, are perceived of increasingly as being necessary to complete efforts directed at reactivating the economy, geographically and structurally diversifying foreign trade, creating new axes of internal accumulation and reinserting the country into 'leading edge' sectors of the current world capitalist economy. Only in this way, from the perspective of the end of the century, can Cuba occupy a new area in the present capitalist international division of labour.

The increased resuscitation of the Cuban economy and the solidification of its capacity to sustain itself obviously have an intricate relationship with the necessities of the defence of national sovereignty and the projection abroad of the socialism being constructed in Cuba. In the same way, this last variable is interwoven with the country's capacity to deepen the democratic workings of all of its institutions. Independent of the internal importance of the issue, Cuban foreign policy will only continue being successful if – as until now – it continues counting on the conscious, organized and democratic support of the majority of its citizenry and of the various institutions of civil society.

AN INCOMPLETE ACCOUNTING OF A POLICY

All the data necessary to undertake a detailed accounting of the achievements and failures of the foreign policy developed in Cuba during the 'special period' are still not available to social and political researchers. However, there is not the least doubt that its principal success has been its contribution to the island's ability to conserve importance spaces within the world system, despite the geopolitical and geoeconomic crises created by the disappearance of the USSR and the strengthening of the policy of blockade and aggression by the American government.

This is above all because, also in this period,[15] the Cuban political and state leadership managed to avoid the geopolitical and economic crisis affecting the island expanding into a social, societal, political or ideological crisis that would – as occurred in the countries of Eastern Europe – put the self-perpetuation of Cuban socialism in danger. Perhaps the verification of this fact, together with the successes of some of the programmes promoted by the Cuban government to overcome the crisis, is what has made the official media and President Fidel Castro himself claim that 'in resistance lies the route to victory'.[16]

Beyond the value judgements that might inspire this assertion from some analysts of the Cuban situation, what is certain is that the period under analysis has been satisfactory for the completion of the immediate objects and priorities of the foreign projection of the Cuban Revolution. Despite (or perhaps because of) all of the international changes and its numerous domestic difficulties, the island continues to be seen by many of the world's state and non-state actors as a symbol of the defence of the principle of self-determination against the attacks of the unipolar and North-centric world system to which reference has been made above. This has contributed to avoiding the dangers of the ideological isolation of the leadership of the island that were created by the collapse of European socialism. In the same way, the traumatic transition towards capitalism of the countries of Eastern Europe (and of the USSR itself) has relegitimated, in the eyes of many international actors (above all from the left), the critical position assumed by Cuba towards what, initially, appeared to be a way to overcome the errors and non-functional aspects of *real* European socialism.

All of this – plus the US obsession with destroying the Cuban 'bad example' while going beyond the obligatory territoriality of its domestic laws – is expressed in the growing significance to Cuba of displays of solidarity with it, and in the favourable nature of the island's recent inter-state relations.

On the other hand, the successes of Cuba in its multilateral relations have been expressed in the government's decision, by 103 votes, to remain part of the Economic and Social Council (ECOSOC) of the UN; by the passing by the UN General Assembly of a resolution condemning the blockade imposed by the United States on the island; by the support of Cuban grievances by the Indonesia Summit of the Non-Aligned Countries Movement; by significant international rejection of the Torricelli Bill; by the positive welcome received by President Fidel Castro at the Earth Summit and at the Third Ibero-American Summit, both in Brazil; as well as by the positive Cuban participation in the World Conference on Human Rights held in Austria in June 1993. All of this contributed to dissipating the unpleasantness created by the position of ambivalence towards Cuba of the Spanish government during the Second Ibero-American Summit in Madrid.

These facts were accompanied by the development, on the part of the island's authorities, of a wide range of bilateral actions with different countries (including the new republics arising from the disintegration of the USSR) of Europe, Asia, Africa and the Middle East, and Latin America and the Caribbean, and with Canada. Within these sub-regions – despite US pressures and the existence of some areas of conflict in bilateral relations with Cuba – there has been a predominant rejection of American actions directed at hardening the diplomatic and economic blockade of the island, as well as more or less explicit calls on the administration of William Clinton to modify the legal–political framework that continues to govern American policy against Cuba.

In this way, the European Economic Community (now Union) (as well as Canada) rejected the passing of the Torricelli Bill. Within the European and Canadian perspectives, beyond resistance to the extraterritorial presumptions of the said act, of decisive influence was the identification of Cuba as an area of new opportunities for business and the development of economic relations, with the added benefit of not having to confront American and (until now) Japanese competition.

This recognition of reciprocal interests is also expressed in the conduct towards Cuba of the republics that made up the now defunct Soviet Union. Within a brief time period, Cuba managed to re-establish its diplomatic and commercial relations with the majority of these countries. The government of the Russian Federation, modifying some of its anti-Cuban ideological statements, finally recognized the importance of normalizing its links with the island. For 1994 and the remaining part of 1993, the two countries have arrived at agreements on economic and scientific/technical cooperation, on matters of trade and on the transport of goods. They also agreed that the Lourdes electronic monitoring base would remain on the island. What remained for further study, on both sides, was the possibility of continuing some joint investments, like that of the Juraguá Nuclear Power Center, and what investments would be necessary to protect what has already been built. Seemingly, some projects of joint cooperation were also reactivated.

With respect to Asia, Cuban economic, political, scientific/technical and military relations have continued to develop with the People's Republic of China, the Democratic Republic of Korea and Vietnam. In addition, Cuban political relations with Indonesia have been re-established and increased, relations with India have been maintained at a good level, commerce with South Korea has increased, and new steps have been made (including a visit to Japan by then Foreign Minister Ricardo Alarcón) in seeking solutions to the problems of debt that continue to limit Cuba's relations with Japan.

In the case of Sub-Saharan Africa, the Cuban government has maintained tight links of economic, scientific/technical and cultural cooperation with Angola, Ghana, Zimbabwe, Botswana, Namibia, Zambia, Nigeria, Guinea-Bissau, Burkina Faso and others. With respect to the Middle East, beyond ratifying its position in relation to the struggle of the Palestinian people and against the hardened position of the UN against Iraq, Cuba has taken new steps directed at increasing its economic links of different types with Iran, Egypt, Syria and Algeria.

Relations with Latin America have continued with their positive dynamic of previous years. The anti-Cuban votes of some of the region's governments (such as Argentina, Chile, Uruguay and Costa Rica) in the UN Human Rights Commission, although generating unease within the official media of the island, have not been an obstacle to Cuba's continued development of multifaceted links in the areas of politics, economics and trade, culture, science and technology and sports. Nor have they prevented the region's private capital from continuing its interest in associating itself in different ways with Cuban firms. All of this explains the support, in the UN General Assembly, of the majority of the countries in the region for the Cuban resolution against the blockade, and their general repudiation of the Torricelli Bill.

Support for this resolution was also offered by various countries of the Caribbean. At the heart of this attitude is the growing movement of CARICOM towards Cuba. During the 'special period', this has been favoured by, among other factors, the re-establishing of diplomatic relations between Cuba and Saint Lucia, San Vicente and the Grenadines, by the overcoming of the disagreement with Grenada and by the re-establishing of consular and commercial relations with Belize. All of this facilitated the induction of Cuba into the Tourism Organization of the Caribbean and the positive welcome given to Cuba's application to be admitted as an observer in CARICOM.

This scheme of relations at the bilateral and multilateral levels has acted positively in the global development of Cuban external economic interactions. Cuba has been able to diversify or sustain its markets for nickel, tobacco and other traditional Cuban products, such as shellfish. Growth registered in investment and production in the country's tourist industry has also been praised, as has the signing of new agreements with foreign private capital (European, Latin American and Canadian) for prospecting and exploiting oil and for the reactivation of previously inactive aspects of the Cuban textile industry.[17]

Despite all of the aforementioned, it cannot be ignored that the period under study has also produced some problems for Cuban foreign policy makers. Obviously, the most resonant of these has been Cuba's latest setback in the UN Human Rights Commission. Not even the high level of abstention registered in the voting on the declaration concerning Cuba, the political and technical justification of the Cuban position given the discriminatory and disproportionate treatment implicit in the resolution, or the normal relations maintained by Cuba with all of the members of the Human Rights Commission can erase the complications caused to the country by the Commission's repudiation. This was once again revealed in the minority position in which Cuba found itself in the voting on the issue during sessions of the Human Rights Commission at the beginning of 1993.

To the above are added the difficulties confronted in the Cuban government's relations with some governments from within the region (such as Argentina and Mexico) and outside (such as Spain) that have agreed to receive officially representatives of right-wing organizations (like the National Cuban-American Foundation and the so-called *Plataforma Democrática*) acting among Cuban exiles. The prudence of the official Cuban response to these issues has not managed to hide the disgruntlement produced by them. This is, above all, because, in the case of Mexico, the reception does not given to these groups fit in with the traditional development of Mexican foreign policy and Cuban–Mexican relations; and in the Spanish case, because this type of reception contributed to reducing the effectiveness of the visit made to Spain by President Fidel Castro on the occasions of the second Ibero-American Summit, the Seville World's Fair and the Olympic Games. However, certain developments since that time have worked to eliminate acrimony in the intense relations between Cuba and Spain.

Only the impressive performance of Cuba in the Olympic Games (the island occupied fifth place in world competition) and positive developments at the Third Ibero-American Summit in Bahía have helped to dissipate the disgruntlement produced in some Cuban circles by the indelicate nature of Spanish protocol and the pressured approval of the Declaration of the Second Ibero-American Summit.[18] This statement, in keeping with the ideological times in which we live, canonized representative democracy (in the bourgeois context) as the only form of government acceptable to the members of this particular community of nations, thus ignoring the ambience of ideological and political pluralism that presided over the birth of the Conferences of Heads of State and Government of Ibero-American Countries, in Guadalajara, Mexico. This was rectified, however, in the Third Ibero-American Summit, which took place in Bahía, Brazil.

The aforementioned political developments cannot hide the difficulties that continue to confront the island in the development of its international economic relations. Although, as has already been indicated, Cuba has advanced rapidly in the process of geographically relocating its principal traditional exports (but not yet all of its imports) and has even opened new markets for its non-traditional products and services, the economic authorities of the country are not able to transcend the many asymmetries that characterize international trade. Nor have they been able to resolve the problem of stability in the production of products (such as sugar and tobacco) with an especially strong presence among Cuban exports.

A LOOK AT THE FUTURE

Based on the above, the challenge that will continue weighing on Cuba's reinsertion into the world (more than the aforementioned changes in its foreign policy or domestic political/economic ordering) in the foreseeable future will be the efficient and competitive construction of new economic complementarities and/or dynamic comparative advantages that would allow the country to occupy a different place in the prevailing international capitalist division of labour. However, for this to occur, what will also be required, along with wise and intelligent economic strategies and policies, is the preservation of the conscious and organized support of the majority of the populace for the strategic objectives of the foreign policy that will be implicit in any mode of independent economic, social and political development of the island. Moreover, this support will guarantee internal consensus that will allow for the political time necessary for the consolidation of the alternatives that today are being developed to overcome the crisis, and restructure the economy of the country.

This is all the more true because, in the immediate future, Cuban society will continue to confront a situation of external adversities and internal complexities. The internal difficulties, despite all the increased social and political costs, could be resolved, as they have been until now, by an adequate political and economic process that would conserve the variables of equality and social justice that are the basis of the ideology and practice of the Cuban Revolution, and of the majority support enjoyed by the political leadership of the country.

However, the external adversities escape the control of Cuban authorities. None of the elements which characterize the hardening of the international context in which Cuba finds itself could be reversed in the short term. The continuation of the application of the Torricelli Bill could create renewed difficulties for the country. Furthermore, the atmosphere of instability within the former Soviet republics (in particular in the Russian Federation) could make even the newly adopted agreements unfulfillable. At the same time, there is no reason to suppose that there will be any modification of the economic and political asymmetries that today characterize the workings of the world system. As a result of this, it is predicted that, at least in the short term, there will be no substantial changes in either the objectives or the priorities that at present characterize the projection of Cuba abroad.

The only variation that could arise within this context would have to come from a change in the anti-Cuban policy of the United States. The administration of William Clinton, without doubt, theoretically has the possibility of producing it, given that he is not directly committed to the aggressive policies previously implemented by successive Republican governments, and much less so to those of the former president, George Bush. This change is demanded of Clinton by the international community and some sectors of domestic public opinion, including prominent members of the Democratic Party.

However, a change of policy toward Cuba does not appear to be among the priorities of the present administration. As expressed to me by a respected American colleague, it could perhaps occur before the end of the first thousand days of an administration that wants to use, in its favour, the rehabilitated image of the late President John F. Kennedy, and give a second chance to those who designed the inconsistent foreign policy of former president James Carter.

This possible change would only occur if the Cuban government and people continued to demonstrate their capacities for resisting the present adversities and achieve, by their own efforts, the necessary economic, political and ideological rejuvenation of the socialist project being constructed in Cuba. Otherwise, what sense would it make for a US administration, of any political denomination, to negotiate with a historic adversary that it perceives as being on the verge of collapsing under its own weight and that, moreover, is not inclined to make unilateral concessions to the American 'right'?

It is recognized, however, that this prediction could be wrong. At least in theory, it is possible that, seeking the longer-term collapse of the Cuban regime, the new administration could produce (as some have recommended) significant amendments to the failed policy of blockade and aggressions that, until now, have been implemented against Cuba by US circles of power.

In the event of a unilateral and surprising lifting of the blockade (or of some of its stipulations), the challenge to Cuba would be considerable. The Cuban political and state leadership would have to confront a change in US tactics for which, perhaps, it is not sufficiently prepared. New and hitherto unknown contradictions would appear within the system, ideology and political culture of the Cuban people. It is possible that solutions to some of the problems at present affecting the nation would appear simultaneously with new challenges that would be produced by the loss of an enemy that has contributed to the domestic cohesion of Cuban society and its political leadership.

In any of these cases what would prevail is the historic necessity for the domestic and foreign policy of this small island in the Caribbean to continue defending, at all costs, its sovereignty, right to self-determination and will to insert itself in a favourable and worthy manner into the world of the approaching twenty-first century.

Notes

1. Fidel Castro, closing words of the XII Period of Ordinary Sessions of the Asamblea Nacional del Poder Popular (National Assembly of Popular Power), published in *Granma*, 31 October 1992, pp.5–6.
2. See Luis Suárez Salazar, 'Crisis, reestructuración y democracia en Cuba', in *Cuadernos de Nuestra América*, No. 20, Havana, January–June 1993, pp.66–82.
3. See Luis Carranza Valdés, 'Cuba: los retos de la economía', in *Cuadernos de Nuestra América*, No. 19, July–December 1992, Havana, pp.132–58; José Luis Rdríguez, 'La economía cubana: Algunos problemas actuales y perspectivas', paper presented to the *XVII Congreso de Latin American Studies Association (LASA)*, Los Angeles, 24–6 September 1992.
4. It is well known that Russia voted against Cuba in the forty-eighth Period of Sessions of the United Nations Human Rights Commission, in March 1992, and again in the ECOSOC meeting where the same issue was debated. Russia abstained from voting on the Cuban resolution (passed by the UN General Assembly) condemning the American blockade against the island, and once again voted against Cuba in the forty-ninth Period of Sessions of the UN Human Rights Commission, in February and March 1992.
5. See Andrew Zimbalist, 'The US Blockade Policy and Its Implications for Cuba', text submitted to the Department of Economics, Smith College, Northampton Massachusetts, October 1992. For an official Cuban version, see *Bloqueo (Documentos sobre la política de cerco desplegada por gobiernos estadounidenses contra Cuba)* (Havana: Editora Cultural Popular, 1992).
6. In January 1992, a group from the organization *Comandos L* was infiltrated into Cuba from the United States, with the objective of committing acts of terrorism against the Cuban civil population. In October of the same year, a counterrevolutionary commando fired on facilities of the Hotel Meliá Varadero. The intellectual and material authors of these suprisings do their

training in the areas surrounding Miami, as has been publicly recognized. The Cuban government has denounced the absence of measures against these groups on the part of the United States, despite their violation of American federal laws concerning neutrality and their well-known historic link to US official agencies.

7. See *National Military Strategy of the United States*, January 1992. A synopsis of this strategy was published by General Colin Powell in the article, 'US Force: Challenges Ahead', in *Foreign Affairs*, Winter 1992/3. The threats to which I refer have also been present in various speeches by former US President George Bush, who even reached the point of affirming, in the midst of his post-Persian Gulf War euphoria, that he would be the first US president to visit a 'free and democratic Cuba'. The entire mechanism for an eventual military aggression against Cuba is being kept at the ready.
8. In the author's opinion, the manner in which the issue of human rights is approached in Cuba shows the extent to which the government there has still not sufficiently recognized changes that have occurred in the global ideological context. Something similar occurs with information about Cuba itself which is sent towards the outside world; Cuba does not always understand the code with which messages emitted concerning current realities in Cuba are deciphered. This sometimes generates areas of miscommunication, even with sectors that maintain an attitude of respect and/or sympathy towards the Cuban Revolution.
9. The term 'differentiated relations' with central capitalist countries is explained by Carlos Rafael Rodríguez in his article, 'Fundamentos Estratégicos de la Política Exterior Cubana', in *Cuba Socialista*, no. 1, Havana.
10. In the reforms introduced within the constitutional precepts of Cuban foreign policy, the island's goal of achieving 'integration and collaboration with the countries of Latin America and the Caribbean' was reaffirmed. This did not appear explicitly in the text of the constitution passed in 1976.
11. See Ricardo Alarcón de Quesada, Cuban Minister of Foreign Affairs, speech in the forty-seventh Period of Sessions of the General Assembly of the UN, September 1992.
12. See the Asamblea Nacional del Poder Popular, *Modificaciones a la Constitución de la República de Cuba*, passed by the XI Period of Sessions of the Asamblea Nacional del Poder Popular. In its new statement, Article 8 indicates that 'The state recognizes, respects and guarantees religious freedom. In the Republic of Cuba, religious institutions are separate from the state. The various beliefs and religions enjoy equal consideration.' In this way, the atheist character attributed to the state in the constitution approved in 1976 was eliminated.
13. In the new statement, Article 23 of the Constitution of the Republic of Cuba indicates that 'The state recognizes the property of mixed firms, corporations and economic associations that conform to the law. The use, enjoyment and disposition of goods pertaining to the aforementioned entities are under rule of law and of agreements, as well as of statutes and regulations specific to those that direct them.'
14. In the period under study, Cuba, together with the firm Euromoney, has promoted the presentation of two seminars on investment in Cuba. More

than half of the participant firms were from the United States, indicating the important growth registered in Cuban trade with subsidiaries of American firms and the expectations generated among these of potential relations should the blockade be eliminated.

15. I have indicated this in an earlier work: see Luis Salazar Suárez, 'La crisis cubana actual: un enfoque desde La Habana', *Nueva Sociedad*, no. 121, September–October 1992, Caracas Venezuela, pp.164–173.
16. *Granma*, October 1992.
17. Beyond this, during the 'special period', Cuba has signed a joint investment agreement with Mexican business groups from the area of Monterrey, for the amount of US$ 1 billion. This will put 15 textile plants on the island back to work, giving employment to 33 000 workers and producing 370 million square metres of different types of cloth, most of which will be destined for export.
18. See 'Declaración de la Segunda Cumbre Iberoamericana', in *Cuadernos de Nuestra América*, no. 19, July–December 1992, Havana.

7 The International Reinsertion of Cuba: Emerging Scenarios

Francisco León Delgado*

INTRODUCTION

The reinsertion of Cuba into the international system is taking place in a period of reorganization and globalization of the international and, particularly, the Inter-American economies. The Cuban economy being one which, traditionally, has been open, this reinsertion will transform the basis of Cuba's social and political system and national sovereignty. The processes of national independence (1898–1902) and post-revolutionary international realignment (1959–62) constitute historic precedents for the reintegration currently in progress.

The reinsertion process is not occurring in the midst of the collapse of the current regime and government, and evidence indicates that the international, and particularly the Inter-American, communities would be prepared to accept a rejuvenated version of this government in order to ensure an orderly transition. This possibility reinforces the importance of, and opportunity for, analysis of the scenarios for international reinsertion being considered as preferences and possibilities by the actors currently in power in Cuba. Three of these, in particular, will be the focus of my attention: plural insertion, the Latin American option for international insertion and direct Inter-American insertion.

Particularly since 1986, out of preference and necessity, the Cuban strategy has consisted of maintaining or gaining access to markets and financial sources, and attempting to make the most of all existing opportunities (Russian, Chinese, Spanish, Canadian, Mexican, Colombian, South African and so on). On the basis of past political investments or superficial changes in the political and economic regime, the government has accumulated some partial and precarious successes in the external sector. In the internal

* Cuban, sociologist, vice-president of the Cuban Studies Institute and social affairs official in the Economic Commission for Latin America and the Caribbean since 1971. This chapter expresses the author's personal analysis and is part of a larger research developed independently of his ECLAC work programme.

sector, through not excluding any options, it has been possible for it to maintain or recreate unity between defensive trends and the most diverse aspects of international insertion. Although this has been useful for gaining ground at a crucial moment, it has not served the purpose either of overcoming the current crisis or of maintaining it within manageable limits.

The Latin American option for international insertion has been revealing itself as an alternative since 1993. Until that time, the about-turn of socialist internationalism towards nationalism had favoured Cuban Latin-Americanism, but had not been able to defeat doubts concerning the real potential of interregional commerce, or resistance to adopting the model (Bolivian, Chilean, Colombian, Mexican, Argentinian and so on). From Guadalajara to Bahía, and before long in Cartagena, Cuba has agreed to presidential meetings, no longer to present its commercial and investment preferences to its Latin American brothers, but to solicit, and give thanks for, a return to full integration into the interregional economy. This option is less demanding in its political conditionality – at least in terms of time limits for and means of democratization – and more open to diplomatic recognition, as well as more likely to receive the sympathy of important sectors in the United States and Canada, and various governments of the European Community (EC).

Finally, direct Inter-American insertion arises from the increase in the presence of the United States in the region and, especially, of Miami as an Inter-American centre. At the same time, it arises from the rejection of Cuba by the United States, a factor which links the Cuban government and population to the US administration and Cuban community. Strangely enough, the more convinced Cuban authorities become that the embargo will continue, the more difficult it becomes to resist the direct alternative of Inter-American insertion, which they assume will allow for improved relations with the numerous and powerful Cuban community abroad, bringing with it some economic relief. However, the de facto intensification of economic relations between both parts of the greater Cuban nation, the refusal of the present government to accept political opposition and the necessity for national reconciliation, as well as the continuance both on and away from the island of a distinct Cuban national identity, constitute elements of a puzzle with no easy solutions.

PLURAL INSERTION

It is normal to associate the adoption of this strategy for international insertion with the culmination of the crisis in international socialism, and in particular with the disappearance of COMECON and the USSR. This insertion strategy arises as part of the process of the gradual reformulation of Cuban foreign policy that began with the end of the Brezhnev era and doctrine.

Given the prolonged crisis of succession in the Soviet Union, increased autonomy within the socialist camp – as a result of the diversification and reinforcement of relations with countries outside it – allowed the government in Havana to increase its capacity to negotiate, along with the political and economic benefits it received from the USSR and COMECON. From the beginning of the 1980s a change in foreign policy was obvious, with the increase in Cuba's diversification and liberalization.[1]

The existence of changes in foreign policy that were already under way, and their characteristics at the beginning of the deterioration of relations with Eastern Europe and – especially – the USSR allow us to put the unexpected nature of this situation in relative terms, and evaluate the Cuban capacity to respond to it. Contemporary and recent evaluations reveal the failure of efforts, throughout the 1980s, to increase exports and reverse the deterioration of financial flows from non-socialist countries, and also the stagnation of trade with socialist countries (1986–91) after vigorous growth (10 per cent) during the first half of the decade. Despite measures adopted during the rectification process, the Cuban government did not achieve its strategic economic objectives. Because of the worsening of the steady dissolution of economic relations with the socialist countries, it could not prevent a heavy fall in foreign trade and the paralysis of many of the country's firms.[2]

It is clear that the success of the Cuban government in diversifying its international political relations throughout the 1980s – within the context of the Cold War – represented very important capital for negotiation, but that this suffered a considerable loss in real value with the end of East–West conflict. In this decapitalized position, the Cuban government could hardly attempt to compensate politically for economic weakness (internal and external) with regard to its foreign creditors or territorial neighbours (the United States, Mexico, Colombia, Venezuela) without this being at the price of a radical change in its economic and political model. The rejection of this option, frequently interpreted as the personal and historic stubbornness of the Cuban revolutionary leadership, also corresponded to a large extent to confidence in its potential for international reinsertion, especially considering that this had already occurred, to a certain degree, during the 1980s.

Throughout the present decade, and especially since the former Soviet republics' breaking off of economic relations with Cuba in 1991, the Cuban government has laid out its strategy of plural insertion. Given the impossibility of finding a commercial counterpart capable of replacing the ex-socialist camp in terms of quantities of money or advantages, the government has accepted the challenge of 'geographically relocating all its integrationist, commercial, financial, scientific/technical, and development/cooperative links, with the goal of preserving national sovereignty and the principal achievements of the revolution, and constructing a renewed space for security in the global system'.[3] The primary instrument chosen to achieve this is economic diplomacy, the success of which will be assisted by the country's political links and international solidarity.

From its inception, international reinsertion has been seen as a process with vast internal repercussions 'on economic and other social relations, and on the ideology and way of living of socialists'.[4] These changes, as well as the debate surrounding them, have been accepted within the framework of 'the preservation of the backing . . . of the majority of the population for the strategic objectives of foreign policy' and 'the guarantee of the internal consensus that will lend us the necessary political time . . . to overcome the crisis and restructure the country's economy'.[5] In this sense, the strategy of plural insertion, implemented through widespread national mobilization and participation, has favoured the achievement of internal backing and consensus by not excluding any positions or actors, so long as they respect the motto: 'Everything within the revolution, nothing against the revolution'.[6]

At the same time, clearly surpassing the framework established in the rectification (1987), a process has been initiated for reforms of the productive, institutional and legal apparatus, among them the following: the introduction of private property in association with the state, the decriminalization of the possession of foreign exchange, the authorization of independent work and the formation of fiscal and financial units to control the public deficit. The reorientation of the economy and foreign economic relations is to be achieved 'through the use of instruments and criteria of market efficiency and, at the same time, maintaining the achievements of the revolution with respect to national independence [and] the satisfaction of social necessities in health, education, nutrition and social justice'.[7]

Since the end of 1993, however, evidence has begun to accumulate showing that, beyond the changes in the style of foreign policy and the advances and failures of economic reforms, the problems in the nature and implementation of the strategy of plural insertion demand a change or redefinition of it in the short term. I will now analyse some of the most important of these problems.

The Limits of Diversity

Cuban policy of international reinsertion does not exclude commercial firms or relations, and seeks the utmost flexibility even at the cost of lack of clarity in the regulatory framework for such relations. The formation of joint ventures between the state and foreign capital is illustrative in the respect that now, beyond previously established options, 'any proposition, in the most convenient form for mutual benefit that can be identified by both sides, will be considered'. Furthermore, still recognizing the challenge that confronts the government in inspiring confidence among foreign business leaders and the efforts that it has made to create a legislative and institutional body, it has been declared that 'the Cuban state is assuming this process of liberalization with new flexibility and pragmatism, avoiding all schemes, and has not opted for establishing a complex system of regulations, but for allowing experience itself to set the rules'.[8]

Conflicts between Economic Management and the Mechanism for the Generation of Internal Consensus

The perfection of the generation of internal consensus with respect to external liberalization and economic reform has realized great changes to the National Assembly, through the addition of consultation with workplace constituencies in cases of the passing of economic policy measures. This new form of decision-making is at odds with the demands of managing a process of adjustment and stabilization like that which is currently under way in Cuba. The deferment from January to May, 1994, of decisions concerning fiscal and financial reform, and the dictation of retroactive measures for controlling and punishing large earnings through informal activities are examples of the conflicts generated by this form of operation among those in charge of economic management.

The Economic Inadequacy of the Measures Undertaken

The reorientation of exports and the liberalization of associations with foreign capital, although they have been produced in areas which are dynamic in terms of growth and investment, have been only partial. In particular, the sugar industry has not been included, with the exception of the refining and derivatives industries.[9] Furthermore, it appears that it is precisely the lack of production and export of sugar, and of the exchange of sugar for petroleum with the Soviet Union, that are factors which have generated the most uncertainty and contributed to the decrease in available foreign exchange.[10]

The sector of firms that has benefited from the opening of the Cuban economy to foreign capital 'has been able to maintain an active and growing domestic link within foreign trade, and has begun to generate a new entrepreneurial and labor culture. This has given rise to the appearance of a type of dual economy, with a distinct set of rules for this new emerging sector and for the traditional sector.' Furthermore, although the presence of the emerging sector 'has been essential to the maintaining of a certain (diminishing) level of functioning of the economy, its weight has proved insufficient for inspiring a general process of recuperation'.[11]

The opening up to foreign capital of firms from the traditional industrial sector has been very conscientiously pursued, because of its possible superior effect on the economy from the standpoint of efficiency and competitiveness.[12] Even so, the reorganization of the sector has not been achieved, and its most dynamic firms have been extracted from it. These firms, functioning with rules of exception (concerning labour, credit and so on) lack incentives to seek out complementarity with others from the traditional sector, and incorporate them into their new-found dynamism.

The Weakening of Revolutionary Achievements in Employment, Nutrition, Health and Education

Since the end of 1991 the Cuban economy has entered into a process of adjustment similar to those applied in Latin America during the 1980s. Osvaldo Martínez, current President of the *Comisión de Economia de la Asamblea Popular* (Economic Commission of the Popular Assembly), has already warned that, although political will has worked to protect social achievements in the face of economic contraction, it is impossible to project what will be the course of future events.[13]

Estimates made in 1993 indicated that around one million people, or about one in three workers, were underemployed.[14] The financing of the wages of these workers, as well as 60 per cent of the salaries of the unemployed (plus or minus 10 per cent), is through the issuing of currency which cannot be indefinitely continued, as was recognized in May 1994 through the adoption of measures for the reduction of excess money supply in the hands of the population, and the elimination of subsidies.[15]

Since the beginning of 1993, food scarcity has meant that the government must aim its supply efforts at satisfying the minimal nutritional requirements for maintaining normal health levels.[16] Despite an increase in rationing aimed at ensuring equality of access, there already was a fringe of about one-quarter of the population, made up of the most vulnerable groups, whose income did not equal the cost of their basic food needs.[17] Of these families, 50 per cent are found in the eastern provinces, many living in cities and headed by pensioners.[18]

There has been much discussion in Cuba in recent years concerning the difference between poverty measured in terms of insufficient monetary income and the conditions of education and health which perpetuate poverty, with the conclusion that, at present, access to the latter factors is still guaranteed. However, it is equally assured that the worsening of food and nutritional scarcities, the decline in levels of hygiene and sanitation – especially the quality and quantity of the water supply – and the deterioration and scarcity of housing have caused an increase in sickness and death and a reduction of the efficiency of schooling.

The economic measures adopted in May 1994 constitute the first experience in revolutionary Cuba in which an attempt has been made to absorb almost 11 billion pesos of excess money supply with a view to making changes in the functioning of the economy, affecting subsidies, prices and savings accounts (59 per cent of excess money supply) and embarking on the road towards the elimination or drastic reduction of free services (water) and rights (full or semi-room and board at schools, medical treatment with sophisticated technologies and so on). There remains to be seen not only the internal consistency of a plan 'whose characteristic is its flexibility (nothing is immobile)',[19] but especially – in an open economy like Cuba's – its performance in an external sector whose principal contributor (sugar) remains in weak condition, with no signs of short-term recuperation.

Austerity Reaches Economic Diplomacy

In the context of the economic crisis, the closing down and expansion of diplomatic representations, related to changes in priorities associated with geographic relocation, were to be expected, and have occurred without necessarily implying a reduction of the wealth of opportunities of plural insertion. With the increase of restrictions it was also logical to relocate some of the most experienced diplomats in other areas of external representation, such as tourism.[20] In future, the development of economic diplomacy will have to be based still more on the increasing productivity of its officials, as prolonged financing of the Instituto de Relaciones Internacionales (Institute for International Relations) is relatively uncertain.

THE LATIN AMERICAN OPTION FOR INTERNATIONAL INSERTION

At the beginning of the 1990s, suppositions in vogue concerned the mutual necessities of maintaining trade with the countries of the ex-Soviet camp (especially Russia),[21] the relative advantages of increasing economic relations with countries holding the foreign debt,[22] or the necessity of countries of Latin America and the Caribbean inserting themselves in a subordinate role with, and consolidating their growing dependency on, the United States.[23] The Latin American and Caribbean model for reinsertion or international insertion were not considered as options for Cuba. Moreover, the experiences of debt negotiations in the regions, the clear rejection of the debtors' club mechanism and the accepting of bilateral negotiation were still fresh and, perhaps, had not been adequately enough evaluated by those specialists in Cuba who saw them as another demonstration of weakness before the United States.

Changes in Cuban Perception

Within the last three years, Cuban government specialists and authorities have changed their suppositions and expectations of the beginning of the decade, in particular the following.

(1) While in 1990/91, the possibility was accepted of recuperating a level of relations with the countries of the ex-COMECON, a recent evaluation,[24] emphasized the possibilities with the relatively less developed countries (Bulgaria and Rumania).

(2) Similarly, in the case of China, some analysts do not consider it possible, because of problems in the supply process, that Cuba could take advantage of the growing Chinese market, or guarantee equal exchange with that country.[25] In addition, Vietnam, the Democratic Republic of Korea and Mongolia are recognized as trading areas with which it would be difficult to move beyond traditional levels of trade.[26]

(3) While the 1990/91 analysis displayed concern about the negative effect of political conditionality,[27] relations with the European Community are today appreciated for 'the decisive contribution that they could make for confronting the clear tendencies of unipolarity under the hegemony of the United States'.[28] In contrast, present fears arise more from the greater difficulties of exporting to a unified Europe, and competition from European exporters, especially in the area of

sugar.[29] Japan, meanwhile, maintained its importance as Cuba's second largest Asian trading partner, after China.

(4) The increased importance of Inter-American trade, especially with Latin America and the Caribbean, is without doubt the central feature in Cuban foreign trade in recent years.[30] The proportion of total Cuban exports that are Inter-American doubled (7 per cent to 14 per cent) between 1990 and 1993.[31] At the same time, this shows the growing independence of Canada, and Latin America and the Caribbean, with respect to the United States, in their economic and political relations.

New Regional Scenarios

The radical change of Cuba's external policy towards the Latin American option for international insertion[32] is associated with a combination of will and political realities, which might be summarized as follows.

(1) In 1993, the economy of Latin America grew for the third consecutive year, continued the reduction of inflation rates and the growth of imports and exports, and maintained its net financial capital inflows.

(2) Regional participation in the global market, after more than two decades of decline, is on the rise, awakening a renewed and growing interest among traditional and emerging enterprises attracted by the liberalization of imports and the success of export efforts.[33]

(3) In recent years, the degree of economic independence of the countries of Latin America has strengthened, measured with respect to trade and investment. This is not only due to formal agreements which have been ratified and applied, but also to the de facto integration that has been possible thanks to geographic proximity and existent markets, in a new context of liberalization, deregulation and globalization.[34] Far from counteracting one another, interregional and extraregional trade have reinforced each other. This is good news for Cuban officials interested in maintaining and increasing their opportunities in extraregional markets. In fact, in the case of Russia, one area of recent interest is joint production with Cuba for export to Latin America and the Caribbean.

(4) With respect to the asymmetry of economic relations with the United States in the context of the Enterprise for the Americas Initiative, which has been a source of much concern for Cuban authorities and specialists, a situation favourable to reducing the economic and political impacts of this unequal relation is found in the process of Latin American regional integration and in the growing Latin American

orientation of Canada. The present freedom with which Chile has decided to confront simultaneously the initiation of negotiations with the United States and with the countries of Mercosur (Argentina, Brazil, Paraguay and Uruguay) is a good example of the wider margins for action towards regional integration.

(5) Although this is happening concurrently with the US 'reassertion of hegemony' in Latin America and the Caribbean, at the same time we see that the United States will use instruments of approach and pursuit with important countries, reserving coercion for those that, in its estimation, are problematic.[35] Among these, without doubt, is Cuba, against which economic sanctions continue to be applied even in the post-Cold War period, reinforced by the Torricelli Bill which, reminiscent of the Platt Amendment, leaves judgement over democracy in Cuba in the hands of Congress and the President of the United States.

The arbitrary and anachronistic nature of the sanctions and the illegitimate nature of the US judgement of Cuba are recognized in the rejection of these measures by the General Assembly of the United Nations and the Ibero-American presidents. At the same time, the Cuban government sustains, on the basis of ideological pluralism, its definitions of democracy and human rights, resisting international efforts by achieving and guarding its own social norms.[36] This goes against the present current of the tendency to consecrate the principle of limited sovereignty and the criterion of 'qualified' intervention under certain conditions,[37] especially based on petitions by international (the United Nations Security Council) or regional consensus (The Council of the Organization of American States).

The changes of the last few years have consisted fundamentally of recognizing the Inter-American character of both the problem between Cuba and the United States and that of its solution.[38] At the operative level, it has been proposed to make use of the good offices of a wide range of ad hoc groups, especially El Grupo de Los Tres (Colombia, Mexico and Venezuela), to achieve the economic and political reintegration of Cuba into the Inter-American community.[39] The idea of an agenda for transition, replacing the conditionality previously established by the Organization of American States, is the centrepiece of the informal dialogue now under way, in which extraregional interests and governments are also playing a part.

Conditionality and Transition

Seemingly, the Latin American option for international insertion arises with the replacement of *conditionality* by *transition*. This brings us to the analysis of the obstacles (conditionality) and the objectives and means (transition): among the former, mutual distrust, the speed of changes in the scenario and the rigidity of the principle actors; among the aspects of transition, only economic and political factors will be considered.

The framework for this option has been the enthusiastic attitude and varied menu of options and alternatives put forward by the Latin American and extraregional participants, influenced by their own experiences (Spain, Chile, El Salvador, Nicaragua and so on) and those of other countries (such as Israel/Palestine, South Africa). It is surprising that, despite frustrations in Russia and Eastern Europe, the majority of participants continue to believe in the possibility of making a transition while maintaining achievements in employment, health and education, thanks to the development of human capital over the last 30 years. Preventing the failures of post-socialist Russia and Eastern Europe constitutes a major motivating factor.

Within this framework, what stands out in the official discourse of Cuban authorities and, to a lesser extent, specialists both within and outside the island is the resistance to renouncing their radical specificity and to learning from other experiences. In the same way, they are afraid of repeating the errors of the reforms undergone in the socialist camp – rapid changes under conditions of economic contraction divisions between the political class and the party, the renunciation of the party and its guiding role, allowing anti-socialist forces access to means of communication, and so on.[40] Both resistance to learning from successful experiences of transition and fear of repeating mistakes favour immobility, as much as or more than the difficulties of undergoing reforms and simultaneously maintaining the unity and discipline of forces and interests that make possible the continuation of revolutionary power on the island.

Within the United States and the Cuban community abroad, it is almost a matter of faith that a change will occur which will allow the creation of a socioeconomic milieu favourable to free enterprise and a reduced role of the state,[41] opening up to a market economy and the integration of the island into the global economic system. The orientation and form of political change, however, are the object of speculation with a number of possible variants, and no consensus among specialists[42] or political actors. Implicitly or explicitly (the Torricelli Bill), the United States and the Cuban American Community will make effective their conditionality on the subjects of human rights, freedom of the press, political pluralism and other issues through formal international mechanisms (the United Nations Human Rights Commission, for example). Obviously, the result will be a transition towards an uncertain situation.

It is this growing impasse in relations between the principal actors that brings them to solicit, accept and allow other Latin American actors to expand their presence in the Cuban transition. This presence, however, has tended to be justified less and less by reasons of regional or sub-regional security – associated with a possible civil war in Cuba or massive exodus to the countries of the Caribbean Basin – and, along with this, military–political solutions and measures have lost their moment of usefulness. In their place, commercial agreements, trade and measures to accelerate economic reforms which could speed Cuba's international economic reinsertion become of greater importance. Behind this, no doubt, is the undisguised assumption that economic transformations will facilitate political transformations.

The change in the approach to the problem is radical in the extent to which it associates conditionalities, the speed of economic reforms and commercial integration with the ability to respond of the Cuban government, economy and society. However, this is not a transition, a route, to an unknown destination. Well-meaning groups, dialogue in presidential meetings and day-to-day relations cause the political climate of Cuba and its Latin American spokesmen to evolve. In the short term, a real induction of Cuba into any of the sub-groups of regional integration is not probable. At its rate of change and level of internal and external economic and financial deterioration, it would be difficult for Cuba to achieve macroeconomic stability, the stabilization of adequate mechanisms for payment, the reduction of impenetrable non-tariff barriers and other elements[43] which would allow meaningful participation in integration schemes.

For Cuba, the most important aspect of the Latin American option is that it constitutes an opportune and efficient solution to the pernicious effects of economic sanctions imposed by other states. As is known, the combination of the embargo and the moratorium on Cuban foreign debt in convertible currency[44] has limited Cuba's access to the world's most important markets (such as the United States, EC/EU and Japan) and, in particular, to financial markets. Cuba has been limited to the unpredictable attraction of private foreign direct investment under exceptional conditions (high profit rates, tax exemptions, immediate repatriation of profits and so on) in order to compensate for risks[45] and the limited possibilities for expansion of foreign exchange earnings. Obviously, in the external sector, the Cuban economy, like no other before it in Latin America, cannot surmount its current crisis without an increase in the net flow of foreign capital and a sustained expansion of its foreign trade, particularly exports.[46]

Given that Cuban interregional trade has recently reached the same levels as before the crisis of the 1980s – 14 per cent of the total – how could Latin America and the Caribbean provide a solution for Cuba to the embargo problem? Some factors which would permit this are the following.

(1) Cuban imports from Latin America and the Caribbean, to a great extent favoured by the embargo, satisfy a greater and growing part of the demand for imports generated by international tourism and remittances from the Cuban community abroad. The expansion of tourist income, which may have reached US$ 1 billion in 1993, has been the principal attraction for Mexican, Colombian, Panamanian, Dominican and Chilean trade with Cuba. In general, to make such exports to Cuba possible, governments have created ad hoc foreign trade financing mechanisms.

(2) The expansion of sectors of the Cuban economy functioning in foreign exchange has increased possibilities for import-substituting production, which is generated by income from tourism and remittances. Some Latin American investors and enterprises are becoming involved in import-substituting activities.

(3) Since the end of the 1980s, Latin American business leaders have been attracted to opportunities in Cuba by their own experiences in working within economies in crisis, and in the development of exports. Their efforts went initially into activities directed at reorienting exports from the Soviet and East European markets towards the West (citric fruits, for example), but are at present expanding into exports to Latin America and the Caribbean (for example, pharmaceutical products, medical and tourist services).

(4) Petroleum-producing countries in the Caribbean Basin (Colombia, Mexico, Venezuela) offer particular advantages for the supply of oil to Cuba, including triangular trade operations with Russia. With respect to two of these (Mexico and Venezuela) Cuba has a relative advantage in sugar production and, with all of them, there exist clear complementarities in the development of multi-destination tourism flows from Europe, North and Latin America.

(5) The importance of foreign trade, investment and financing, generated through activities like those noted above, now constitutes a critical mass capable of playing a decisive role in Cuban international reinsertion and transition.

(6) The Latin American option is complementary to other opportunities for Cuban international reinsertion and thus moves the Cuban economy towards conforming itself to this model. This would involve, in the external sector, the combination of special trading agreements of a

preferential nature and activities driven by market signals, as well as, in the internal economy, the achievement of economic equilibrium through structural reform and productive transformation in areas which are most dynamic in international trade, and the increase in complementarity between internal production and production for export.[47]

(7) The governments and societies of Latin America and the Caribbean share with Cuba the objectives of associating economic growth and international insertion with the simultaneous achievement of social equality. In order to bring these together, Cuba lacks only a project of democratization and full recognition of human rights, within the relatively specific nature of national processes. Now that Latin America and the Caribbean have had to understand that these are internal and external preconditions for economic growth and international reinsertion, why should Cuba not have to understand it as well?

DIRECT INTER-AMERICAN INSERTION

The idea that the lifting of US economic sanctions on Cuba and the normalization of relations between the Cuban communities on and away from the island would rapidly solve the present economic crisis is dominant among the principal actors in the crisis as well as in public opinion generally. These actors, however, differ radically on the feasibility of this. In contrast, the general public that observes and listens to them retains the false, or at least biased, impression that the will of the various parties involved is all that is required to achieve a solution. Beyond this superficial impression lie persistent and difficult realities.

The Communities and the Nation

Seen from the perspective of early 1994, the lifting of the embargo and normalization of relations between the Cuban community at home and abroad appear more distant today than in the last four years. However, at the same time, there have been some concessions without the embargo being lifted, and relations of solidarity and cooperation have intensified between the two Cuban communities. These results are the consequence of the development of actions which, although giving a very different impression, are oriented towards the direct commercial integration of the Cuban economy into the Inter-American and, especially, US economies.

Without doubt, the most active of all the actors promoting this strategy has been the Cuban government itself, increasing its efforts in favour of the lifting of the embargo, including declarations in the press announcing Cuba's willingness to negotiate on the issue of payments for expropriations. However, the government's most important and successful front has been the intensification of family, political and cultural contacts with, and economic assistance (remittances) from, the Cuban community abroad. Moreover, the Cuban government recently invited exiles to a conference directed specifically at the community abroad, entitled 'The Cuban Nation and Emigration'.[48] Many will have noted that this invitation appeared close to the time of the hundredth anniversary of the beginning of the final process of independence, and that, some weeks beforehand, Vice Minister of Foreign Affairs Isabel Allende had received members of the community abroad as *part of the nation.*

In the conference, individuals and organizations invited were treated as representatives of the majority of émigrés, who had not renounced their links with the country, and who were against the counterrevolutionary minority. In making the invitation, the Cuban government was intervening once again in the ongoing discussion on the nature of Cuban identity. Within this same discussion, *Miami Herald* writer Mirta Ojito had added that Miami is today more Cuban than the island itself. The day before the conference, María de los Angeles Torres had concluded – commenting on the exhibition 'Arte Cubana' of both 'island-Cuban' and 'diaspora-Cuban' artists – that 'Accepting that Cuban culture can be created outside of the national borders is equivalent to accepting that the nation overflows the borders of the state. The state has lost control of the nation.'[49]

It is possible that, within the Cuban government, the arguments which will have taken precedence are those oriented towards obtaining increases in remittances and investments from the community abroad, by giving its members the same treatment made legendary by the national apostle José Martí, in his dealings with Cuban communities in Tampa, Cayo Hueso, Ibor City, New York and Philadelphia that cooperated in the financing of the war of independence from Spain. In doing so, Martí surely appealed to the national feeling and identity of people 'who had not renounced their links to the country', seeking to repay their services with similar recognition. Thus, for the present Cuban government, it is of utmost importance that it not lose control of the nation, including its influence on that part of it that lives abroad.

To define the problem in terms of *control of the greater nation*, as opposed to *who is Cuban*, shows how far we have come from the original policy of revolutionary power which rejected the nationality of those who established themselves abroad after 1959. It also shows how strong national identity is among members of the Cuban community abroad and on the island.

In a clear revision of past policy, the Cuban government has widened the authorization for temporary exit from the country to include all citizens over 18 years old,[50] authorized visiting rights to the island for anyone who has more than two years of permanent residence abroad, and liberalized authorization to live outside the country, especially for technicians, professionals, artists and students, at the same time making official and more common contacts with potential investors abroad. In this sense, the new policy seems to have been inspired by the reformist model of the People's Republic of China in its relations with Hong Kong and the rest of the international Chinese community.[51]

However, the advances in the recognition of the 'Cuban identity' and in the 'equal treatment' of non-resident Cuban investors (in the form of joint ventures with the state) have been accompanied by a refusal to recognize them politically. The Cuban constitutional reform of 1992 prohibits dual citizenship.

To the changes in government policy, the community abroad has responded with great efficacy, if not deliberately, through three basic instruments:

(1) solidarity with relatives and friends or acquaintances on the island, showing in these relationships an attitude of immediate and unbiased reconciliation that explains the speed and extent of the process of reunion between family and friends;
(2) pressure through the governments of their countries of residence, especially that of the United States, for the negotiation of 'rules of play' to establish norms for relations between members of the communities on the island and those of the diaspora, demonstrating great efficiency with the achievement of special treatment for Cubans in the immigration policies of their countries of residence and the prevention of the unilateral establishment by the Cuban state of regulations regarding travel and stay on the island; and
(3) constant vigilance over and reporting of human rights and political violations in Cuba, as well as signs of internal economic, political and social deterioration associated with the crisis in the economy and in the socialist regime.

The Communities and the Economy

The confrontations over the question of nation between the community in Cuba and that of the diaspora will continue for years. However, they occupy today only the background of relations between the communities, and are largely expressed through the problem of economic survival – of the regime, of the country and of families and individuals. These three dimensions of economic survival could not constitute equally shared objectives of the principal actors within the two Cuban communities without the possibility of there arising some conflict and competition between them.

Since the beginning of the economic reforms in July 1993, the dynamism of these relations, until then concealed, has made itself known with all of its expansive force. For example, the decriminalization of the dollar increased transfers by way of foreign remittances and government foreign exchange income, but, simultaneously, has accelerated the dollarization of the economy and the expansion of the informal sector and black market. The government 'was not able to lessen the excess supply of pesos in circulation; could not cut the budget deficit without a revision on the basis of fiscal policy; and could not promote the internal market without great alterations in the property regime'.[52] Furthermore, at the same time, individuals and families abroad assumed or increased their obligation to those on the island. Morally, they could only be liberated from this obligation by those on the island overcoming their crisis of survival or leaving the country permanently. The failure of the dollarization policy as an instrument of economic adjustment without structural reforms, and the institutionalization of remittances, is changing the relation between the state and the Cuban household from one of an administrative nature (based on rationing books) to one of taxation and a commercial nature.

Faced with households as economic subjects, thanks to the excess supply of pesos and the availability of dollars, both formal economic actors (the 'basic units of cooperative production'[53] and own-account workers) and informal (*jineteros* and *macetas*[54]) may expand their production of goods and services. These actors are characterized by autonomy in management and profitability which are the necessary conditions for the existence of their activities, with or without the implicit subsidy of the formal or state sector (through the theft of raw materials and products, or double employment). What may be developing is an all-encompassing process of the privatization of the domestic economy. This is occurring with or without the participation of the state, which may be in the process of ceding part of its official function of the generation of employment and the paying of salaries, and assuming a role of tax collector and the collector of payments for public services (water, electricity, refuse collection and so on).

The recent adjustment programme – this time with some structural and policy reforms – although it incorporates measures of administrative control such as the freezing of bank deposits and expropriation of goods from those who have become rich 'illicitly', places priority on measures for the regulation of autonomous economic actors and for the reduction of households' free or rationed access to products and services. In this context, one may expect an increase in households' pressure to obtain greater incomes through family remittances, and to be able to handle them more efficiently. This may increase the influence of the community abroad on the economy and on the success of the adjustment programme.

The American Administration's Costs and Alternatives

Economists that have been interested in recent years in estimating the aid that the United States would have to give directly or indirectly, through international organizations, in order to resolve the crisis have not generally included all of the items listed by R. Dornbusch, but have included substantial numbers of them. In the Dornbusch proposal, the American administration would have to assume a direct economic cost of US$ 2 or 3 billion annually, deal with the interests of foreign corporations in order to restore Cuba's sugar quota, confront US firms in forming an agreement with the Cuban government on compensation for properties expropriated in Cuba in the 1960s, and confront Cuban-American exiles so that they accept the definitive loss of their old properties on the island.

Various analysts have signalled that, in the light of recent experience (Panama, Nicaragua and so on), of US failures in providing economic aid to governments arising from changes inspired by such promises, it would be difficult to imagine much different behaviour in the hypothetical Cuban case. The basic issue, given present reality, is even more transparent: the United States does not have to assume economic and political costs, like those mentioned above, for the simple reason that there would be no argument of national security or of immediate convenience to its foreign policy that would justify them. Furthermore, the United States would be satisfied with discreetly cooperating in a solution built on the basis of the efforts of the Cuban government and community (domestic and abroad) and third-party countries of the Inter-American system and the EC.

In the realm of internal policy, moreover, a progressive evolution from the present hostile status quo towards the Cuban government may have fewer political costs than continuing in the anti-Castro struggle. Finally, there is something to the suggestion that the US administration should stop supporting President Castro by mobilizing popular nationalism in favour of his government and, at the international level, giving him the attractive image of David struggling against Goliath, which he has used effectively for more than three decades.

The International Context of Direct Inter-American Insertion

Sugar and security, which were the bases of the pre-revolutionary US–Cuban relationship, have ceased to play this role, and are unlikely to do so in future. In the views of some analysts[55] the US market will be, in the best of circumstances, complementary to the Russian, Chinese and Japanese ones. Recently, Marifeli Pérez-Stable (1993)[56] argued that, since the post-Second World War period, sugar has been incapable of guaranteeing the country's sustained development. Furthermore, attempts to base this process on industrial, tourist and services deregulation have been equally unsuccessful. The sale of sugar at the end of the 1960s, following the entrance into COMECON, is a policy that not even the Cuban officials who adopted it would repeat. The return to tourism and services, the search for advances in technology, and the re-evaluation of non-sugar agriculture for export, among other things, indicate a route for the productive transformation of the island on which there is wide consensus between Cuban investors and business leaders and non-Cubans interested in the future development of the country.

A similar consensus exists concerning the importance of the US market for Cuban foreign trade, and it is this commercial argument that reinforces the rejection, in principle, of the economic sanctions imposed on Cuba by the United States. Whoever invests and develops commercial activities in as open an economy as Cuba's will do so looking also to the US market, but will not necessarily be an entrepreneur or investor from the United States. The same occurred in Mexico, both before and after NAFTA, and in the Dominican Republic and Costa Rica, to cite just a few examples.

By its past experience on the island, by its financial and business activities in Latin America and the Caribbean Basin, and by its knowledge of the US market, the Cuban community abroad possesses relative advantages for identifying and developing investment and business opportunities in Cuba. It would be an error, however, to presume that 'big money', after decades of efforts to establish dealings and accumulate experience within a wide diversity of geographic areas and activities, is going to give priority to undertakings on the island, based on motives of national identity. This priority could be given in the case of small and medium-sized investors, and entrepreneurs with family ties on the island or an interest in returning there to retire. In fact, it has been these groups which, so far, have shown the greatest interest in Cuba, and received the preferential treatment of the Cuban government.

With greater influence than the community of foreign business leaders and investors (from the United States, Venezuela, Mexico, Spain, Puerto

Rico and so on), Miami will carry decisive weight in the direct Inter-American insertion, as one of the principal financial, commercial and business centres of Latin America. Who could doubt that a good part of the financial and commercial activities on the island, in both of the schemes that have been analysed here, will be developed in connection with, or by subsidies of banks and corporations based in this city? Is it not, in part, in recognition of this reality that the ruling government has attempted to assert its presence in Miami and attract the attention of the business community there? Can anyone imagine that the business leaders of many Latin American or Caribbean countries, or from other latitudes, would prefer to act in Cuba through New York, Mexico City, Madrid or from their own national bases, when they could use the facilities that would be available to them in Miami?

The international insertion of Cuba in the political realm, in security and in important aspects of the area of economics – be they the present transition or future stages of stability – will be linked to other international centres. Madrid, Mexico City, Oslo or Santiago offer places for political negotiations, and Washington, DC or Paris for those concerning multilateral or bilateral financing and the renegotiation of the debt. The thematic diversity and, even more, the complexity of the problems of international insertion will demand that Cuba swiftly attain the maximum of support in these centres.

In this respect, very little support would be furnished by Miami. Instead, the solidarity and reciprocity that the Cuban authorities and people have gained through the last 30 years would constitute a factor capable of gaining support in other centres.

The greater the future internationalization of Miami in the economic, cultural and political realms, the less serious will be the problems that the presence there of the most important Cuban community outside the island will generate for the process of reconciliation, and for the reaffirmation of Cuban national sovereignty. Many are those who worry about the influence that the differing claims of Havana and Miami will have on the future of the Cuban nation, and how each will deal with the rivalries and complementarities of their international vocations.

Within any of the presumptions that one could make, the future situation shows that what once was a confrontation between the 'continental' nation and the 'island' nation will be consistently converted into a closer, but not necessarily less difficult, relationship through the influence of two cities.

CONCLUSIONS

The group *Nos y Otros*, with the assistance of Jesús Díaz, has produced a version of *Alice in Wonderland* in which, in our Wonderland, the exacerbation of idleness, bureaucracy, the profit motive and similar problems culminate in a terrifying stampede of its residents.[57] It is this vision, presented in all the media, that a growing number of compatriots have taken up. This option, in some cases, responds to the belief that socialism is not viable, that its experience in Cuba is not worth saving, and that its objects are fantasies. For others, it reflects a feeling that there is no future for them on the island, and that it would not be bearable for them to stay through a transition towards some still undetermined end.[58] There are still others who, faced with the deterioration of so worthy, humane, clean and just a reality, lack the minimum of incentive and desire to work like heroes, instead opting for absenteeism and slovenliness in their work.

In order to overcome what many consider to be the deepest crisis of the Cuban nation this century, it would be necessary to achieve a social harmonization of goals similar to that with which, also in this century, the ideals of our political culture were consecrated in the constitution of 1940, and in the revolutionary transformation of 1959.[59] The international reinsertion of Cuba is, at the same time, imperative for the survival of the nation, families and individuals, and one of the corner-stones of the consensus necessary for overcoming the crisis.

In this chapter I have, first, systematized the arguments and evidence that point to the necessity for change in the means of the international reinsertion that has been urged by Cuban authorities since the end of the 1980s. Secondly, I have oriented the analysis towards the alternatives which hold the attention of officials and of analysts on and away from the island, as well as of investors, entrepreneurs and governments interested in a solution to the present Cuban crisis.

Together with those who believe that, from exhaustion or conviction, an immediate end to the US sanctions against Cuba would not be unexpected, and that it is not possible to continue the interminable debate over economic and political conditionalities, we seek a Latin American option as a viable alternative. Our region offers an economic space and a model for international reinsertion that is already under way, with a success that is growing, although still modest, and that could serve as a basis of support and inspiration for Cuba to maintain a more positive perspective as it continues with the painful apprenticeship of economic and political reform, through which the economies and societies of Latin America and the Caribbean have also travelled in recent years.

This Latin American option has the attraction of being possibly implemented under the present conditions of the Cuban economy, at the same time that, by commitment to a process of Inter-American insertion in the medium and long run, it would be complementary to the efforts at direct inter-American integration undergone by Cubans on and away from the island. However, in order to overcome present obstacles and, especially, to achieve the full reinsertion of Cuba into the Inter-American system, this latter option would require more time, greater convergence of goals among the various actors, and consensus on issues still highly controversial among Cubans. Moreover, I believe I share with many Cuban and other Latin American and Caribbean people a conviction that the Inter-American integration already under way must be a process which consolidates national sovereignties within a framework different from the Pan-Americanism dominant during the century that is now coming to a close.

Notes

1. During his recent testimony before the United States Senate Select Committee on Intelligence, Jorge I. Domínguez listed the principles of these changes, from the increased willingness to negotiate, the liberalization to foreign investment and the breaking with international isolation. See J.I. Domínguez, 'Cuba y la Comunidad Internacional en los noventa: soberanía, derechos humanos y democracia', *Estudios Internacionales*, 1994. Similarly, consult work from the period (1980–84), among which of particular interest are the presentations to the Cuban–United States discussions, organized in May 1983 by the Friederich Ebert Foundation in Bonn: J.G. Tokatlián (editor y compilador), *Cuba–Estados Unidos: Dos Enfoques* (Bogotá: CEREC y Grupo editor latino-americano, 1984).
2. Nancy Madrigal and Hiram Marquetti, 'El comercio internacional: Desafíos para el comercio exterior de Cuba', in *Economía Internacional: Revista del Centro de Investigaciones de Economía Internacional de la Universidad de La Habana*, vol. 1, no. 1, (1993) pp.64–82.
3. Luis Suárez, 'Cuba: La política exterior en el período especial', *Estudios Internacionales*, 1994.
4. See Fernando Martínez, 'Tres notas y dos debates', *La Gaceta de Cuba*, May/June 1992, pp.16–20.
5. L. Suárez, 'Cuba'.
6. '*Dentro de la revolución todo, contra la revolución nada*', a motto incorporated into Cuban political culture during the 1971 Education and Culture Conference, in order clearly to define the extent of permitted cultural freedom.
7. Georges Carriazo, 'Las relaciones econónicas Cuba–Estados Unidos: Una mirada al futuro', *Estudios Internacionales*, 1993.

8. Eduardo Klinger, 'Cuba se abre al capital extranjero con condiciones exceptionales', *Prensa Latina*, 3 May 1994.
9. Pedro Monreal, 'Apertura y reforma de la economía cubana: Las transformaciones institucionales (1990–93)', *Estudios Internacionales*, 1994.
10. It has been estimated that, to raise sugar production to 6.4 million tons – that is, to recover 50 per cent of the drop in production since 1989 – would require an investment of US$ 1.5–2 million, without including improvements to agricultural and transport equipment. See Nicolás Rivero, 'Cuba's Sugar Industry: Transition Where?', in *Sugar y Azucar*, March 1994, pp.30–8.
11. Alfredo González, 'Los retos de la transición', *Prisma*, December 1993, pp.4–7.
12. Ibid.
13. Osvaldo Martínez, 'Desarrollo humano: la experiencia cubana', *Revista Cuba Económica*, April–June 1991, pp.16–36.
14. Alfredo González, 'Los retos de la transición'.
15. At present, the excess money supply is more than 11 billion pesos, providing workers with their salaries; and subsidies for losses by firms have increased by 73 per cent since 1989, reaching 4.6 billion pesos, a number greater than the state budgetary deficit of 4.2 billion pesos. See L. Tabares and E. Balari, 'Cuba: Situación Economíca, Política y Social', *Revista Situación Latinoamericana* (Spain, 1994).
16. See Estela Espinosa, testimony before INIE, 1993.
17. A. Feriol and A. González, *Cuba: Política social en el ajuste económico* (Havana: Instituto de Investigaciones Económicas, 1993).
18. Victoria Pérez, testimony before INIE, 1993.
19. José Dos Santos, 'Cuba: Nuevos precios y tarifas, medidas sin sorpresas y pocos sustos', *Prensa Latina*, 23 May 1993.
20. For example, in April 1994 the ex-ambassadors to Italy and Mexico moved over to directing hotel chains (Gran Caribe, Grupo Horizonte) oriented towards international tourism, both of which grew out of the disappearance of the Instituto de Turismo (INTUR – Tourism Institute).
21. José Luis Rodríguez, 'Cuba en la economia international, nuevos mercados y desafíos en los años noventa', *Estudios Internacionales*, 1993.
22. Georges Carriazo, 'Cuba: Apertura y adaptación a una nueva realidad', paper presented at the seminar, *Cuba in the International System: Normalization and Integration*, Ottawa, 1993.
23. Pedro Monreal, 'Estados Unidos y América Latina y el Caribe: Geoeconomía, conflicto y coexistencia', paper presented at the *Congreso de Especialistas de Estudios del Caribe*, Havana, June 1991.
24. N. Madrigal and H. Marquetti, 'El comercio internacional'.
25. Ibid.
26. Ibid.; L. Suárez, 'Cuba'.
27. P. Monreal, 'Cuba y América Latina y el Caribe: Apuntes sobre un caso de inserción internacional', *Estudios Internacionales*, 1993.
28. L. Suárez, 'Cuba'.
29. N. Madrigal and H. Marquetti, 'El comercio internacional'.
30. L. Suárez, 'Cuba'; C. Lage, interviewed in Susana Lee, 'Entrevista a Carlos Lage', *Granma*, 1993, pp.3–8; M. Madrigal and H. Marquetti, 'El comercio internacional'.

31. C. Lage in Susana Lee, 'Entrevista'.
32. Francisco León, 'Cuba: Una opción latinoamericana de inserción internacional', *Estudios Internacionales*, 1994.
33. Ibid.
34. ECLAC, *El regionalismo abierto en América Latina y el Caribe. La integración económica al servicio de la transformación productiva con equidad* (Santiago, Chile: 1994).
35. S. Tokliatán and D. Cardona, 'El grupo de los tres y la política exterior de Colombia', *Estudios Internacionales*, 1993.
36. While Cuban specialists continue to speak of the reaffirmed principle of ideological pluralism, their Latin American colleagues recognize that this has been eclipsed. See L. Suárez, 'Cuba', cit.
37. S. Tokliatán and D. Cardona, 'El grupo de los tres'.
38. Interamerican Dialogue, *Cuba in the Americas: Reciprocal Challenges* (Washington, DC, October 1992).
39. Jorge I. Domínguez, 'Cuba y la Comunidad Internacional en los noventa: soberanía, derechos humanos y democracia', *Estudios Internacionales*, 1994.
40. J. Valdés, *La transición socialista en Cuba: Continuidad y Cambio en los 90s* (Ciudad Habana, September 1993).
41. Carlos Quijano, 'The Role of International Organizations in Cuba's Early Transition', statement at the *Cuba Transition Workshop* (Washington, DC: Shaw, Petman, Potts & Thornbridge and The Association for the Study of the Cuban Economy, Inc., 27 January 1994).
42. Lisandro Pérez, 'Introduction', in *Transition in Cuba: New Challenges for US Policy* (Miami, The Cuban Research Institute, Latin American and Caribbean Center, Florida International University, 1993).
43. ECLAC, *Balance preliminar de la Economía de América Latina y el Caribe 1993, en Notas sobre la economia y el desarrollo* (Santiago, Chile, December 1993).
44. Excluding debt contracted with countries of the former COMECON, especially with those making up the former Soviet Union.
45. Commercial sanctions by the US government and firms, as well as possible expropriations with a change of government in Cuba.
46. In 1992, in Latin America and the Caribbean, foreign direct investment represented US$ 14.08 billion of the US$ 54.0 billion net total movement of capital. See ECLAC, *El regionalismo*.
47. ECLAC, *Políticas para mejorar la inserción en la economía mundial* (Santiago, Chile: 1994).
48. See 'Convocatoria', *Granma Internacional*, 23 February 1994.
49. See M.A. Torres, 'Dreaming in Cuba', *The Nation*, 24, 1994.
50. Those below this age only have the right to leave permanently.
51. The People's Republic of China has always recognized the nationality of residents outside China and promoted among them the maintaining of Chinese identity.
52. Rafael Rojas, 'Una reforma lenta y silenciosa', *La Opinión*, January–March, 1994, pp.1–4.
53. *Unidades básicas de producción cooperativa* (*UBPC*).
54. That is, 'hustlers' and 'blackmarketeers'.
55. N. Rivero, 'Cuba's Sugar Industry . . .'.

56. *The Cuban Revolution Origins, Course and Legacy* (New York: Oxford University Press).
57. Jesús Díaz, Cuban writer and film maker, central figure in the editorial team of the magazine *Pensamiento Crítico* (Critical Thought) of the 1960s, in revolutionary intellectualism and in the national model of socialism, has lived in exile since 1992. *Alicia en el Pueblo de Maravillas* provoked strong debate during its first performances, which culminated in the suspension of its presentation on the island. Roxana Pollo, from the pages of *Granma*, rechristened the film 'Alice, a Feast of Swine', affirming that 'our future will not be decided by the impassive or those who would provoke scepticism and distrust in the revolutionary process that, with all its imperfections, has allowed us to live in one of the most worthy, humane, clean and just places on the planet'. See Roxana Pollo, 'Alicia, un festín para los rajados', in *Granma*, 19 June 1991.
58. J. Domínguez, 'Cuba y la Communidad Internacional'.
59. Anthony Maingot, 'The Ideal and the Real in Cuban Political Culture: Identifying preconditions for democratic consolidation', in *Transition in Cuba: New Challenges for US Policy* (The Cuban Research Institute, Latin American and Caribbean Center, Florida International University, 1993).

8 Cuba's Evolving CARICOM Connection

H. Michael Erisman

Cuba, like most other smaller countries, has always been vulnerable to external domination. In Havana's case, this general trait has been exacerbated by two geopolitical factors – the island's strategic location and its proximity to a great power (the United States) that has traditionally defined its international role in highly messianic terms. The Caribbean has long been recognized as one of the world's premier crossroads; through it and into it have flowed goods, people and cultural influences from Europe, Africa, North America, Latin America and, to a somewhat lesser extent, the Near and Far East. Unfortunately, all this attention has likewise functioned to make the Caribbean a cockpit of great power competition. This centuries-old struggle, which has raged from almost the very moment that Columbus first set foot in the New World, initially involved a wild scramble for colonies among such major powers as France, Britain and Spain. This European pre-eminence was, however, gradually displaced by the growing power and influence of the United States. Standing at the epicentre of this maelstrom has been Cuba, the Pearl of the Antilles, which has passed through cycles of depending upon Spain, the United States and the former Soviet Union to its present situation, where it struggles to survive.

As its connections with the former Soviet bloc have unravelled, Cuba has sought to build new bridges to (or at least strengthen existing ones with) various segments of the international community. One aspect of this campaign has been to explore more vigorously the South–South option. Although admittedly a simplification, the South–South option can be seen as encompassing two basic (and often interrelated) dimensions. The first involves expanding Cuba's socioeconomic relations with its less developed country (LDC) counterparts as a means to increase its developmental capabilities while the second, and perhaps more important, focuses upon policy coordination among developing nations as a means to enhance their (collective) bargaining power within the context of evolving North–South ties.

There is, of course, a heavy emphasis within the South–South option on markedly increasing the flow of investment capital, technology, trade, and even aid between LDCs, thereby, it is hoped, strengthening their joint capability to achieve significant socioeconomic progress. In particular, a major concern is to determine the 'best fit' among nations with regard to their human and natural resources in order to create the economies of scale (both in terms of productive facilities and markets) normally associated with high rates of growth. It is, however, recognized that such exercises, no matter how far removed from the political arena in a purely technocratic sense, do not and cannot occur in a power vacuum. Thus attention is also devoted to the question of Third World vulnerability to external penetration or domination.

Horizontal collaboration is seen as an essential first step for uncoupling developing countries from existing patterns of dependency. Once this has been accomplished, new patterns of North–South ties will have to be established, with the most likely profile entailing negotiations by groups of LDCs in an effort to create a diversified network of developmental relationships with multiple centres of metropole power. In short, the key goal of the South–South approach to counterdependency politics is to acquire the political–economic space and the bargaining power necessary to be able to exert some coordinated control over their dealings with the already highly modernized nations within an ongoing context of North–South interdependence.

The specific aspects of Havana's South–South bridge building to be surveyed here concerns its evolving relations with the English-speaking nations of the Caribbean, which are commonly referred to as the CARICOM countries (CARICOM being the Caribbean Common Market and Community, a regional organization formed in 1973 to promote economic integration, cooperation in various functional areas and foreign policy coordination among its members).[1] Within this larger scenario, special attention will be devoted to exploring the impact of the human rights issue.

CUBA'S EVOLVING RELATIONS WITH THE CARICOM STATES

The early 1970s saw Havana launch an effort to normalize its relations across a broad spectrum of countries. In the CARICOM region, this initiative led to diplomatic ties with Barbados, Guyana, Jamaica and Trinidad/Tobago in 1972. The most cordial links were forged with Jamaica following Michael Manley's election as prime minister in 1972. Although a democratic socialist rather than a Marxist, Manley nevertheless displayed considerable admiration for the Cuban Revolution (particularly following his 1976 re-election landslide).

Beyond the progress registered by these normalization endeavours, a major breakthrough (at least from Havana's perspective) occurred in the radicalization of the area's politics when a group of young leftists led by Maurice Bishop staged the Commonwealth Caribbean's first successful armed insurrection in Grenada in March 1979 and proceeded to begin to implement their brand of radical socialism on the small island. Although the Cubans had played no direct role in Bishop's coup, they had maintained strong fraternal relations with his New Jewel Movement over the years and moved very quickly to demonstrate their ongoing solidarity with his new government by providing arms, security advisers and various types of developmental assistance.

Ironically, just as it appeared that Cuba's increased Caribbean assertiveness was beginning to pay major dividends, the political waters suddenly became more murky as the prevailing flow of the ideological tides shifted. The emergence of Bishop's regime in Grenada as well as the triumph of Nicaragua's Sandinistas in July 1979 were obviously bright spots for Havana, but elsewhere in the Caribbean moderates and indeed often strongly anti-communist conservatives scored a series of electoral victories over left-wing parties. The most important race occurred in Jamaica (October 1980) where Harvard-educated Edward Seaga won convincingly with 57.6 per cent of the vote over incumbent Michael Manley.[2] Shortly thereafter, following the lead of the new Reagan administration in Washington, Kingston adopted a hardline anti-Cuba stance; diplomatic relations were severed in October 1981 and practically all Cubans were expelled from the island.

The emergence of this increasingly inhospitable environment was accelerated by developments in Washington, where Ronald Reagan assumed office determined not only to pursue the containment concept much more vigorously than many of his predecessors, but also to incorporate into his foreign policy an idea long dear to the radical right in the United States, the rolling back of communism. Accordingly the Reagan doctrine, which committed Washington to providing strong material/logistical support for insurgent movements fighting to overthrow (Third-World) Marxist regimes, began to be implemented, with the Caribbean/Central American region being a major theatre of operations. Such intransigence, especially when combined with the 1983 Grenadian invasion which demonstrated that the US was willing to use its own troops to move against Caribbean governments which it perceived as being too radical and perhaps too closely aligned with Cuba, had a sobering effect in many quarters, causing some who otherwise might have been inclined towards cordial relations to begin to put some distance between themselves and Havana. Such tendencies were reinforced by the fact that Cuba did not always assign the Caribbean a very prominent place on its international agenda during the 1980s, preferring instead to give higher priority to Central America and non-hemispheric Third-World affairs. This situation was summarized by Cuban Deputy Foreign Minister for American Affairs Ramón Sánchez Parody when he stated in a December 1989 interview that

> Washington's hostile policy against the Cuban government has been a very important factor in the links with countries that are economically dependent on the United States. But we must also acknowledge that there was a lack of diplomatic work [on our part] and our foreign policy didn't give the [CARICOM] area adequate priority.[3]

Having made this admission, Sánchez Parody indicated that Havana was inclined to try to re-energize the Caribbean dimension of its foreign policy. Driven by the growing need to diversify its economic relationships as the Soviet bloc crumbled around it, Havana began to devote serious attention in the early 1990s to building new or stronger bridges to the anglophone Caribbean.

This processes began to gain momentum in 1990 when, in response to Cuban overtures as well as CARICOM's desire to expand participation in the organization, the CARICOM heads of state decided at their eleventh summit conference (Jamaica, August 1990) to launch serious discussions with Havana regarding the possibilities for increased economic cooperation. A series of meetings followed in which progress was made towards an agreement covering a wide range of topics, but complications then developed when objections were raised by some CARICOM members to expanding contacts and collaboration with Havana as long as tensions continued between Cuba and Grenada (which had severed all relations with the Fidelistas as a result of the 1983 crisis). Havana, once again demonstrating its interest in strengthening its CARICOM connections, responded by launching a campaign to resolve its differences with the Grenadian authorities. Following discussions highlighted by high-level meetings at the twelfth CARICOM summit (July 1991, St. Kitts–Nevis) and a February 1992 CARICOM conference in Jamaica, the two parties finally announced in May 1992 that they were re-establishing normal diplomatic ties.[4]

With this obstacle removed, the bridge-building process moved forward swiftly on a variety of fronts. In late May 1992, for example, Havana established diplomatic relations with St. Vincent and the Grenadines. More important, however, from both an economic and even a symbolic perspective, was the June 1992 decision by the 31-member Caribbean

Tourism Organization (CTO) to approve Havana's application for admission. Cuba, of course, had dominated the Caribbean tourism industry in the pre-revolutionary period. It was only after the rupture of the island's relations with the United States and Havana's subsequent de-emphasis of tourism as it concentrated on establishing alternative economic linkages with the socialist bloc that other Caribbean countries began to develop a truly significant presence in the industry. The disintegration of the socialist bloc and with it Havana's preferential arrangements forced Cuba to reassess its entire economic posture, including its position on tourism.

The basic problem that Havana faced was both simple and terrifying: it now had to conduct practically all of its foreign trade on a hard currency basis, a commodity of which it had little in the way of readily available reserves. In short, Cuba was confronted with the daunting prospect of having to acquire large amounts of dollars, pounds, francs, marks and the like in order to be able to service its extensive import needs. Hence tourism, which was perceived as an extremely productive source of such funds, once again moved to the forefront of the island's economic agenda. This development was viewed with some trepidation in the CARICOM area, for it was recognized that Cuba could emerge as a formidable competitor in the highly lucrative Western European and Canadian markets (although the main prize – the United States – remained beyond its reach). Faced with the question of whether to close ranks against the island in an effort to frustrate its tourism aspirations or to enter what would, it was hoped, be a mutually beneficial cooperative relationship with it, the CTO (wherein the CARICOM countries are the most influential bloc) chose the latter course.[5]

Although CARICOM has traditionally restricted its membership to territories that were formerly part of the British empire, it has in recent years become increasingly committed to broadening its scope. Thus far this effort has been limited to granting official observer status to interested parties (with Haiti and the Dominican Republic being most frequently mentioned as leading candidates for eventual full membership). The thirteenth CARICOM summit conference (June 1992, Trinidad) saw similar initiatives taken on the Cuban front. While Havana's request for official observer status was not approved (owing, it was reported, in large part to intense counterlobbying by the United States), CARICOM did take what was generally seen as an important first step towards eventual Cuban membership by voting to establish a joint commission to exlore the prospects for greater CARICOM–Cuban cooperation in the areas of trade, developmental programmes and cultural exchanges.[6]

This new tolerance was apparent in the increasing criticism levelled by

CARICOM leaders at Washington's economic blockade of the island. The immediate catalyst for their displeasure was the Torricelli Bill (passed by Congress and embraced by President Clinton) which prohibited the overseas subsidiaries of US corporations from dealing with Cuba as well as imposing other restrictions designed to discourage countries from trading with the island. Perhaps the most vivid illustration of such sentiment came when Eugenia Charles, the leader of Dominica who had previously been one of the Caribbean's most fervent supporters of the Reagan administration's intransigent anti-Castroism, said in February 1993, 'I don't think that the embargo should continue – they should let people trade with Cuba if they want to . . . .'[7] She reiterated this position the following month, declaring that Dominica would trade with Havana as long as it remained profitable to do so and that 'the US must realize that we [in the CARICOM region] are independent countries and in the same way that they choose their friends we must be allowed to choose ours. . . . If they haven't realized that the Cold War is over, we have.'[8]

Buoyed by such shifts in the political/economic winds, Cuba reciprocated with various gestures to advance its courtship of the CARICOM countries. In early April 1993, for example, Havana hosted a special seminar for Caribbean business leaders designed to spur their interest in taking advantage of the extremely liberal reforms that had been instituted in the island's joint venture and foreign investment laws.[9] During these meetings the Cubans stressed the significant growth that had already occurred in their trade with the Caribbean area (rising from 8.7 million dollars in 1987 to 17.7 million in 1992) and their intense interest in maintaining such upward trends.[10]

A temporary disruption in the process of setting up the joint CARICOM–Cuba Cooperation Commission (initiated at the 1992 CARICOM summit) occurred in May 1993 when Havana objected to the inclusion in the draft document of a clause stating that CARICOM endorsed the OAS (Organization of American States) philosophy regarding questions of government and politics in the hemisphere. A key issue here was an autumn 1992 vote taken in the OAS that accepted the restoration of democracy as a legitimate rationale for approving regional military interventions.[11] Ultimately, this problem was resolved to Havana's satisfaction when the fourteenth CARICOM summit (July 1993, The Bahamas) accepted an agreement setting up the Commission that made no mention of democracy, human rights or any similar item as a precondition for cooperation between the two parties. Instead, responding to Cuban suggestions, the document was modelled on similar CARICOM accords with Mexico and Venezuela wherein such matters were not raised.[12]

Washington was certainly less than enthralled by this turn of events. Clinton administration officials had lobbied participants in the Nassau summit hard to adopt the US tactic of employing economic tools to force political/ideological concessions from Havana and were extremely unhappy when these entreaties were ignored. The response by some elements in Congress was even more heavy-handed. Led by vehemently anti-Fidelista Representative Robert Torricelli (Democrat, New Jersey and Chair of the Foreign Affairs Subcommittee on Western Hemisphere Affairs), several members of the House sent letters to CARICOM leaders threatening to deny their countries any future trade concessions (especially under the aegis of NAFTA, the North American Free Trade Agreement) if they did not rescind their decision to delete the human rights provisions from their agreement with Cuba.[13] Given the fact that Havana had made its position clear that such preconditions were unacceptable, these letters in effect represented demands or ultimatums that CARICOM abandon its efforts to expand trade and economic cooperation with the island.

These letters (which were widely perceived as nothing less than blatant economic blackmail) infuriated many CARICOM government officials. The general consensus was that evolving CARICOM relations with Havana were a purely intraregional matter and that the process would proceed regardless of any misgivings on Washington's part. Representative of such sentiment was the statment by Trinidad's foreign minister, Ralp Maraj, that 'the community made [its] decision and that decision stands'.[14] This posture was maintained when five CARICOM leaders (Cheddi Jagan of Guyana, Erskine Sandiford of Barbados, Patrick Manning of Trinidad/Tobago, P.J. Patterson of Jamaica and Hubert Ingraham of The Bahamas) held a meeting with President Clinton in Washington on 30 August 1993. In the press conference following this gathering, it was apparent that both sides had quietly 'agreed to disagree' on the Cuban question and preferred to avoid as much as possible any public comment on the issue.[15] However, what should not be overshadowed by such diplomatic politeness was the fact that the CARICOM delegation *had not* bowed to US pressure, but instead remained committed to developing a closer, more cooperative relationship with Havana.

BRIDGE BUILDING AND CUBAN–CARICOM PERSPECTIVES ON HUMAN RIGHTS

Human rights questions are often controversial. Beyond the fact that all governments consider such issues sensitive, the debate is complicated in the Cuban case by basic conceptual discrepancies in the sense that the Western liberal democratic tradition tends to accord top priority to civil/procedural rights (such as freedom of speech and religion, legal due process and regularly scheduled multi-party elections) which serve primarily to protect the individual against the government, while the Marxist/Leninist perspective emphasizes the socioeconomic obligations (housing, jobs, medical care and so on) which the society has to the people as a whole. These philosophical differences will almost inevitably produce diametrically opposed responses to situations where these two sets of rights come into conflict, with communist countries like Cuba seeing nothing particularly wrong with policies and practices which subordinate what is in their eyes the selfish interests of the individual to the exigencies of promoting socioeconomic egalitarianism. This collectivist conception of rights was graphically illustrated when Castro, having been accused of violating human rights by refusing to allow those who did not embrace the government's Marxist ethos to express their views publicly, responded by explaining that the basic rule of thumb in Cuba was 'Within the Revolution – anything; outside the Revolution – nothing'. The problem, of course, is that such dictums may function to tarnish Cuba's image in places like the English-speaking Caribbean where the prevailing political culture places a very high premium on maximizing the individual's civil liberties.

The CARICOM states, given their Westminster-style political culture, naturally have a greater affinity for countries which operate along pluralistic, Western liberal lines. Conversely, they have always been leery about the advisability of becoming closely associated with the kind of military dictatorships and brutal oligarchies that too often in the past have characterized the Latin American political scene. Sometimes this aversion has been rooted in noble human rights principles, while in other instances it was probably more a matter of either not trusting such governments to keep their word or believing that they would not survive long enough to do so. In any case, it has long been accepted that differences in ideological/cultural perspectives (with human rights and political civil liberties issues being especially salient) have operated as a significant variable hindering the establishment of close, cooperative relations between the CARICOM region and hemisphere's dominant Hispanic community.

There are, however, some nuances that need to be factored into the equation when probing CARICOM attitudes towards the Cuban Revolution that may very well function to soften what initially appears to be a stark dichotomy between the two parties. For instance, while it is true that the CARICOM countries endorse in principle a party-competitive type of political system modelled along Western European/North American lines, it has not been uncommon in the region for a single party (often built around a charismatic leader) to monopolize power for long periods of time. (An excellent example is the PNM – People's National Movement – in Trinidad/Tobago.) Basically, then, while the two situations are certainly not identical, both the anglophone Caribbean and the Cuban Revolution have, irrespective of what their 'official models' might be, experienced the functional reality of single-party systems. Consequently, although rejecting the legitimacy of the Cuban political model in a theoretical/intellectual sense, there is at the practical level probably less of an inclination in the CARICOM region (than, for example, in the United States) to condemn it as an ipso facto violation of human rights.

Turning to socioeconomic questions, there has always been a strong current of egalitarianism in CARICOM's cultural tradition. Many of the leading political parties in the region grew out of labour unions that had strong ties to various branches of the European socialist movement, particularly the Fabianists in England. There does, therefore, tend to be considerable West Indian empathy with those such as the Fidelistas who seek to create societies characterized by a high level of equity in the distribution of wealth and related social benefits. Revolutionary Cuba has, of course, registered remarkable achievements along these lines.

Placing the human rights question in an even broader perspective, the CARICOM countries have in the past been willing in some cases to assume a posture of what they have called 'tolerance for ideological pluralism' (including divergent views of human rights). While admittedly something of a simplification, it would appear that such a stance is most likely to be adopted when the system of highly centralized political power involved is devoid of any patterns of endemic brutality and is tempered by a firm commitment to promoting socioeconomic egalitarianism (two tests which the Central American countries, for example, have historically been unable to pass). The first time that CARICOM officially embraced the ideological pluralism principle came in response to the New Jewel Revolution in Grenada. Confronted with the problem of whether (and how) to reconcile themselves to the abandonment of the Westminister model by Maurice Bishop's government, which came to power in March 1979 as a result of the anglophone Caribbean's first auccessful armed coup,

> The CARICOM foreign ministers' meeting in Saint Lucia in February 1980 declared that 'ideological pluralism is an irreversible fact of international relations and should not, therefore, be permitted to constitute a barrier to the strengthening of the mechanism of CARICOM', a position

which was reinforced by a similar declaration by CARICOM heads of government two years later.[16]

Recognizing that Bishop's New Jewel Movement was heavily influenced by Fidelista thinking and that the Cuban Revolution seems to fall within the acceptable limits of ideological diversity mentioned above, it would be reasonable to expect that CARICOM would be willing to apply this tolerance principle in its current dealings with Havana.

CONCLUSION

Based on the above analysis and the dynamics of evolving relations between the two parties, it does not appear that the human rights issue poses an insurmountable obstacle to Cuban bridge-building efforts vis-à-vis CARICOM. This does not mean, of course, that problems will not arise. Given the different philosophical perspectives between the two parties, there is always the possibility that serious disagreements will erupt that could derail the normalization process. At this juncture, however, it seems likely that more pragmatic considerations will be the key factors influencing the prospects for closer, more cooperative Cuban–CARICOM ties.

Perhaps the most important potential disincentive to improved relations as far as the CARICOM countries are concerned centres on the reaction of the United States and particularly the extent to which Washington is inclined to link NAFTA/CBI (Caribbean Basin Initiative) concessions to the Cuban question. What CARICOM would prefer, irrespective of its relationship with Havana, is at least some revision of the proposed NAFTA agreement that would serve to protect and enhance the economic advantages accruing to the region under the CBI programme. Ideally, of course, the CARICOM group would like to be offered full NAFTA membership under conditions that would maintain its CBI benefits.

Reports following the 30 August 1993 meeting between President Clinton and five CARICOM heads of state suggested that the US was sending mixed signals on the linkage issue:

> US administration sources told the press after the White House meeting that the Caribbean states were informed that the improvement of relations with the US will be tied to an effort in favor of the democratization of Cuba. But they also were given a guarantee that no Caribbean state will be economically sanctioned for adopting measures to improve their relations with Cuba.[17]

This linkage question could, however, be moot since Washington had previously indicated that no NAFTA concessions would be made to CARICOM in any case. Certainly, this was the position taken by David Malpass, the Bush administration's Deputy Secretary of State for Inter–American Affairs, when he declared in an August 1992 interview that a special arrangement for CARICOM was 'simply not the direction that we [the United States] see our policy heading.' He went on to say that he did not 'think it works to the benefit of the [Caribbean] countries to be in a dependency relationship where they get better access to the US markets than the US gets into their markets', advising instead that they move decisively towards full trade liberalization by removing all barriers to the free flow of goods, services and capital between themselves and the outside world (particularly the United States).[18] President Clinton did little to refute this hard line in his August 1993 meeting with CARICOM leaders, conceding only that he recognized that they were concerned that NAFTA might negatively affect them and promising to consult them after an impact study had been made.

Assuming that this situation does not change radically and that the CARICOM states will therefore remain receptive to Cuban overtures, one can pinpoint a number of incentives that should prove to be sufficient to assure a continuation of Havana's bridge-building efforts. Surprisingly, given the fact that almost all discussions of future cooperation have revolved around economic themes, it is questionable whether CARICOM in and of itself has much to offer Havana in terms of such things as *direct* trade benefits. The total CARICOM population is rougly 5.8–5.9 million, which is not a particularly large market (although per capita income figures for the region are fairly high by LDC standards). It is true that Cuban trade with the Caribbean (which includes such countries as the Dominican Republic, the Netherlands Antilles, Guadeloupe/Martinique and St. Martin as well as the CARICOM community) has been growing rapidly, the total figure doubling from 8.7 million dollars in 1987 to 17.7 million in 1992.[19] Realistically, however, 17.7 million dollars is a relative drop in the bucket in terms of the island's overall foreign trade. Consequently, apart from collaboration in the field of multi-destination tourism, where the prospects for mutual benefits would appear to be considerable, one must move beyond trade issues to the broader aspects of Cuban–CARICOM rapprochement. Here special attention will be focused on the extent to which a CARICOM link might provide access to other bridges that Havana might find useful in its quest to maximize its economic space and/or to enhance its international bargaining power.

One fascinating dimension of this topic is its implications with regard to possible Cuban involvement in the Lomé process. The genesis of Lomé can be traced to Britain's decision to join the European Community (EC). London's pending entry sent shock waves through the Third-World members of the British Commonwealth, who feared that their privileged access to English markets was now in jeopardy. Consequently, when given the opportunity under the provisions of the January 1972 Treaty of Accession which ushered London into the EC to establish an institutionalized association with the entire European Community, the developing Commonwealth nations formed the ACP (Africa, Caribbean and Pacific) Group to serve as their agent. ACP membership was quickly expanded to include the former colonies of other European powers (especially France) and the 45 participating governments then proceeded to enter into discussions in pursuit of a comprehensive new relationship with the EC. The result was the 1975 Lomé (I) Convention, which has subsequently been renegotiated every five years – Lomé II–1980, Lomé III–1985 and Lomé IV–1990.[20] While the Lomé experience has not, as perhaps should have been expected, always lived up to the initial ACP expectations, it nevertheless represents a major accomplishment on the part of the Third-World nations – specifically, the acquisition and exercise of collective bargaining power within the context of periodic negotiations over the exact terms of at least some important aspects of the North–South economic relationships.

Since the CARICOM countries have long played a highly influential role in ACP/Lomé affairs and since Cuba, as a former colony of one of the EC countries (Spain) would appear to have the basic credentials to join the ACP and become a party to the Lomé accords, significantly improved Cuban–CARICOM ties could markedly enhance Havana's membership prospects. Such a move could contribute greatly to Havana's efforts not only to stabilize, but also, it is hoped, to expand its trade/aid with Western Europe. Perhaps even more intriguing, however, are the possibilities which arise with respect to restructuring some of Havana's badly battered Eastern European connections. Practically all of the old COMECON nations want, as part of their transformation towards more Western-style market economies, to become incorporated in some capacity into the EC framework. The former GDR (East Germany) has, of course, already gained entry as a result of reunification with an existing EC member. Moveover, in late 1991, the EC agreed to extend associate membership status to Czechoslovakia, Hungary and Poland.[21] The remaining COMECON countries will almost undoubtedly have to wait for several years before any action is taken on their behalf and even then associate rather than full membership is most likely. In any case, whatever specific version of this Cuban/ACP and COMECON/EC/EU scenario might transpire, it could very well provide a useful mechanism for Havana to get its Eastern European relations on a much more even keel.

A more recent development in terms of 'secondary bridges' is the CARICOM/Venezuela free trade accord. Caracas has long been interested in playing a more active, influential role in Caribbean affairs and hence has undertaken various initiatives to cement a closer association with CARICOM. One key outcome of these efforts emerged from the twelfth CARICOM summit (St. Kitts, July 1991) when it was announced that a preliminary agreement had been reached that opened the way for West Indian exports to enjoy duty-free access to the Venezuelan market. A formal treaty to this effect was signed on 13 October 1992, its main provisions being as follows: approximately 1300 CARICOM products will be afforded duty-free access to Venezuela for a five-year period (1993–8), with some items on the list being phased in more slowly than others; collaboration in trade financing and transportation as well as the promotion of joint ventures will be undertaken; and two-way free trade will replace the one-way arrangement at the end of the initial five-year period (that is, after 1998, Venezuelan exports will be allowed duty-free entry by the CARICOM countries).[22] The possibility of participating in such a free trade agreement should be extremely attractive to Havana, especially if it offers the prospect of ameliorating the island's desperate situation with regard to petroleum imports. Moreover, in early 1993, the CARICOM leaders announced that they had accepted a Colombian proposal to launch free trade negotiations. Although details regarding what was being suggested were not provided, it would appear that certain concessions for the CARICOM countries were being anticipated since Bogota said that it recognized the need to take into consideration the differnces in economic development of the parties involved.[23]

In conclusion, then, given the fact that the human rights issue seems unlikely to function as an impediment and that there are considerable potential advantages involved for Cuba, it can be expected that Havana will move forward energetically in its attempts to establish a closer, more cooperative relationship with CARICOM. While this process will in all likelihood focus initially on specific collaborative programmes (for example, in the tourism sector), CARICOM membership represents the optimal means to assure access to such major benefits as participation in the Lomé accords and the various CARICOM free trade agreements. Thus Cuba would be well advised to go beyond simple bridge building to full-fledged integration with its Caribbean neighbours.

Notes

1. The thirteen members of CARICOM, with their dates of independence from Great Britain in parentheses, are Jamaica (1962), Trinidad and Tobago (1962), Barbados (1966), Guyana (1966), The Bahamas (1973), Grenada (1974), Dominica (1978), St. Lucia (1979), St. Vincent and the Grenadines (1979), Antigua and Barbuda (1981), Belize (1981), St. Kitts-Nevis (1983) and Montserrat (the only non-independent member of the organization).
2. Other moderate–conservative leaders who were elected in the late 1970s early 1980s were Milton Cato in St. Vincent (December 1979), Kennedy Simmonds in St. Kitts-Nevis (February 1980), Vere Bird in Antigua (April 1980), Eugenia Charles in Dominica (July 1980), George Chambers in Trinidad/Tobago (Novemeber 1981), John Compton in St. Lucia (May 1982) and Lynden Pindling in The Bahamas (June 1982).
3. Quoted in John Walton Cotman, 'Cuba and the CARICOM States: The Last Decade', in Donna Rich Kaplowitz (ed.), *Cuba's Ties To A Changing World* (Boulder, Col.: Lynne Rienner Publishers, 1993) p.146.
4. For details, see *CubaINFO Newsletter*, vol. 3, no. 12, 2 August 1991, p.4 and vol. 4, no. 6 (18 May 1992) p.4; and Cotman 'Cuba and the CARICOM States' pp.146–7.
5. *CubaINFO Newsletter*, vol. 4, no. 8, 21 July 1992, p.4.
6. These developments are discussed in *CubaINFO Newsletter*, vol. 4, no. 8, 21 July 1992, p.4; *Caribbean Contact*, July/August 1992, p.10; and 'CARICOM Considers Closer Trade Relations With Cuba', a synopsis of Inter Press Service reports provided via electronic mail by PeaceNet, 2 April 1993.
7. Quoted in *CubaINFO*, vol. 5, no. 3, 26 February 1993, p.3.
8. Quoted in *CubaINFO*, vol . 5, no. 5, 12 April 1993, p.4.
9. Discussions of these laws can be found in Donna Rich Kaplowitz and Michael Kaplowitz, *New Opportunities for US–Cuban Trade* (Washington, DC: Johns Hopkins University, 1992) and in David Jessop, *Cuba: New Opportunities For British Business* (London: 1992), a report prepared for the Caribbean Trade Advisory Group, the Anglo-Cuban Trade Council, and the West India Committee. See also the following articles in the *Granma Weekly Review*: 'Doing Business With Cuba', 7 October 1990, p.8; 'Joint Ventures In Cuba', 25 November 1990, p.12.
10. This information was provided in 'Cozying Up To The Caribbean', a summary of *Granma* news reports provided via electronic mail from Havana by the Grupo de Video, Joven Club, 26 April 1993.
11. This development is summarized in CubaINFO, vol. 5, no. 7, 21 May 1993, p.4.
12. See *CubaINFO*, vol. 5, no. 9, 16 July 1993, p.7.
13. Reported in an Associated Press news item, 11 August 1993, provided via electronic mail, entitled 'Cuba–Caribbean Commission Gains Support Despite US Threats'.
14. Quoted in ibid.
15. See The White House, Office of the Press Secretary, 'Press Availability By The President And Caribbean Heads Of States', 30 August 1993, transcript provided via electronic mail; and Caribbean Countries Won't Exclude Cuba

From Regional Matters', a news report from *La Prensa*, 3 September 1993, provided via electronic mail by the NY Transfer News Collective.

16. Quoted in Lloyd Searwar, 'The Caribbean Conundrum', in Thomas G. Weiss and James G. Blight (eds), *The Suffering Grass: Supperpowers and Regional Conflict in Southern Africa and The Caribbean* (Boulder, Col.: Lynne Rienner Publishers, 1992), p.30. Regarding the CARICOM summit declaration, see also Anthony Thorndike, *Grenada: Politics, Economics, and Society* (London: Francis Pinter Publishers, 1985), p.120.
17. 'Caribbean Countries Won't Exclude Cuba From Regional Matters' Additional information regarding the US government's perspective on the Clinton meeting with CARICOM leaders can be found in The White House, Office of the Press Secretary, 'Background Briefing By Senior Administration Official', 30 August 1993, transcript provided via ėlectronic mail.
18. These quotations and related material can be found in 'US Against Special Trade Treatment For The Caribbean', *Latin American Regional Reports/ Caribbean Report*, 1 October 1992, p.8.
19. The trade information comes from 'Cozying Up To The Caribbean'.
20. For information about the Lomé process, see John Ravenhill, *Collective Clientelism: The Lomé Conventions and North–South Relations* (New York: Colombia University Press, 1985); Ellen Frey-Wouters, *The European Community and The Third World: The Lomé Convention and its Impact*, Praeger Special Studies (New York: Praeger Publishers, 1980). By 1985, the ACP's ranks had grown from the original 45 members to 66 participants.
21. Reported via electronic mail by the Technology Transfer in International Development newsgroup. Subject: EC And Eastern Europe, 12 December 1991.
22. This CARICOM/Venezuela free trade agreement is discussed in *Latin American Regional Reports/Caribbean Report*, 26 July 1991, p.1 and 5 November 1992, p.5. The full text of the agreement is provided in a special supplement to *Caribbean Affairs*, vol. 6, no. 1, January–March 1993.
23. This Colombian proposal is reported in *Latin American Regional Reports/ Caribbean and Central American Report*, 13 May 1993, p.4.

9 Unravelling the Paradox: The Canadian Position on Cuba

John M. Kirk

The Canadian presence in Cuba is unmistakable. From the moment that one arrives there (either at the new Varadero air terminal or the revamped one in Havana – both built by Canadian companies) it is impossible not to be aware of Canada's role. Largely it can be seen in the number of holidaymakers (more than 130 000 of whom travelled to Cuba in 1993). Increasingly, however, Canadian inroads are being built in mineral and petroleum production. Also Canadian consumer goods can be spotted in the hard currency shops. At the same time, however, and despite significant changes since the end of the Cold War, Ottawa has done little to amend its official views on the Cuban revolution: bilateral development assistance (cut off in the late 1970s at the time of Cuban incursions into Angola) is still unavailable for Cuba; humanitarian assistance following the March 1993 'storm of the century' was remarkably late arriving; and export trade credits are still obtained with great difficulty by Canadian companies wanting to trade with Cuba.

This chapter examines what appear to be the common denominators in the bilateral relationship. It is based upon the concept that there has indeed been paradoxical behaviour in this bilateral relationship.[1] Based upon a long-term project analysing Canadian–Cuban relations, and following significant research in the archives of the Department of External Affairs in Ottawa and the Ministerio de Relaciones Exteriores in Havana, some thoughts are presented on the nature of Canadian–Cuban ties.

In 1970 the late Assistant Under-Secretary of State for External Affairs, John Holmes, noted that 'a sound foreign policy must be based on an acceptance of paradox. This is true for great powers, but it is especially true for a middle power whose reach ought not to exceed its grasp.'[2] An analysis of 34 years of the Canadian view of events in Havana shows clearly that, whether by design or by accident, Ottawa's position in large part has revolved around this tenet.

Four key concepts are necessary to understand the dynamic of Canadian–

Cuban relations during their evolution over the last 34 years. They can be defined in the following manner:

(1) misunderstanding and miscommunication – although this feature is clearly less obvious now;
(2) diplomatic pragmatism and the recognition of an established government, whether Ottawa is pleased with it or not;
(3) traditional deference to Washington, particularly noticeable during the last (Mulroney) government from 1984 to 1993;
(4) a determination to coexist with Cuba and, at certain times, to pursue a mutually advantageous bilateral relationship.

Dealing with the first of these concepts, the archives of both foreign ministries are full of examples of cultural faux pas, misunderstandings and communication that – often despite the best of intentions – simply went awry. Consider, for example, the anguished plea for help from Cuban Ambassador Américo Cruz to his Foreign Minister Raúl Roa in the spring of 1961. Cruz urgently asked for instructions since he was fearful that, unwittingly, he had caused a major international incident. This particular episode revolved around two boxes of cigars which he had sent to the Secretary of State for External Affairs, Howard Green, and to Prime Minister John Diefenbaker. Green had enjoyed his cigars, yet Diefenbaker had returned his box to the Cuban embassy, declaring that he simply could not accept the gift because of the sentiments expressed in the accompanying note. The letter in question stated:

> Dear Prime Minister,
> I ask you to accept this box of Cuban cigars with our best wishes.
> I hope that, while you smoke them, you will have 'the name of Cuba on your lips', and that your thoughts will be with the courageous people of my country who are resisting firmly the imperialist aggression.[3]

Miscommunication and difficulties in transcultural communication were not restricted to Cuban diplomats, however. Indeed, the diplomatic archives of both countries are replete with embarrassing incidents that were largely the result of a lack of appreciation of the target culture. In 1969, for instance, the awkward-sounding title of a memo, 'Municipal Regulations concerning Fires and the Cuban Embassy', prepared at the Department of External Affairs, revealed a clear breakdown of communication over a remarkably minor incident.

On 26 May 1969, Cuban officials decided to burn some confidential documents in the backyard of the embassy. Unfortunately a neighbour, after noticing the smoke, alerted the local fire brigade, after which there ensued a Chaplinesque sequence involving 'a massive descent of fire-fighters armed with axes' upon the Embassy, arm-waving Cuban officials informing them about the nature of the fire, and an officious fire-fighter informing them that they had committed an infraction against municipal air pollution regulations (burning paper in the open). The Cuban Ambassador subsequently informed External Affairs that in future all confidential documents would be burned in the furnace. ('The idea of a paper-shredder had still not occurred to them,' noted drily the author of the memo.)[4]

Two years later an incident involving the renowned Canadian photographer Youssef Karsh also speaks volumes of the triumph of bureaucracy over meaningful communication. Karsh had recently returned from Havana, where he had undertaken a series of portraits of Fidel Castro. During his trip he had praised a particular Cuban palm tree (the 'palma macana'), whereupon Fidel Castro promised to send him one. True to his word the Cuban leader did so – an event which caused grave concern in Ottawa because of the resulting infraction of regulations which the spontaneous gesture of goodwill involved. Indeed, as an enterprising bureaucrat in the Department of Agriculture informed the Canadian Embassy in Havana, there was a significant amount of red tape involved: '1) Plant must come completely free of soil as import of soil is prohibited from all countries except continental US. 2) Plant must be accompanied by phytosanitary certificate (i.e. plant health certificate) issued by plant quarantine authorities of Dirección Nacional de Sanidad Vegetal.'[5]

Amusing those these incidents are, it is important to bear in mind that they – and many others like them – reveal a glaring lack of awareness of one culture for another. In these three cases parties from the Canadian and Cuban sides acted wth the best of intentions and yet in all three a clear cultural communication breakdown occurred. The ensuing misunderstandings compounded the lack of appreciation for the other culture, thereby perpetuating stereotypical images about the other.

In many ways more serious, however, was the misinformation provided by diplomats in the field to their superiors. Cuban officials, for example, waxed eloquent in the early 1960s about the level of oppression encountered by the Québécois at the hands of their anglophone masters (which was why, it was claimed, they were ready to seek independence, and looked with longing at the Cuban model). In 1992, Canada's Ambassador to the OAS (and a former diplomat in Cuba) told me that 'both Canada and the United States viewed Cuba as a rotten apple. The only difference between Canadian and US policy towards Cuba was that, while Ottawa is waiting for the rotten apple to fall with its own weight, Washington is shaking the tree.' Hardly a diplomatic position, and incidentally one not shared by many colleagues at the Department of External Affairs.

Why dwell on these incidents? Basically this is done to reveal that miscommunication is a self-perpetuating act, eventually developing into a 'leyenda negra' or 'black legend' which is extremely difficult to break. The late 1950s and early 1960s are particularly good examples of Canadian officials misinterpreting Cuba and providing a steady stream of anti-Castro invective. If, for example, one were to have accepted at face value the interpretations of Canadian diplomats in the field at the time, one would have surmised that Fidel Castro would never beat Fulgencio Batista's army; Fidel Castro would have been overthrown within a year; the revolutionary government lacked popular support at that time; and the United States would have invaded to protect US investment.

It is significant that an evolution has indeed taken place in the manner in which Ottawa and Havana now view each other, as would be expected some 35 years after the revolutionary government took over. That said, it has indeed been an uphill struggle to arrive at the current state of diplomatic relations, a process not helped by Cuban intelligence-gathering operations in Canada, the infamous 'spy school' at the Montreal consulate in the mid-1970s, misinformation about Cuba deliberately spread by Canadian security officials and politicians cashing in on red-baiting activities. The bilateral dynamic has, in sum, undergone some severe strains which have in no small part been due to an unfortunate level of miscommunication. Some outstanding diplomats from both countries have slowly turned this current around, but it has clearly not been easy to overcome this tradition of suspicion.

The second feature of this bilateral relationship has been Ottawa's pragmatism, supported by its standard policy of recognizing the established government in virtually any country. Clearly the revolutionary government of Fidel Castro has been firmly in control over the past three decades, and accordingly the Canadian government has pursued a normal policy of correct and cordial relations.

It is also important to bear in mind two further factors which have contributed to solidifying this relationship: Canada's refusal to break with revolutionary Cuba, despite significant pressure from Washington, and the value of the Trudeau initative in the 1970s. These two factors, allied with the standard Canadian diplomatic practice, have contributed significantly to the establishment of a reasonably firm bilateral dynamic.

The first point is worth emphasizing, since the value of this factor is often not appreciated sufficiently in international diplomatic circles, including Ottawa itself. Indeed, only two countries of the Americas – Mexico and Canada – refused to go along with US pressure in the early 1960s after Cuba was suspended from the OAS. The nationalistic government of John Diefenbaker at the time steadfastly refused to accept the browbeating of John F. Kennedy. In part the Canadian prime minister hoped to take advantage of the US blockade of Cuba by selling Canadian products to replace US goods no longer available in Cuba. But there was also a strong degree of nationalism involved, as Diefenbaker sought to demonstrate that Ottawa would make its own foreign policy in a sovereign, independent way. (In addition, the personal animosity and indeed mutual antipathy between the two North American leaders was also a contributing factor.)

The 1976 visit of Prime Minister Pierre Trudeau, accompanied by his family, was also extremely important in developing the relationship between Ottawa and Havana. Trudeau ran a significant risk in domestic politics by making the trip, which significantly was the first made by the leader of a NATO country. His personal friendship with Fidel Castro (which continues nearly 20 years later) and a determination to pursue a 'third option' in Canadian foreign policy (that is, one which was independent of the two traditional thrusts of Canadian foreign policy towards the United States and the British Commonwealth) were beneficial for both countries. Indeed, by 1980 Canada was exporting some $400 million worth of goods to Cuba.

Trudeau firmly believed that the way to influence other governments was by trade. He was also convinced that, despite fundamental differences of opinion over the Cuban role in Angola, it was indeed possible to establish a fruitful dialogue with the revolutionary government. In short, the bluster of Washington (as well as its armed support for the UNITA guerrillas) was rejected by Trudeau as being decidedly unhelpful. It was during his term in office, and particularly during the 1970–79 period, that Canadian–Cuban relations developed a firm basis, both politically and commercially.

The third constant in seeking to explain the dynamic of the Canadian–Cuban relationship revolves around the exremely close ties between Canada and the United States. Culturally, there are significant similarities between both nations, with a constant flow of television, music, film, sports and media influences from the south. In addition to popular culture, however, the immense undefended border is another useful symbol of the extremely close ties. Finally (and perhaps most importantly), the interlocking of business elites from both countries, the impact of the Free Trade Agreement and a clear commercial dependence of Canada upon the US market are major influences upon Ottawa's foreign policy. This was the case particularly during the leadership of Prime Minister Brian Mulroney (1984–93), when a closer relationship with Washington was set out as a fundamental goal of the Canadian leader.

The commercial dependency can be explained by a variety of statistics. All reveal Canada's status in essence as a 'branch plant' of US industry. Some 80 per cent of Canada's exports go to the United States, an extraordinary (and clearly unhealthy) situation. Over a century ago José Martí urged Cuba to diversify its trading partners since, as he noted with some foresight, 'El que que compra, manda' ('In business, the buyer is always the person in control'). The resulting deference to Washington is quite understandable, given this context. Indeed, the clear streaks of economic nationalism shown by prime ministers such as Diefenbaker and Trudeau are quite unusual, given the overwhelming influence of Washington. Over 20 years ago Trudeau put it well when he commented: 'Living next to the United States is in some ways like sleeping with an elephant. No matter how friendly or even-tempered is the beast, one is affected by every twitch and grunt.'[6]

A close reading of the archives of the Department of External Affairs shows how even trivial decisions or transactions were often impeded or thwarted by cautious Canadian diplomats who sought to avoid offending or slighting their US counterparts. Examples abound, but one will perhaps suffice. The sale of 5000 head of cattle (at a cost of some $10 million) to Cuba was clearly a good commercial enterprise for Canada, yet led to much diplomatic hand-wringing as Ottawa tried to think of various explanations which it could provide to Washington as a justification for the sale. A confidential memo of 29 April 1969 to the Under-Secretary of State for External Affairs by J.C. Langley sought to justify the extension of export insurance credits to Cuba for this venture, noting that the sale of cattle to Cuba was in fact a modest change by Canada in a market where Japanese and West European countries were now extending more generous terms. That said, Langley hastened to add, 'it will be necessary to have available a fairly convincing rationale to use in explaining this move' in Washington, and he suggested connecting it with the ongoing review of Canadian foreign policy.[7] Significantly, US diplomats seemed studiously uninterested in the export of Canadian cattle – while Ottawa was clearly on diplomatic tenterhooks.

More recently this uncertainty as to how to proceed, defending Canadian interests, on the one hand, while dealing with US pressure on the other, can be seen in Ottawa's reaction to the Cuban Democracy Act of 1992 (commonly referred to as the Torricelli Bill). The Act prohibits the sale of goods produced by US subsidiaries in third countries to Cuba. Ottawa responded firmly to this piece of legislation (clearly passed in the heat of the 1992 presidential campaign in the United States), condemning it for its infringement upon Canadian sovereignty. On 13 October 1992, Secretary of State for External Affairs Barbara McDougall condemned the bill and introduced blocking legislation in Canada. At the same time Minister of Justice (and later Prime Minister) Kim Campbell defended Ottawa's blocking order: 'This order is intended to protect the primacy of Canadian trade law and policy. If left unchallenged, the measures passed by Congress on October 5, 1992 would be an unacceptable intrusion of US law into Canada and could adversely affect significant Canadian interests in relation to international trade or commerce.'

Ms. Campbell sounded a sternly nationalistic note in her reactions to the Torricelli Bill: 'Canadian companies will carry out business under the laws and regulations of Canada, not those of a foreign country.'[8] Prison terms and fines would be imposed upon those who did not respect Canadian law, the government warned. A year later, however, approximately a dozen subsidiaries of US-based companies have ignored the Canadian legislation. Indeed the Department of External Affairs has referred these cases of alleged violations to the Department of Justice for investigation. To date not a single prosecution under the Foreign Extraterritoriality Measures Act has been made – in no small measure because of the same defensive approach which affected the sale of Canadian cattle some 20 years ago. Put simply, Ottawa does not know how to extricate itself with diplomatic grace from what is, after all, the law of the land.

The fourth, and final, common denominator in this enigmatic bilateral dynamic has to do with a firm, albeit occasionally wavering, attempt to actually strengthen Canadian–Cuban relations. Largely this is the result of initiatives taken by a variety of sources, to which Ottawa has responded. The federal government clearly wants to coexist with Cuba, and indeed recognizes that there is something of value to be gained (in commercial and political terms) by so doing. That said, it is clearly not out to pursue some trail-blazing activities and in general plays a role reacting to initiatives undertaken by others.

It is important to point out that there have indeed been significant developments on this front – by parliamentarians themselves, provincial governments (and in particular the visit of Premier John Savage of Nova Scotia, heading a delegation of 25 business people in January of 1994, should be mentioned), entrepreneurs, non-governmental organizations (NGOs) and solidarity groups (a dozen of which have developed across Canada since 1991). In 1993, for example, some 21 members of Parliament and senators formed the 'Canada–Cuba Friendship Group'. Legislators from the Ontario legislature (and in particular its speaker, David Warner, and Member of the Provincial Parliament, Jim Henderson) have pursued a variety of tacks: approximately 100 buses and dozens of crates of medicine have been donated as a result of the efforts of these members of the provincial Parliament, and several delegations of Canadian business leaders have been led by Henderson in the search for mutually beneficial joint ventures.[9]

Trade missions have been led from the provinces of Nova Scotia, Ontario, Saskatchewan, Quebec and New Brunswick in recent years. These trips have proved useful and, while they have produced profitable contracts, they have largely been the result of individual effort – rather than the support of Ottawa. Advice on trade is of course provided by the federal government, and by the trade commissioner in the Canadian embassy in Havana. From interviews with many Canadian entrepreneurs who have been to Cuba, however, it is clear that many potential investors prefer to seek out business ventures for themselves. Give the highly profitable nature of a select group of Cuban industries, it is clear that Canadian entrepreneurs – and indeed provincial governments – will continue to seek out investment opportunities. It is unfortunate, however, that Ottawa still refuses to take any leadership by providing substantial trade credits to potential Canadian exporters.

Ottawa's position on supporting commercial ventures can accurately be termed both cautious and lukewarm. There are, however, some encouraging signs which should be highlighted. In 1993, Canada provided some $250 000 in food aid to Cuba, and a further $250 000 in medicine (a further $300 000 in humanitarian aid was given in 1994, and in that year Cuba was put back on the list of countries eligible to receive government support). Significantly, these donations were not a bilateral grant, and the first two were (somewhat tardy) responses to Cuba's appeal to the international community for humanitarian assistance in the wake of the March 1993 storm which devastated Cuba. Nevertheless, it was an important gesture – more than a decade after development assistance through the Canadian International Development Agency (CIDA) was cut off to Cuba – which was appreciated by Havana.

GENERAL OBSERVATIONS AND MORE PARADOXES

Canadians, not being burdened with the responsibility of being the last surviving superpower, clearly do not fear the Cuban revolution as a threat.

Indeed, more than 100 000 of them sought to escape the long Canadian winter last year, a large increase on the 20 000 who visited just a decade ago. (The current figure, expressed in terms of the US population, would be about 2.5 million North Americans – clearly a staggering number.)

These figures increased to 130 000 for the 1993 season. Possibly this amount would be even higher, were it not for the dire warnings found in 1993 travel bulletins issued by the Department of External Affairs on the risks involved in venturing on Cuban soil. Clearly the current financial crisis in Cuba has led to a massive increase in petty crime (and robbery in particular has reached previously unheard-of levels). That said, travelling in Cuba remains far safer than it is in Nicaragua, El Salvador or even Jamaica – something which would not be clear from the official Canadian government travel advisory bulletins, which paint an alarming picture of Cuba and do not differentiate between it and other countries.

The traditional 'hands-off' policy of Ottawa can in general be contrasted with the 'hands-on' policy of NGOs, individuals, provincial governments, entrepreneurs and holidaymakers who continue to press for increased communication with Cuba. The trade missions led by people like Ontario legislator Jim Henderson, humanitarian assistance sought by OXFAM, CUSO and the churches, and individual business people undertaking (profitable) commercial activities in Cuba are clearly the trailblazers – from whom Ottawa can learn a lot. There are signs that the official position might indeed be starting to change, as closer ties between Canada and Latin America become inevitable, and as Latin America, the CARICOM nations and Europe develop closer commercial ties with Cuba. This process will be slow, however, and the federal government will once again probably react to changing circumstances rather than actively pursuing such changes.

The paradox of Canadian–Cuban bilateral relations is seen clearly in their commercial relations. Recent reports from Havana point to the increases in bilateral trade, despite Cuba's current crisis, yet Ottawa still provides only limited export credits to Canadian exporters, unlike our main competitors – Mexico, Spain and France – which do ensure such credits. (In actual fact, while Cuban exports to Canada have risen from $44.3 million in 1985 to $171.4 million in 1993, Canadian exports have shrunk steadily from $330 million to $133 million over the same period. When put in the appropriate perspective, and not allowing for inflation, this represents approximately one-quarter of Canadian exports in 1980.)

Canadians have a relatively important role in Cuba: they constitute 28 per cent of all foreign tourists and have the largest single foreign investment in Cuba. Canadian companies have been increasing their involvement in the tourist sector and are active in petroleum exploration, gold mining and nickel smelting. In total, among all foreign investors in Cuba, Canada holds first place for the number of joint ventures with Cuban business.

Given this involvement, and the traditional recognition of revolutionary Cuba, one is at a loss to explain why Ottawa did not respond more quickly to Cuba's request for aid following the March 1993 'storm of the century'. (The official explanation given in Ottawa, namely that a cabinet shuffle saw a new secretary of state for external affairs, explains in part this tardiness, but clearly is not a significant factor.) Most countries of the Americas, the Caribbean and Europe provided humanitarian assistance, while Ottawa dragged its feet, despite a request for assistance from Canadian diplomats in Havana. The subsequent support for medical assistance ($250 000) with a similar amount in food assistance (approved five months after the storm) is useful. It is unfortunate, however, that 'too little, too late' was given – and then after countries throughout the world, most far poorer than Canada, and without our commercial involvement, has already done so.

In 1992, Canada's roving ambassador to Latin America, Richard Gorham, outlined the bilateral dynamic well. Bilateral relations, he explained, 'have been, and continue to be, correct, cordial and as close as can be expected between two nations which have important differences on foreign policy issues, security questions, political and economic structure, and political philosophy'.[10]

Therein lies the rub, however, for in the light of changes on the world stage and in Cuba itself, those 'important differences' are nowhere nearly as great as they were just four years ago. This is a development of which official Ottawa is not yet fully aware, and which it needs to appreciate as soon as possible.

THE FUTURE

The basic position for Canada, then, is largely based upon a sense of 'business as usual' with Cuba, accompanied by the stolid and occasionally boring (but not to be underestimated) 'Canadian compromise'. Slowly, however, policy-makers are realizing that the world *is* different with the demise of the Cold War. Cuba, which is having grave difficulties even feeding itself, is no longer a threat to inter-American security. Moreover, changes in Cuba since 1991 (and indeed over the summer of 1993) have produced a vastly different economic situation. Indeed, as Canadian investors have been informing Ottawa, business prospects in Cuba are exceptionally promising, with or without government financial assistance. As a result the Canadian perspective, which has been rather unfocused in the last few years, badly needs to be sharpened and brought up to date.

Canada which, unlike the United States, has traditionally sought a policy of *engagement* with Cuba, now needs to realize that Cuba is indeed changing, and rapidly. Moreover, mandarins in Ottawa need to appreciate that Canadian interests can be better served by developing that engagement, rather than, as has been the case in recent years, merely standing by. Canadian commercial and political interests can be served, and deserve to be served, by taking the initiative in pursuing this policy. Canada has paid its historical dues by developing a policy towards Cuba, and it is time to cash in now, rather than be passed by the Europeans, Latin Americans and, within the next five years, maybe by the United States.

It is indeed true that Mexico, and possibly Venezuela, Brazil and Chile, offer sound investment opportunities which need to be pursued as Canada seeks to develop a reinvigorated policy towards Latin America. It is also the case that none of these countries is seen as posing a problem by Washington (which continues to look askance at foreign investments in Cuba). At the same time, a fresh Canadian policy for the Americas cannot ignore the political weight of Cuba among the inter-American and Caribbean communities (where its comparatively small size has not hindered its high international profile). A decade ago it was generally held that Cuba was a 'Third-World' country with a 'First-World' profile. Much of that has clearly gone for ever, yet much respect still remains, as can be seen from the attention focused on Fidel Castro at presidential inaugurations in Latin America and Ibero-American summits.

But in addition to recognizing both significant domestic changes in political and economic matters, and in the international fora (such as the 1992 and 1993 UN General Assembly condemnations of the US blockade of Cuba, or the 1993 rejection of the same by the European Parliament) it is also clear that it is extremely profitable to invest in Cuba at present. The Spanish hotel chain Sol-Meliá has clearly learned that lesson and is now making significant profits after already recouping its investments from its two flagship hotels at Varadero. Canadians too are learning that Cuba is worth investing in, especially at this time of such dramatic transition.

Some encouraging signs are beginning to emerge in Canadian policy towards Cuba. The highly regarded International Development Research Centre (IDRC) and the Foundation for Canada and Latin America (FOCAL) are pursuing some useful initiatives in the island. In particular IDRC, whose former director Ivan Head refused all attempts from the Canadian government to cut funds for research in Cuba, deserves to be commended for pursuing an apolitical programme. Its support for the delivery of an MA programme of a Canadian University (Carleton) for junior faculty members of Cuban universities at the University of Havana, in order to facilitate the renewal of research and of the teaching of economics in Cuba, is an interesting initiative. Moreover, the findings in medical research undertaken at the Institute for Tropical Medicine in Havana – also supported by IDRC – have been of benefit to tropical countries.

The prime minister of Canada, Jean Chrétien (elected in October 1993) has also pursued some useful initiatives. In the spring of 1994 his minister of foreign affairs, André Ouellet, meeting his Mexican counterpart, called upon Washington to 'turn the page' and resolve its difficulties with Cuba. The heightened interest of Canadian investors (particularly in the mining sector), the steadily increasing number of Canadian tourists travelling to Cuba and the decision to place Cuba back on the list of countries eligible to receive Canadian development assistance are all encouraging signs.

The successful January 1994 visit to Cuba of Premier John Savage (the first official visit by a Canadian premier in nearly 20 years) and a 25-person business delegation from Nova Scotia, a highly visible Canadian contingent at various trade shows in Havana, the steady flow of Canadian joint ventures with Cuba and the volume of tourists augur well for the growth of bilateral relations. The investment factor is particularly interesting, since Canadians rank second only to their Spanish counterparts. Indeed, from the first joint venture developed in 1992, with nine more following in 1993 and 17 in various stages of negotiation as of May 1994, it is clear that the Canadian private sector is pleased with doing business in Cuba.

Perhaps the most important indication of the new 'business as usual' approach of the Canadian government came from the official statement of Canada's secretary of state for Latin America and Africa, Ms. Christine Stewart, in her opening address to delegates at a conference on business opportunities in Cuba organized by *The Economist* in the summer of 1994. Ms. Stewart announced several important innovations in Canada's bilateral relationship with Cuba: high-level government exchanges are to start in the near future, probably with a visit to Ottawa of Cuban Foreign Minister Robaina; senior officials in the Department of Foreign Affairs and International Trade are to initiate a series of formal consultations with their Cuban counterparts (a structure which was set up by Pierre Trudeau but which was disbanded many years ago); Ottawa also seeks to examine with other countries the manner in which Cuba could be readmitted to the OAS; development assistance – cut off by Ottawa to Havana following Cuban incursions into Angola – will now be available for Canadian NGOs seeking to undertake projects in Cuba ($1 million has been earmarked for the initial phase of this programme); a further $500 000 in humanitarian assistance – through the World Food Programme – is to be donated; and Canadian companies seeking business opportunities in Cuba will now be eligible for funding provided by the Industrial Cooperation Program of CIDA. I prefaced my remarks with observations by the great Canadian political scientist John Holmes on the need for an element of paradox in the foreign policy of a middle power. That element clearly abounds in Canada's policy towards Cuba. But Holmes also had some wise words about the limits of paradox, which we would do well to consider. Writing almost a quarter of a century ago, he noted that 'The constant contemplation of paradox can produce hypnosis. The besetting sin of diplomats, and ex-diplomats, is creeping paralysis.'[11]

Within the broad sweep of reform, it is clearly time to revisit our Cuba policy – to outline attainable goals and to pursue them. The policy, particularly when compared with that followed by our powerful southern neighbour, is surprisingly balanced, yet it still needs to be proactive rather than reactive. The important initiatives undertaken by the Trudeau government in the 1970s, and the early indications of a changing policy under the Chrétien government, show that it is possible to pursue a commercial and political bilateral policy that is constructive. Canadians therefore, to paraphrase Holmes, need to look at their future foreign policy 'with hard realism but without cynicism'. And, lest we become overambitious, it is important to remember that 'the danger of delusions of grandeur is, on the whole, to be feared less than the danger of paralyzing abnegation'.[12]

Notes

1. I am employing here the definition of paradox found in the *American Heritage Dictionary of the English Language*, which explains that the term comes from the Greek *paradoxos* ('conflicting with expectations') and refers to it as 'one exhibiting inexplicable or contradictory aspects.'
2. John W. Holmes, *The Better Part of Valour: Essays on Canadian Diplomacy* (Toronto: McClelland and Stewart, 1970) p.vii. He continued in a similar vein: 'Discretion in diplomacy is not incompatible with boldness of initiative in foreign policy or even with dramatic moves in international politics. The discretion is in the calculation of the issues at stake and the forces which can be mustered. Above all it lies in the recognition of contradiction and the acceptance of paradox.'
3. See the letter of Ambassador Cruz to the Canadian Prime Minister, 3 May 1961, Archives, MINREX, Havana.

4. See the memo, 'Le règlement municipal contre les incendies et la chancellerie de Cuba', 27 May 1969, 20-1-2-CUBA, 2, Archives, Department of External Affairs, Ottawa.
5. See the memo from the Department of Agriculture to the Canadian Embassy in Havana, 'Cable re: Karsh', 22 October 1971, File 20-1-2-Cuba, vol. 14, 1 October 1971–30 November 1971, Archives, Department of External Affairs, Ottawa.
6. Pierre Elliot Trudeau, *Conversation with Canadians* (Toronto: University of Toronto Press, 1972) p.176.
7. See the memo of J.C. Langley prepared for the Under-Secretary of State for External Affairs, and sent on 29 April 1969 to the Canadian embassy in Washington. Archives of the Department of External Affairs, 20-1-2-Cuba, p.2.
8. Government of Canada, 'News Release', no. 199, 13 October 1992, 'Canada issues order blocking US trade restrictions', p.1.
9. For an account of a recent trip of David Warner, see his article, 'A Speaker's Diary: Parliamentary Visit to Cuba', *Canadian Parliamentary Review*, vol. 15, no. 4, Winter 1992–3, pp.11–13.
10. Richard V. Gorham, 'Canada–Cuba Relations: A Brief Overview', in H. Michael Erisman and John M. Kirk (eds), *Cuban Foreign Policy Confronts a New International Order* (Boulder, Col.: Lynne Rienner, 1992) p.203.
11. Holmes, *The Better Part of Valour*, pp.vii–viii.
12. Ibid., p.27.

Part III

Resolving the US–Cuban Impasse

10 Cuban Security in the Post-Cold War World: Old and New Challenges and Opportunities[1]

Carlos Alzugaray

CONCEPTUAL FRAMEWORK

As Raymond Aron argued in his classic *Paix et Guerre entre les nations*, 'toute unité politique aspire à survivre'.[2] Herein lies the reason for security, in terms of the ability of any nation to survive, becoming the main objective of national strategy. However, defining national security has always been a difficult endeavour, for both policy-makers and scholars. In 1985, the international community recognized this dilemma when the United Nations' secretary general, at the request of the General Assembly, published a report by a group of experts about the concepts of security, demonstrating that there was substantial confusion about the subject.

This report confirmed what Arnold Wolfers had pointed out as early as 1952, in a well known article published in the *Political Science Quarterly*, about the ambiguous nature of national security as a symbol more than a substance of policy.[3] More recently, however, especially since the late 1980s, there has been some success in pinpointing the exact content of the concept of security. The Canadian National Defence College, for example, has defined it in the following terms:

> National Security is the preservation of a way of life acceptable to the Canadian people and compatible with the needs and legitimate aspirations of others. It includes freedom from internal subversion and freedom from the erosion of the political, economic and social values which are essential to the quality of life in Canada.[4]

The above definition, applied to the Cuban case, can serve our purposes very well by offering us a proper framework of analysis. However, it must be taken into account that, since the 1960s, there has been a growing consensus that development and security are 'inextricably entwined', as

UN Secretary-General Boutros Boutros-Ghali ascertained in the Winter 1992/3 issue of *Foreign Affairs*.

None other than Robert McNamara, who served as secretary of defence in the Kennedy and Johnson administrations in the 1960s and later became president of the World Bank, explained this linkage in his 1968 book, *The Essence of Security*:

> In a modernizing society security means development. Security is not military hardware, though it may include it; security is not military force, though it may involve it; security is not traditional military activity, though it may encompass it. Security is development, and without development there can be no security. A developing nation that does not, in fact, develop simply cannot remain secure for the intractable reason that its own citizenry cannot shed its human nature.[5]

The Independent Commission on Disarmament and Security Issues, headed by Olof Palme, reaffirmed the concept when it stressed in 1982:

> The present condition of the world economy threatens the security of every country. The Commission believes that just as countries cannot achieve security at each other's expense, so too they cannot achieve security through military strength alone. Common security requires that people live in dignity and peace, that they have enough to eat and are able to find work and live in a world without poverty and destitution.[6]

But the notion of development itself has also been a subject of disagreement. The South Commission in its 1990 report, *Challenge to the South*, argued forcefully for a broad interpretation:

> The South's vision must also embrace a notion of what development ultimately signifies. In our view, development is a process which enables human beings to realize their potential, build self-confidence, and lead lives of dignity and fulfilment. It is a process which frees people from the fear of want and exploitation. It is a movement away from political, economic, or social oppression. Through development, political independence acquires its true significance. And it is a process of growth, a movement essentially springing from within the society that is developing.[7]

HISTORICAL SETTING

For Cuba, the attainment of security and development as described in the above-mentioned terms has been the central goal of national policy for the past 35 years. However, because of her geopolitical setting close to the United States, her geostrategic importance as key to the Caribbean Basin and northern tier of the Latin American continent, and the openness and vulnerability of her economy, the Cuban search for those aims has turned into a very complex and indeed perilous endeavour.

Cuba's history is the history of the Caribbean, and the history of the Caribbean, as former Dominican President Juan Bosch has argued, is 'the history of the struggle of empires against the peoples of the region to take away their rich lands; it is also the history of the struggle of empires against each other, to take away part of what each one of them had conquered; and lastly, it is the history of the struggle of the peoples of the region to liberate themselves from their imperial masters.'[8] Since the early eighteenth century, when Thomas Jefferson advised the British minister in Washington that the United States would not accept the transfer of sovereignty over Cuba from Spain to any other power and John Quincy Adams enunciated his ripe apple doctrine, arguing in a private letter that the Cuban archipelago would inevitably fall under the American sphere of influence as soon as it was torn away from Spain, as surely as an apple would fall to the ground when it ripened, every US government has felt that it had a special responsibility in ordering, organizing and overseeing Cuba's economic and political system.

If there was ever a clear example of the application of the so-called 'doctrine of limited sovereignty', you could find it in the US–Cuban relationship up to 1959. This hegemonic syndrome imperilled Cuba's security and negatively influenced her development. Hence economic and political independence from the United States is perceived in Cuba as a precondition for both. Her previous semi-colonial and dependent status was one of the main causes for the 1959 Cuban Revolution, which is, as Harvard Professor Jorge Domínguez has recently pointed out in 'Castro's Staying Power', in the spring 1993 issue of *Foreign Affairs*, 'an authentic social revolution', a fact very often forgotten when post-Cold War myths about the Cold War become so common.[9]

Just like any other revolution, the Cuban one had to introduce radical change into the economy and society, which in turn could not be done without affecting US economic and political interests. It is this complex problem and none other that lies at the vortex of the 35 year conflict between Havana and Washington.

The Cuban revolutionary leadership has pursued four main objectives throughout all these years: national independence, economic development, social justice and political democracy. Those four objectives, intimately related to each other, are at the centre of Cuba's aspirations today.

The past and present attitude of the US government, which in essence means the hegemonic rejection of an independent and sovereign Cuba, has been and still is the overbearing threat to her security. Because of the asymmetry of power between them, their geographical closeness and the use by the United States of practically every instrument of policy short of a major military invasion, this danger has become a multidimensional menace that the Cuban government has overcome until now, albeit at a high price in material and human terms. With the end of the Cold War, the danger arising from this US hegemonic aspiration has increased substantially.

In defining current policy towards Cuba, American officials stress the advantage that the disappearance of the Soviet Union and the community of European socialist countries gives them, by eliminating this Caribbean nation's main political and military allies, her secure and fair markets and her source of capital goods, spare parts, foodstuffs and investments.

That situation has provided the US government 'with an unprecedented opportunity' to achieve its goals in Cuba, as explained in Section 1701 (Findings), paragraph (6) of the Cuban Democracy Act of 1992. This legislation, also known as the Torricelli Bill, constitutes the most comprehensive formulation of American policy towards the island nation and means that Washington arrogates to itself the right to determine her socio-economic regime, in a typically ideologized Cold War position.

US policy hinges on the effectiveness of the economic, commercial and financial blockade of Cuba in the expectation that it will bring about both the overthrow of the Cuban government and the complete transformation of the economic and political system itself. Some observers have pointed out that what is being sought is a 'pressure cooker effect': to increase the difficulties that the Cuban people face, inducing a social upheaval that would either bring about the demise of the system or a chaotic situation which would legitimize a US military invasion, under the broad umbrella of a humanitarian intervention.

The pressure cooker effect is reinforced by American immigration policy towards Cuba. As is the case with any other country in the region, there has always existed a strong tendency for Cubans to emigrate to the United States. However, Washington persists in putting obstacles in the way of normal and ordered entries into American territory, while stimulating the illegal ones through the Cuban Adjustment Act. It is paradoxical and extremely destabilizing that any Cuban who is denied a normal visa request at the Interest Section in Havana can be admitted into US territory if he or she uses illegal means, even in the case where a crime is committed.

MILITARY SECURITY

The Clinton administration has moderated the rhetoric of the US governments's Cuba policy and has initiated a period of so-called tacit cooperation with Havana in specific and limited areas of common interest. However, there is no basic change in its position as described in the Torricelli Bill, supported by the president himself during the 1992 electoral campaign. In July 1993, the White House approved the regulations for its implementation. The rationale behind such a course is that the Cuban leadership cannot survive the economic crisis without introducing the type of changes that the US government arrogantly demands, as the president himself declared to *The Miami Herald* on 6 September 1993.

Although recently Washington has publicly promised that its armed forces do not threaten Cuba, in line with what the Interamerican Dialogue's special report, *Cuba in the Americas: Reciprocal Challenges*, recommended, Havana cannot feel secure as long as her powerful neighbour seeks the overthrow of her sociopolitical system through the application of coercive economic sanctions. This is clearly the case, despite all protestations of peaceful intent that are included in US official statements on Cuban policy.

The Cuban leadership cannot forget that in 1989 the United States invaded Panama, ignoring the pledges not to do so included in the 1977 Panama Canal Treaties. Moreover, the Chairman of the US Joint Chiefs of Staff declared after the Gulf War that Cuba was one of the few enemies of the United States still around. War manoeuvres resembling activities that the US armed forces would have to undertake to attack Cuba have been conducted over in the early 1990s in the Caribbean Basin.

More recently, in a keynote address to the fourteenth Seminar on International Security, which took place at The Graduate Institute of International Studies in Geneva, US Ambassador to the European Union, James Dobbins, while proposing what he described as a 'new grand strategy' for the United States and the West, mentioned Cuba – together with Iraq, Iran, Libya and Serbia – as one of the countries which had to be contained in the post-Cold War international system.

The world is passing through a unipolar moment, as Charles Krauthammer defined it in a recent issue of *Foreign Affairs*.[10] The United States is the only multidimensional superpower and present discussions at international fora involve such new and sensitive concepts as limited sovereignty, humanitarian intervention and the irrelevance of the principle of self-determination. Given the priority the United States accords its travails to isolate Havana diplomatically and destroy Cuba's image, attempting to portray her as a human rights violator, it would be naive for the Cuban government to trust that these factors could not be combined at a future date to legitimize a military intervention in the island, sanctioned by the UN Security Council, where the American government enjoys paramount power at the moment.

Even though Cuba is undergoing a period of extraordinary economic difficulties, it has no choice but to maintain the necessary defensive resources in order to deter a US invasion. The main tenets of the Cuban military posture (Doctrina de la Guerra de Todo el Pueblo – All People's War Doctrine), first developed in the early 1980s, are still relevant today. Deterrent in essence, its basic underpinnings stress that, if Cuba prepared the whole population for protracted resistance, a future war would become so costly in human and material terms that the hostile country would desist in its aggressive intent.

Cuba's military security policy follows Walter Lippmann's maxim: 'A nation has security when it does not have to sacrifice its legitimate interests to avoid war, and is able, if challenged, to maintain them by war.'[11] Cuban leaders are confident that such a defensive stance is possible under present circumstances, although a special effort must be made to reduce her armed forces to the bare minimum, enhancing their self-reliance without decreasing their deterrent capability. As long as her defense system is perceived to be stable and effective in Washington, the military threats to Cuba's security may remain latent, but cannot be considered immediate.

INTERNAL POLITICAL SECURITY

A second source of danger to Cuba stems from the policy of internal subversion conducted by the United States, through what the government in Washington euphemistically calls public diplomacy, reminiscent of the Low Intensity Conflict (LIC) Theory, typical of the Second Cold War. The proposed objective, as reflected in the Torricelli Bill, is to bring about a 'peaceful transition to democracy'. Behind this formula, what is being pursued is the imposition of a basic systemic change, so as to create a new economic and political regime that would be more amenable to the American hegemonic syndrome towards Cuba.

Although the Cuban government enjoys overwhelming popular support even in the very difficult present circumstances, as was demonstrated in the massive support obtained in the December 1992 and February 1993 elections, the US government insists on questioning its legitimacy and deploys enormous efforts to disprove it, by its destabilization campaign.

The United States Information Agency and the Voice of America (VOA) maintain a two-pronged radio and television programme directed exclusively at Cuba, transmitting anti-government propaganda for the population on the island. Official broadcasts are supplemented by dozens of 'pirate' radio stations. All of them concentrate on providing disinformation and opinion-forming programmes in which Cuba is depicted as a decomposing society, isolated from the world.

A recent example of this destabilizing policy was the way in which the Cuban Service of VOA handled the activities carried out by criminal elements and antisocial individuals, who took advantage of the power cuts in Havana and other towns during the summer months of July and August 1993 to break windows and throw bricks at peaceful bystanders. Artificially giving them a political overtone, the main pirate radio station unsuccessfully attempted to stimulate them, criticizing at the same time the Cuban government when it undertook measures to bring to a halt such acts of indiscriminate violence, which constituted clear violations of social discipline and jeopardized the security of law-abiding citizens.

These broadcasts are paid for by American taxpayers, at a cost of US$ 17 million a year from 1985 to 1990 and around US$ 30 since then, when the TV Martí channel was added. Significantly, this channel has been successfully blocked and is not seen at all inside Cuba.

Through the National Endowment for Democracy, millions of dollars have been funnelled to opposition groups mainly outside, but also inside Cuba, presenting them as allegedly independent human rights activists. None of them has been successful in growing to more than a few individuals without any significant influence among the Cuban people. An important characteristic of these groups is their persistent incapacity to articulate an alternative, credible and comprehensive economic and political programme that would address the historical problems facing the Cuban people: national independence, autonomous economic development, social justice and political democracy.

Other typical traits of these groups are their sectarianism and constant internal squabbling, which keeps them divided into numerous tendencies. Even though they had the opportunity to participate in the elections of December 1992, none was able to muster enough support even to get their candidates on the ballot for the first round of municipal elections.

(Nominations to these elections were made at 24 215 open neighbourhood meetings, where every citizen could propose, or be proposed as, a candidate. Half the national deputies and provincial delegates elected in the February 1993 elections were originally nominated in these meetings.)

American policy has been partially successful in portraying Cuba as 'swimming against the current' because of the uniqueness of her revolutionary democracy and the association of her political system with the failed regimes of the former Soviet Union and Eastern Europe. Even though mistakes were made and certain traits of the system were copied from the Soviet and Eastern European models, the fact is that the essential premises of the Cuban polity evolved basically from the democratic traditions of her own society.

Before 1959, Cuba experimented with two-party and multi-party systems, which guaranteed neither political independence and freedom, democracy, fair elections, economic well-being nor social justice. Moreover, both experiments ended, in 1932 and 1952, with the establishment of cruel dictatorships, subservient to US interests and characterized by their flagrant, systematic and massive human rights violations, anti-democratic essence, widespread electoral frauds and administrative corruption. The existence of more than one political party was totally ineffective in stopping these tragic outcomes.

It was not surprising that, in 1959, practically all of the pre-revolutionary parties disappeared without pain or glory. Their lack of prestige and political authority, because of fraudulent practices and corruption, produced enormous scepticism among the population about their effectiveness and legitimacy. These parties have not even been able to reproduce themselves among the exiled population in Florida or other parts of the world.

For the Cuban political elite, to experiment once again with a multi-party system would not only go against the popular will expressed in the 1976 constitution, but would invite disaster by undermining national independence, basic human rights protection and real social justice acquired and guaranteed under the revolutionary regime established after 1959.

The challenge for today's Cuba is to search for and find ways that would secure a continually growing popular participation in the governance of the country with the necessary plurality, in an increasingly democratic environment, without opening it up to the manipulation of the anti-national elements, who are trying to come back from Miami and restore the pre-revolutionary dictatorial regime. Their supporters in the US government, which have traditionally taken advantage of any factional or political division in Cuba to impose their will on the Cuban people, also seek to impose a 'made-in-Washington' form of government.

SECURITY AND FOREIGN POLICY

The Cuban government must neutralize US efforts to isolate it in the international arena since, at this level, the military and internal subversion threats could be combined if it became possible to present Cuba as an outlaw state against whom sanctions should be adopted by the Security Council. Such a scenario is unthinkable at the moment, but cannot be dismissed as long as certain trends prevail. Just recently, the US House of Representatives adopted a non-binding resolution asking President Clinton to 'internationalize the embargo' by presenting Cuba's alleged human rights violations to the Security Council and requesting the imposition of economic, commercial and financial sanctions.

In 1991, the United States imposed a Special Rapporteur for Cuba at the UN Human Rights Commission, even though neither the Secretary-General nor the Latin American and Caribbean Group had requested it. This action was a typical example of the politically motivated manipulation of the human rights issue for the purposes of superpower intervention in the internal affairs of an underdeveloped country, as some observers have pointed out.

The Torricelli Bill, Section 1703 (Statement of Policy), paragraph (3), specifies that it is the policy of the United States 'to make clear to other countries that, in determining its relations with them, the United States will take into account their willingness to cooperate in such a policy [towards Cuba]'. Therefore it is imperative for Cuba to conduct an active foreign policy that would tend to demystify the distorted image that is being projected about her, broadening bilateral and multilateral relations as much as possible.

Cuba's role in United Nations as an active, principled and, at the same time, flexible actor is of the utmost importance. Her recent election as a member of the Economic and Social Council (ECOSOC) and her important contributions to the Vienna World Conference on Human Rights attest to her success. At the UN and other international fora, Cuba is seen as an influential Third-World nation which can be counted on to put forward the positions of the Group of 77 and the Nonaligned Movement. Her contributions to South–South cooperation in Asia, Africa, Latin America and the Caribbean in public health, education and construction are important assets of her multilateral diplomacy.

Cuban foreign policy has entered a new, more active phase as she searches for new alliances. Her natural environment is Latin America and the Caribbean (LAC), where she is seeking some form of cooperation with CARICOM, supporting the creation of the Association of Caribbean States, taking part actively in the three Ibero-American summits (the last one was held in Brazil in late July 1993) and other concertation efforts, and strengthening relations with all the countries of the region. The recent visit of President Fidel Castro to Bolivia, to participate in the inauguration of President Gonzalo Sánchez de Losada and his subsequent conversations with Colombian President César Gaviria at Cartagena de Indias attest to the success of Cuban policy in Latin America.

Although Cuba is encountering opportunities at the regional level, there are also important challenges. Latin American and Caribbean economic integration at present is passing through a period of ambivalence, as was pointed out recently by Cuban economist Osvaldo Martínez, Director of Havana's Centro de Investigaciones sobre la Economía Mundial (Centre for World Economics Research) and President of the Economics Commission of the National Assembly. On the one hand, this economic integration has become more necessary than ever before while, on the other, it is being pushed as part of neoliberal experiments with their high social costs and orientation towards a continental economic bloc with the United States as its central component. For Cuba, this scheme is not completely satisfactory, as long as the American sanctions against Cuba are in place.

The development of relations with Mexico, Colombia, Chile, Brazil and Venezuela, among other Latin American countries, demonstrates the real possibilities of growth, but is not exempt from certain political and economic obstacles. A few governments, mainly in Central America, still refuse to establish full diplomatic relations with Cuba. Some of them, no doubt, fear US reaction to such a step. Nevertheless, the definitive insertion of Cuba into the LAC Commonwealth is already a fact of life. The consolidation of this process is essential in guaranteeing Cuban security. Given the peculiarities of her economic and political system and the crises in some of the most reputedly democratic neighbouring polities, the challenges are both for Cuba and the hemisphere, which has to demonstrate that it will continue nurturing pluralism of political regimes in a difficult social and economic environment, where poverty and huge differences in the standard of living – a phenomenon which Cuba has overcome – can imperil recent democratic advances.

Present challenges to Cuban security and foreign policies are also linked to the development of her relations with other regions of the world. Foremost among them are the industrialized capitalist nations of the North, where there are both opportunities and challenges. The opening of Cuba's economy to foreign investments has attracted businessmen from all over Europe, Canada and Japan, yet relations with most of these governments are clouded from time to time by their coincidence with the United States in their assessment of Cuba's political system and her human rights record.

Of course, not all governments take exactly the same position and it must be recognized that the present impossibility of Cuba's servicing her debt is also a factor affecting the development of closer ties, especially in the fields of aid to development and economic cooperation. Nevertheless, Havana has suceeded in maintaining a working relationship with this group as a whole and in this sense has been able to thwart US isolationist attempts.

Since we are talking about the closest US allies, the maintenance and nurturing of such relationships become a very important counterpoint to American policy of economic sanctions. Harvard University's Jorge Domínguez has rightly pointed out that, in this aspect, the US government has contributed to its own isolation by giving priority to its Cuban policy over the elimination of irritating elements in its ties with some important allies.

Cuba maintains a broad range of relationships with the Asian and African states. A case that merits special consideration is China, which has become a major trading partner and with whom Cuba maintains a high degree of political cooperation. On the other hand, countries such as China, Vietnam, Iran, Ghana and Zimbabwe hold similar positions to Cuba's in resisting the projected new world order where sovereignty and self-determination would be undermined.

Relations with Russia and some of the former Soviet republics are a very special case. There is no doubt that Cuban insistence on maintaining a basically socialist economy must sound irksome to reformist ears. Nevertheless, there are important strategic and economic interests, especially in the case of Moscow. Relations have recently been activated by the signing of several agreements and there is a political will to expand them. The main obstacle lies in the prevailing instability and unpredictability of the Russian political situation.

ECONOMIC SECURITY

Because Cuba had based her development on her relationships with the Soviet Union and the socialist community, integrating her trade, finances and economy in the Council of Mutual Economic Assistance (CMEA) since 1972, the demise of this system has created the most critical situation that the country has faced in recent times. Cuba's import capacity diminished from an estimated US$ 8 billion in 1989 to a little over US$ 2 billion in 1991. From 13 million tons of oil that were imported in 1988, the country now has to survive with only five to six million.

In these very difficult circumstances, the US government has decided opportunistically to tighten its economic, commercial and financial blockade against Cuba through the enactment of the Torricelli Bill, as has already been pointed out. Herein lies the most difficult present challenge to Cuba's national security. To reinsert and reorient the country's external economic relations in a changed world, where capitalist market systems predominate, with the dead weight of American unilateral sanctions hanging over the adoption of a new economic strategy, while at the same time maintaining the social gains acquired during the last 35 years and guaranteeing the society's security and stability, seems an insurmountable task.

Yet over the last three years Cuba has been defying all predictions – surviving in these very adverse conditions and even conducting national elections under new, more democratic rules. Looking at the Cuban government's ability to survive in the four years since 1989, one is reminded of the Italian aphorism: 'Il possibile l'abbiamo gia fatto. L'impossibile lo stiamo facendo. Per i miracoli ci vuole un po' di tempo.'[12]

In order to pull off that miracle in the economic sphere, the government has adopted a programme whose main objectives are:

(1) food self-sufficiency through the extensive cultivation of new crops;
(2) expansion of the tourist sector with the aim of turning it into the second most important source of foreign currency, after the export of sugar;
(3) development of its biotechnological and pharmaceutical industry, based on the country's comparative advantage resulting from the investments that over the years were made to enhance the national health service;
(4) attracting foreign investment to those sectors where the national economy does not have the capital, the markets, the basic products or the technical knowhow to develop;
(5) pushing for an aggressive development of oil exploration and exploitation in order to compensate the loss of import capacity.

What the government has been endeavouring to do is to guarantee a *soft landing* of the economy after the debacle of Cuba's external commercial and financial relations, while creating conditions for the *take-off* of her development process under a new diversified model, including initiatives that could not even be realistically considered a few months or years ago. Each new measure adopted by the government in the economic sphere during 1993 – the legalization of foreign currency, the authorization of self-employment and small private enterprises or the decentralization of the agricultural sector – cannot be taken as final under current circumstances. Other transformations should be expected as Cuban development faces new challenges, such as the ones adopted in mid-1994. The present aims are to increase productivity and stimulate an economic recovery without sacrificing the core social achievements of the revolution.

If Cuba can survive its current economic predicament in the next three to four years, as most of its leaders believe, this will inevitably generate pressure for the lifting of the US economic blockade. In this case, as Edward González and David Ronfeldt, of the Rand Corporation, wrote in their *Cuba Adrift in a Postcommunist World*, the blockade

> would look increasingly anachronistic not only because of the Cold War's end and Cuba's apparent cessation of its 'internationalist' and subversive activities in Africa and Central America, but also because of the end runs by Western investors and traders eager to do business in Cuba. Continued maintenance of the embargo under these circumstances would be subject to international and domestic criticism, including from US investors and other economic interests wanting equal access to the island.[13]

That criticism may have already begun. On 24 November 1992, the United Nations General Assembly adopted Resolution 19/47 on the need to put an end to the economic, commercial and financial blockade imposed against Cuba by the government of the United States. The vote was 59 to three, with 74 abstentions. Many US allies and friends joined the Cuban delegation in supporting the measure. A new resolution on the subject was adopted by an even wider margin in November 1993, and again a year later.

In Latin America and the Caribbean even those few governments who are more critical of Cuba's political system, such as Argentina, have demanded an end to the sanctions. This position was expressed in the final document of the Ibero-American summit in July 1993. Moreover, both the European Commission and Parliament have expressed their disavowal of such a policy and demanded that the United States repudiate the Torricelli Bill.

Inside the United States there is a growing movement against the blockade among religious groups, public health workers, the business sector and even the Cuban-American community. Several important US newspapers, such as *The New York Times* and *The Washington Post* have editorialized against it. Cuba must insist on the elimination of the blockade which has already cost her more than 40 billion dollars, according to the estimates of the *Instituto Nacional de Investigaciones Económicas* (National Institute of Economic Research). Even with the sanctions in place, the government is convinced that by continuing present policies the country will overcome her current predicament and emerge fully integrated into the world capitalist economy without sacrificing its social achievements resulting from the socialist policies followed in the past.

Maintaining a policy of unilateral and extraterritorial sanctions against Cuba, the US administration is damaging its relations with other governments and hurting its own business interests. It is also giving Cuba the possibility of developing a diversified economy without initial American economic and financial presence. This could have a beneficial impact on the long-term prospects of Cuba, since any normalization of relations between the two countries, which is unavoidable in the long run, would inmediately generate enormous pressure for an opening to US investments. The Cuban government would like nothing better than to have the leverage of a broad variety of commercial and financial partners in order to preserve its independence by compensating in advance a future massive influx of US capital and business interests.

It must be taken into account that one of the endemic problems in the pre-revolutionary period was the disproportionate position of US companies and their excessive influence. Future Cuban security and development could be enhanced if the country could develop a diversified economy, both in terms of production and sources of capital.

CONCLUSIONS

Regional security and development would benefit from a détente in Cuban–American relations. Most countries in the Basin feel uneasy about the present state of this 35-year conflict. The Group of 3 (Mexico, Venezuela and Colombia) has appealed both to Cuba and to the United States to put aside their differences and negotiate a normalization of relations. Caribbean leaders feel, as former Jamaican Prime Minister Michael Manley has recently stated, that the US policy is an anachronism which impedes rational economic development for the region.

Cuba is ready to negotiate a normalization of relations if the United States treats her as a sovereign country with equal rights and responsibilities. This is hardly a tough precondition. However, it will take a broad vision for the present or any future American administration to understand that it stands to gain more from a normalization of relations with the current Cuban government, as Robert Pastor recommended in his article on US Latin American policy, published in the autumn 1992 issue of *Foreign Policy*.[14]

With the end of the Cold War, hardly any benefit can be derived from a policy that ignores the fact that no other leadership in the region has been more successful in maintaining peace and stability in its territory under incredibly adverse circumstances and against the challenge of continued American hostility. The probability that such a leadership would surrender, as the US government seems to think, is non-existent. In summary, for Cuba security and development are intimately linked. Paradoxically, the end of the Cold War has not made Cuba's task easier. Old dangers remain or have been enhanced by the new international situation. The US hegemonic altitude towards the island has been accentuated by the 'unipolar moment' resulting from the demise of the Soviet Union, formerly Cuba's main ally. By the same token, she has lost her most significant trading partners and her import capacity has been reduced fourfold over the 1989–92 period. While Cuba is better prepared to overcome the military and political threats arising from the new world order, her most important challenge resides in the economic sphere, where the US blockade complicates an already critical situation.

No matter how difficult Cuba's predicament, there are also new opportunities. The disappearance of the Soviet and Eastern European socialist experiment has liberated Cuba from the need to accept certain alien dogmas and practices with which her political elite never felt fully comfortable. This means she can follow a course of action more in line with her own cultural traditions, closer as they are to Latin American and Caribbean developments. In the economic sphere, she can now adopt a policy that will really bring about an autonomous and diversified development.

In his largely ignored and strongly criticized latest book, *Out of Control: Global Turmoil on the Eve of the 21st Century*, Zbigniew Brzezinski has argued that 'the preoccupation with global inequality is likely to express itself through political receptivity to the appeal of a concrete model and a specific leader that appear effective in defying the richer West and in shaping a social order that is stable and capable of coping internally with massive social injustice'.[15] The former National Security adviser casts China in that role in a world context.

Given the extreme inequalities and poverty prevailing in Latin America and the Caribbean, excellently described in the Interamerican Dialogue's last report, *Convergencia y Comunidad: Las Américas en 1993* (Convergence and Community: The Americas in 1993), in contrast to the *permissive cornucopia*[16] that pervades American culture, Cuba and Fidel Castro could very well fit the part described by Brzezinski at the Western Hemisphere level.

In those circumstances, although Cuba might be adrift, she will certainly neither go away nor sink in the post-Cold War World. Precisely that scenario would present a distinct challenge to Caribbean and Western Hemisphere security if the United States does not finally come to terms with the reality that Cuba attained her independence in 1959 and there is no way that the clock of history can be turned back.

Notes

1. This chapter contains the author's personal opinions and does not necessarily reflect the official position of the Cuban government.
2. Raymond Aron, *Paix et Guerre entre les nations* (Paris: Calmann-Lévy, 1962) p.82.
3. Arnold Wolfers, 'National Security as an "Ambiguous Symbol" ', *Political Science Quarterly*, vol. 64, no. 4, December 1952, pp.481–502.
4. *Divided We Fall: The National Security Implications of Canadian Constitutional Issues* (Toronto, Ontario: The Canadian Institute of Strategic Studies, 1992) p.4.
5. Robert McNamara, *The Essence of Security: Reflections in Office* (New York: Harper & Row, 1968) p.49.
6. *Common Security: A Blueprint for Survival* (New York: Simon & Schuster, 1982) p.182.
7. Comisión Sur, *Desafío al Sur* (Mexico: Fondo de Cultura Económica, 1991) pp.13–14.
8. Juan Bosch, *De Cristóbal Colón a Fidel Castro: el Caribe, frontera imperial* (Madrid: Ediciones Alfaguara, 1970) p.12.
9. Domínguez has consistently sustained this position. In his *To Make a World Safe for Revolution: Cuba's Foreign Policy* (Cambridge Mass.: Harvard University Press, 1989) p.2, he affirmed: 'In spite of foreign policy reverses and domestic opposition, however, Cuba's is one of the twentieth century's authentic revolutions.'
10. Charles Krauthammer, 'The Unipolar Moment', *Foreign Affairs: America and the World 1990/91*, vol. 70, no. 1.
11. Walter Lippmann, *US Foreign Policy: Shield of the Republic* (Boston, Mass.: Little, Brown & Co., 1943) p.51.
12. 'We have already done what is possible. We are working on the impossible. We need a little more time to pull off a miracle.'
13. Edward González and David Rondfelt, *Cuba Adrift in a Postcommunist World* (Santa Monica, Cal.: RAND Corporation, 1992) p.51.
14. Robert Pastor, 'The Latin American Option', *Foreign Policy*, no. 88, Fall 1992, p.51.
15. Zbigniew Brzezinski, *Out of Control: Global Turmoil on the Eve of the 21st Century* (New York: Charles Scribner's Sons, 1993) p.226.
16. A term used also by Brzezinski to describe the prevailing lifestyle in the West, which has as its primary end individual self-gratification, without any moral restraint.

11 'Conflict Resolution' between the United States and Cuba: Clarifications, Premises and Precautions

Rafael Hernández

In an article published in the winter 1991–2 edition of *Foreign Affairs*, and which has passed conspicuously unobserved by the majority of experts on Cuban problems, the secretary of state of the United States expressed the following:

> As our president pointed out at Yale University in June, no nation has yet discovered a way to import the world's goods and services while stopping foreign ideas at the border. It is in our interest that the next generations in *Cuba* be engaged by the Information Age, not isolated from global trends shaping the future . . . Resolving these issues . . . can only be pursued through a policy of active engagement . . . Our experiences in working with *Havana* on *the South West Africa peace process* and on *the migration issue* suggest that our engagement can produce results. In sum we need to recognize that *Cuba* is in a time of transition. An anachronistic regime has alienated us by lashing out, by seeking to repress an irrepressible spirit. A return to hostile confrontation will not help the people of *Cuba* nor serve our national interest.[1]

This quotation is almost exact. The only difference is that I have substituted 'Cuba' (or 'Havana') for 'China' (or 'Beijing'), and 'South West Africa' and 'the migration issue' for 'Cambodia' and 'the Korean Peninsula', so that the Bush administration will have already explained before the public opinion of its own country and the world the strategic basis for re-establishing relations with Cuba, through this speech by the secretary of state.

However, the conflict continues. Why?

THE NATURE OF THE CONFLICT AND THE ATTITUDES OF THE ACTORS

Opposing values and interests have always been at the root of the principal questions that have confronted the United States and Cuba. These values and interests also fall within the more general framework of relations between the United States and Latin America.[2]

According to the logic of classic American geopolitics, countries with values opposed to those of the United States will only allow themselves to be guided by their own interests.[3] From this perspective, these backward countries are not capable of adequately playing the role of objects of domination, and consequently the US must exercise its so-called imperative responsibility. In a few short words, its policy must not be based on the consensus of the dominated, but rather, as Joseph Nye would say, on its duty as a power which is *bound to lead*.[4]

In the tradition of Cuban political thinking, one has always perceived a moral and political duality in the Monroe Doctrine, according to which the United States would preserve the liberty of Latin America against non-hemispheric powers, at the price of exclusivity over the region. For Cubans like José Martí,[5] American values and interests are as distant from those of Latin America as are those of the European powers, and it is contrary to the interests and values of Latin American countries to associate themselves with the United States on the pretext of the technical progress and financing which come from the North.

This aligning of opposing values and interests leads to the following questions. What are the terms of the conflict between Cuba and the United States? To what extent is it reasonable, in the light of the historic tendencies and factors of power at play, to hope for any solution to the conflict? What limits do these factors place on the prospects for change in existing relations?

THE US IMPULSE

American relations with Cuba carry with them a series of enigmas. Why has the United States wasted so much effort on a small island with no great natural resources, and which is so close to it that conventional aircraft could attack it within 15 minutes? How does one explain that this policy has been maintained for so long without substantial results in its stated objective – that of making the present Cuban regime unviable?

In its most general framework, the policy of the United States towards

Cuba is explained by the assumptions of the Monroe Doctrine, by the Cold War and, especially, by 200 years of American influence on the economic, political and cultural destiny of the island. The features which have characterized it can be summarized in terms of national interests, alliances, ideological perceptions and the impact of domestic policies.

The United States has never understood Cuban nationalism. In particular, it has not realized that this nationalism constitutes a force for unifying people that is superior to any ideological or philosophical creed. In its zeal to contain communism and support its Cuban associates, the United States has found allies successively in the Batista regime, the Cuban extreme-right, counterrevolutionary groups fighting in the mountains of the island, terrorist groups in Miami, Latin American military regimes and even the Mafia.

In particular, the United States has proved itself incapable of maintaining an adequate relationship with Cuban exiles with respect to its own national interests. The relationship established with this group was at the heart of the Bay of Pigs fiasco in 1961, and chaotic situations like the exodus from Mariel in 1980. Even today these exiles interfere with the adoption of a rational US policy towards Cuba, thanks to an interweaving of local commitments, links with American political organizations and personal connections which reach as far as Congress. The United States has never understood the extent to which these allies make relations with Cuba impossible.

The United States has always had a limited understanding of the Cuban domestic political situation. The escalation of animosity towards the island, and in general the application of the rule of permanent hostility, have produced results equal and opposite to those which were originally intended. That is, they have produced growing support for the regime, under the banner of a nation threatened by external forces. From the force of Cuban nationalism and from the weakness of American misunderstanding and alliances is derived a strategic imbalance, in Cuba's favour, of greater weight than the technological and quantitative superiority of American power.

As for US domestic politics, Cuba has never been a factor of any influence in dividing American public opinion. The initial sympathy towards the revolution ended rapidly under the weight of the Cold War. The general rejection of Fidel Castro has not ceased, even after monumental errors like that of Playa Girón, or horrors like the threat of nuclear holocaust in 1962. The hatred of the Cuban regime inherent in the dialogue of the Cold War remains intact 30 years later. Hardened by time, it has formed a scab on American public perception, like that which existed towards China for more than 20 years. However, now, unlike the situation in 1960, it is not a factor of any importance in domestic politics, and much less a source of any national consensus.

CUBAN MOTIVATIONS

The Cuban revolutionary impulse of 1959 was the release of one hundred years of frustrated nationalism. In Cuba, revolutionary nationalism was not directed by the communists. However, it was the nationalist revolutionary discourse predominant in Cuba in the early 1960s – and not the language of conventional Soviet Marxism – that caused the political reaction of the United States. If the Cuban Revolution became radical and absorbed Marxist–Leninist ideology, this was due more to the impulse of this revolutionary nationalism, rooted in popular struggles since the wars of independence, than to the influence of historic communist tendencies.

Four months after the triumphant revolution, while the Soviets were still asking themselves who this bearded leader was, Richard Nixon emerged from a conversation with Fidel Castro saying that he must be either 'naive or a communist'. However, Fidel Castro and his fellow collaborators came from the radical wing of the *Partido Ortodoxo* (Orthodox Party), whose ideas were not especially different from those of Perón, Lázaro Cárdenas or Jacobo Arbenz. Whether he was secretly a Marxist or not, the fact is that his politics were not initially in line with those of the USSR. Nonetheless, Eisenhower approved the Playa Girón plan long before the Soviets ever dreamed of one day deploying nuclear missiles on the island.

The question of the true political orientation of the revolution seems to have been a purely academic one for the United States. The American government was not much concerned with establishing a 'subtle difference' between what Cuba did 'by order of the USSR' and what it did on its own account, if – in the US opinion – what Cuba did eventually benefited the East anyway. It seems that the feelings of the East towards the revolutions of the Third World were more clearly defined in Washington than they were in Moscow or Warsaw.

Furthermore, in the end, why would anyone care about these 'subtle differences' concerning Cuba? In other words, who would have had any special political interest in distinguishing rational and legitimate nuances and motivations in the conduct of Fidel Castro? In whose interest is it to explain Cuba's decisions on the basis of its own history, culture, traditions and ideology? It is easier to explain Cuba as a case for Sovietologists, not unlike Hungary or Poland.

The other big problem between the United States and Cuba – perhaps even the greatest – has always been that of the 'exporting of the revolution'. However, despite what the United States may have believed, neither Soviet nor Chinese support has ever been the driving force behind Cuban operations in Latin America or in Africa. Cuba was not 'exporting the revolution' as a 'Soviet satellite' but, more likely, completely of its own accord.

Geopolitical environment played a key role in defining the conflict with Cuba. In the first place, the island is not 20 000 kilometres from the US coast, nor on the border of a socialist power. Consequently, the United States could confine Cuba politically and economically in the 1960s, and separate it from the Inter-American system, reinforcing the objective situation of ideological and geopolitical isolation in which the Cuban socialist regime found itself within the Western Hemisphere.

Secondly, US governments reacted excessively to the Cuban Revolution. In effect, they overestimated the possibility of 'other Cubas' arising in the hemisphere. However, the solution that they hoped to apply to this supposed threat had the potential of creating a self-fulfilling prophesy. Punishing the island was a means of dissuading others from taking the same route, but it had a counterproductive effect. Excluded from the Inter-American system, Cuba felt free to respond by identifying itself with practically all revolutions in the region.

In the end, Cuba has reintegrated into Latin America because other governments ceased to fear it. What is paradoxical is that, without having triumphed in the struggle with the United States, Cuba is today more important in the hemisphere than it ever was before 1959. An important part of this reunion is the result of an international policy which converges with the interests of other countries in the region, and of the Third World in general.

A Third-World component which varies from the more general strategy of Cuban foreign policy has been the rejection of the idea of 'spheres of influence'. Independent of all ideological motivations, the existence of a socialist regime 90 miles from the United States has implied the negation of such geographic fatalism. To a great extent, such a location, exposed to the United States and within the Latin American milieu, has established the Cuban focus in international relations, in contrast to those of other socialist countries.

For Cuban politics, peace represents an object of integral scope, not to be reduced to peace between the superpowers. Particularly on the issue of regional conflicts, Cuba has appreciated that changes at the global scale do not imply the end of regional tensions. To the contrary, since the end of the Cold War, regional conflicts – the Gulf, Bosnia, Somalia – have proliferated.

With respect to national security, its primary problem continues to be the US threat, although many inquire if it is realistic to expect, at this point, a direct military operation against Cuba. In effect, in American military logic the predominant idea does not seem to be to dispose of Cuban socialism in a military manner. Can Cuba assume that it is no longer a target in US contingency plans? Can it be assured that American actions directed at intervening in a Caribbean country will not imply 'cautionary measures' equivalent, in reality, to military operations whose 'secondary' objective will be Cuba? And, above all, would this alternative be discarded if the United States perceived signs of political instability in Cuba? It seems clear that these causes of Cuban concern are a long way from evaporating.[6] In effect, the persistence of destabilization plans, the blockade, the naval base in Guantánamo – together with other, more ambiguous, policies, like the lack of determination against terrorist groups in Miami or New Jersey – and the reaffirming of a policy that seeks to change the political regime in Cuba have been direct threats to Cuba's national security and stability.

With respect to covert activity, from the Cuban perspective one need not conjecture about the recent actions of so conspicuous an organization as the CIA. Self-evidently, propaganda ('Radio Martí', 'Tele Martí') and political action (the support of organizations and groups: 'human rights committees') are maintained in concurrence with *the political culture of covert activity*. Furthermore, under the present circumstances, it is logical to think that not only intelligence activities are undertaken, but also covert operations attacking the stability of the Cuban regime.

While American official discourse does not allow the practice of terrorism, the ambiguity underlying US policy concerning specific sectors of the Cuban community – where terrorist operations against Cuba have typically been initiated – creates a grey area in this respect. In consequence, the majority of Cubans on the island have reason to assume that Cuba effectively constitutes a US target.

Reflecting on the situation as a whole, one must ask oneself: Why – if we except countries like Iraq, against which the United States has launched wars – is the United States more hostile towards Cuba than towards any other country? Why is it more recalcitrant in its relations with Cuba than with China? Thirty years after the imposition of the embargo and the diplomatic break, Cubans perceive a perpetual self-reproduction of these gestures of animosity.

All these factors tend to reaffirm the idea that the relationship between

Cuba and the United States is part of a structural situation which responds to the nature of the conflict and to attitudes which are not easily reduced to terms of negotiation. Does this mean that there exists no room at all for politics or for a diplomatic solution?

THE INTERNATIONAL AND REGIONAL SITUATIONS: THEIR IMPACTS ON THE DYNAMIC OF THE CONFLICT

Let us now examine a series of problems which derive from global changes and are relevant to discussion concerning policy alternatives between the two countries.

The Impact of the Collapse of European 'Real Socialism' and the End of the Cold War

Clearly seen, the lessons for the United States from the fall of socialism in the East should be that economic and diplomatic relationships, cultural exchange and contact in general give greater results than economic blockades and isolation. In effect, the present situations in Hungary, Poland and Czechoslovakia conform more with US objectives than those in Vietnam, the Democratic Republic of Korea and Cuba.

Seen from Cuba, the lessons of the East are a little different. It is strange for Cubans to put themselves in the position of the people of Poland and Czechoslovakia. They were never model political societies for those who knew them directly. Nor did there exist a particular Cuban affinity with their foreign policies towards the Third World or Latin America.

Among the criticisms of foreign policy that could exist in Cuba, it is not common to find oneself reproaching the government for having followed the guidelines of Moscow, as was commonly heard in Eastern Europe. Cubans did not feel themselves to be satellites of the Soviet Union, and thus the fall of the Berlin Wall did not seem to them to be a liberation. In fact, some have found it to be exactly the opposite.

Seen from Cuba, the experience of the USSR and Eastern Europe could be summed up in the following manner. Some policy of reform of socialism being necessary, a poorly conducted process could lead to the demise of the system which it is attempting to reform – and not only of the system, but of the very cohesion of the civil society on which it is built. If changes to the system are really necessary, under conditions of economic crisis and social tensions these must be conducted with the utmost caution and moderation, with the goal of consolidating a new model and overcoming present problems.

Paradoxically, Cubans today could learn more from the successive reforms undergone by the United States itself – preserving the essential integrity of its system despite profound economic crises and formidable social challenges – than from the chaos in which have fallen the societies of the European East.

Naturally, the launching of a far-reaching, controlled, stable and integral process of reform requires not being trapped in a struggle to satisfy one's most immediate necessities. In other words, the present sharp economic crisis does not add to the speed of reform.

National Insecurity

The disappearance of the 'Soviet threat' has clearly raised Cuba's level of exposure to the United States. The impact of the crisis, not only on productive sectors of the economy, but on other aspects like health, education, services and information, and its effect on Cubans' general standard of living, has created a heightened state of social tension, unpredictability and sensitivity over future supplies of necessities – as much from abroad as from within – that borders on a national emergency.

Secondly, the continuance and, in certain aspects, the recrudescence of classic US policy against Cuba, combined with the preceding factors, has increased the feeling of exposure, vulnerability and strategic imbalance in the face of a renewed threat, not only to the economic order and political regime, but also to the social system of the country.

As shown, in strictly military terms, the question of security continues to have a marked influence on Cuban perceptions. In effect, despite the fact that a military attack against Cuba could not guarantee the supposed object – that is, provoke a change in the country's political regime – the persistence of a strategic deployment directed towards the island keeps Cuban precautionary measures intact. These are based, as is logical in military terms, not on the intentions of the enemy, but on its real capacity.

In this context, US policy, contrary to its own interests, contributes to strengthening the Cuban perception of being a *besieged fortress*, with the consequent effect of increasing internal mobilization and cohesion. In this situation, this implies an extension of security measures, special economic controls, greater centralization of decision making, mobilization and so on, and, of course, the maintaining of a certain level of attention to defence.

This image of a besieged fortress is neither solely military, nor merely a perception. The domestic significance of the relationship with the United

States has increased in recent years. Cubans look around themselves and see American footprints in various domestic situations:

(1) the economic crisis experienced by the country sharpens the real significance of the blockade;
(2) the relative reduction of domestic consensus resulting, above all, from the crisis, exacerbates sensitivity to the destabilizing factors introduced by the US government, like radio and television propaganda designed to encourage discontent, and the fostering of opposition groups;
(3) under the conditions of international ideological isolation suffered by socialist ideas owing to the collapse of the USSR and Eastern Europe, campaigns of isolation and discredit directed at representing the Cuban regime as the principal violator of human rights in the hemisphere gain more weight, especially in international forums, using political and economic pressure upon other governments to gain their ends;
(4) in the restorationist climate emerging from the experiences of Eastern Europe, the level of expectations of exiled counterrevolutionary groups in Miami has increased, counting on the promising encouragement of the American administration and creating an atmosphere comparable to that of the White Terror – all of which is perfectly understood in Cuba.

On this last issue it is worth pointing out that the emigration of exiles is a phenomenon which has been highly politicized by both sides. The majority of Cubans want to have more normal relations with their relatives in the United States. However, they do not believe that these relatives have influence that could change US policy towards Cuba. They know that the majority of exiles are not counterrevolutionary militants. However, for the majority of the Cuban population on the island, including those who propose changes to the system, the prevailing discussion among exiles appears authoritarian, conservative and pro-American.

Alliances and Compromise

With the end of Cuba's African wars towards the end of the 1980s and the quieting down of Central American conflicts at the *military level*, as well as with the disappearance of *economic* links with the Socialist bloc, it is logical that *diplomatic* resources should now carry increased weight in Cuban foreign policy. It could only be expected that the Cuba of today would conduct itself with greater diplomatic realism. However, as the Cold War tone has been kept up in relations with the United States, a fourth factor – *ideology* – has tended to acquire greater weight.

The inflammation of the ideological confrontation, in effect, has been converted into an adverse factor for Cuba's reintegration with the rest of the hemisphere. However, this process has not been completely blocked, despite pressure from the United States. At the same time, Cuba is far from being the thorn in the side of Inter-American relations. To a certain extent, the Cuban Revolution has clearly fallen in what could be identified as the hierarchy of regional concerns.

In its conflict with the United States, Cuba found favourable situations in the multilateral forums of the 1970s and the early 1980s, as part of the more general North–South conflict. These forums were characterized by the adoption of the problems of the Third World. Today the international system is characterized by economic crisis within the Third World, processes of integration centred around advanced capitalism, and the well-known collapse of international socialism, all of which continue to be reflected by changes within the institutions of the United Nations system. Among these effects, the internationalization of domestic political problems has been especially significant. This naturally creates a growing margin for Cuban distrust towards multilateral mechanisms.

However, Cuban relations with the Latin American and Caribbean region, and with other countries such as Canada, have improved, as much in economic as in political terms. The rest of the hemisphere, in general, promotes understanding between Cuba and the United States.

THE MARKET AND GEOPOLITICS

The manner in which the United States has failed to recognize the changes seen in the international context of its relations with Cuba as well as the changes within Cuba in recent years, presages that Americans will be content with nothing less than the return of capitalism to Cuba.

Cuban foreign investment policy and the search for markets, as well as relations with business interests from all parts of the world – including those of Mexico, Canada and the United States itself – reflect the point that its present policy is not to go against *geoeconomic factors* or to counteract market forces. The difference between Cuba and other countries of the Caribbean Basin region is that these countries have not been able to separate themselves sufficiently, in their political systems, from the geopolitical conditions imposed by the close proximity of the United States –

conditions which are, by nature, distinct from the logic of the market. Cuba would not necessarily counteract international market relations led by non-state or transnational actors, but would act against subjection to the dictates of the American state. Economic interdependence is not what contradicts the assumptions of Cuban development, but the political regression implied by having the American state as an internal factor in the Cuban system, reigning like a demigod over foreign policy – as it did for more than half a century. Do the logic of the market and the geoeconomic factors of the Caribbean area necessarily imply subjection to the interests of the United States, in terms of domestic political options or of the selling out of national security?

On the other hand, is it not precisely the logic of the market which makes American geopolitics an aberration? If it is geoeconomic logic which is to preside over relations between the United States and the Caribbean Basin, would it not be logical that business leaders prevail over geopoliticians? Or is it that the post-Cold War period will be a return to the pre-Cold War period?

In geopolitical terms, the construction of an international security structure in the Caribbean area would be a necessary, although insufficient, condition for the stability needed to develop economic relations in the area. To guarantee its functioning, in the shadow of the North American Free Trade Agreement, there should be no wars or military operations which would interrupt the free and peaceful course of commerce and transnational productive links. One of the basic promises of free trade is that the problem societies of the Caribbean and Central America would find themselves less troubled by exogenous causes, such as those which at present exacerbate inter-state conflicts or provoke interventions. For this to be true, it would be useful if some rules, accords and cooperation were established between states, facilitating not only free trade but also peace and stability. Without this, the geoeconomic logic of integration between the – at least for the moment – distinct countries and nations of any given area will be like that which was once believed characteristic of the socialist revolution – something inevitable, but which lamentably has not yet occurred completely.

If, in addition to the above condition, states also share the ideas of respect for sovereignty and self-determination, military non-intervention, democracy and human rights, the best means for preserving the free market would be through preventing tensions. Obviously, the question of the market and integration appears as something more complex than the irresistible ascent of certain actors and of a certain geopolitical logic; it also imposes a framework of pluralism and tolerance as *sine qua non* conditions. In another way, all types of differences – ideological, ethnic, national, cultural – confound the transparent dynamics of even the greatest of economic tendencies.

US POLICY TOWARDS CUBA: A HALF-FILLED CUP?

The process of US policy making with respect to Cuba is at present passing through a kind of change. The international circumstances which have decisively marked the course of this policy for 30 years have been radically transformed. The extinction of the Soviet–Cuban alliance and the changing tide of processes of national liberalization in Latin America and Africa in a global context emerging from the end of the Cold War have substantially modified the scenario for policy towards Cuba.

The objectives of this policy continue to be the same as those with which the United States confronted the revolution in 1959 and 1960. Its fundamental ingredients remain unaltered. However, the new global context and its manifestation in political changes in the United States create the conditions for a new logic. This is currently reflected in political statements of intent, in which the ideas of the radical right and moderate liberals converge. The basic continuity and gradualist character of this tendency impede one from clearly appreciating its steady advance. A tendency towards small changes can display, in international and domestic circumstances like those of the present, new conditions which might facilitate decisive changes in future American policy.

OFFICIAL POLITICAL DISCOURSE CONCERNING CUBA

The official American position has not moved much since the Bush administration. Firstly, Cuba must establish a *certified democracy* through 'internationally' observed and qualified elections. This is to say, implementing changes to the electoral system is not enough, but popular power must be made more efficient and democratic, more participatory and pluralist. This means an 'international' organization – like Amnesty International or the Carter Center – and the government of the United States would judge and endorse the change. Secondly, Cuba must abandon its 'closed economic model', given that the failure of the 'statist model' in Latin America has been proved and that 'strong central governments' are a thing of the past. In other words, it is not sufficient that the Cuban economy straighten its path and open itself up to collaboration with foreign capital – by, among other actions, liberalizing the circulation of foreign exchange, independent work and the private use of agriculture – but the reforms must have a radical neoliberal edge, erasing the role of the state in the economy.

This process would permit a 'peaceful transfer, through democratic institutionality, towards a successor government'. In sum, democratic elections, human rights and market economics are conceived of by the US government as a plan to change Cuba's political and social regime peacefully.

Under the Clinton administration, Cuba continues to be an issue of little importance to US foreign policy. It still carries with it the inertia of Cold War discourse, but has ceased to have the strategic value or influence on the dynamic of power of other regions that it had in a bipolar world. This discourse continues to codify Cuba in an old language, with the addition of a new expectation – the inevitability of the collapse of socialism. It is an antiquated outlook, but one not entirely removed from the pragmatism of the post-Cold War period. Why negotiate with a regime which could be incapable of sustaining itself? Why hurry decisions on an issue that is not a foreign policy priority? As a result, official treatment of Cuba in political discourse gives the impression of an issue become stagnant, or 'put on the back burner'.

The principles of this discourse are well known. The United States does not feel obliged to change its policy by bringing it in line with the tendency, predominant in the hemisphere, of maintaining normal relations with Cuba. It qualifies all changes that have occurred in Cuba in recent years as 'cosmetic'. It admits that there exists no military threat to the United States from Cuba, now that the Soviet military presence there is non-existent. It claims to have no hostile military intentions towards the island. However, the full extent of US policy is not contained in this discourse.

THE CLINTON ADMINISTRATION AND FACTORS OF DOMESTIC POLICY

Many experts expect that Clinton will do nothing within his first year with respect to policy towards Cuba. This does not fall within his priorities. The scant references he has made to the subject, such as reiterating his support of the Torricelli Bill, have not been hopeful. The best possible scenario would be if Clinton did not have strictly to follow the letter of these few references. However, this is only a possibility, and by no means assured.

Apparently, other factors continue to be influential. As long as the Cuban

American National Foundation (CANF) is the best organized group in Washington – with all the necessary financial resources – and the only one with any real presence, it will continue to have influence. Other Cuban-American groups appear not to have the same capabilities, nor has there emerged any economic interest group exerting pressure in favour of open relations. It can only be expected that CANF will attempt to block initiatives for change with respect to Cuba. It is also possible that they will manoeuvre to provoke a premature reaction on the part of the administration, committing it to continuing hostilities against the island.

The weight and influence of the group cannot be underestimated. However, it would be an error to think that US policy toward Cuba is maintained only, or even primarily, by CANF. The prevailing policy has been sustained for three decades because the political elite and the permanent bureaucracy of the national security administration have supported it. The existence of CANF itself has been made possible thanks to the continued interests and objectives of these sectors. Today, CANF is a type of Frankenstein which cannot be as useful to many influential elements of the present administration as it was to the previous one, particularly to those needing room to manoeuvre. Furthermore, it is privately considered to be a domestic nuisance by the new foreign policy establishment. At the present time, the key political question with respect to CANF is whether it would have the strength to counter a governmental initiative introducing policy changes concerning Cuba.

To what extent, up to the moment, has the present administration reflected a proclivity towards change? Firstly, it is evident that, as opposed to all other administrations since that of Carter, the Clinton administration has been relatively silent with respect to Cuba. As pointed out earlier, this relative silence could be interpreted as good, inasmuch as early references to the subject would have reflected a pre-established policy on the issue.[7] Secondly, certain members of the new administration have stated that the Torricelli Bill does not tie the hands of the executive. In effect, despite the laws of the blockade, including the recent Torricelli Bill, the executive retains a fundamental decisive power with respect to policy towards Cuba. In fact, the administration could emphasize the 'positive' aspects of these laws, like their allowing for the donation of medicine and food to Cuba. Thirdly, it is obvious that, whatever its real power, CANF and the anti-Cuban extreme right do not possess the same avenues of access to the highest levels of the present administration as they had during Republican administrations. Finally, the logic underlying documents about Cuba at present in circulation carries a different tone, reflecting a critical focus on the efficiency of the inherited policy.

A SCENARIO FOR CHANGE

Looking at present official discourse and the situation as it was under Republican administrations, or assuming that the Torricelli Bill expresses a consensus for possible policy towards Cuba, one would have to assume that the current policy will remain static. It is necessary to analyse the question of the probability of change as a dynamic political process.

Although up to the moment there has been no pressure group, equivalent to CANF, in favour of dialogue with Cuba, the question of the position of the business sector with respect to interests in Cuba should not be seen as a closed book. In fact, the threshold for greater business activity could be determined, definitively, by reading the signs emitted by official policy.

These signs could consist of small movements, such as the showing of some proclivity towards conceding licences for the sale of medicines and food. In terms of authority, the present administration is capable of repealing the presidential proclamation prohibiting American citizens from spending money in Cuba, without modifying the blockade legislation. It is not possible to say what would be the short-term consequences of such a movement. With all certainty, it would modify the domestic political context, in particular attracting the attention of commercial sectors interested in business with Cuba, and creating a framework of expectations enough to cause the rise of pressure groups and lobbies in powerful sectors like those of petroleum, biomedicine and agroindustry, whose power in Congress could greatly surpass that of CANF and the anti-Cuba extreme right. This new configuration would give the Clinton administration an adequate opportunity to openly present the adoption of a new strategy towards Cuba, with a minimum of political cost. In conclusion, these small movements could be produced without changing the overall framework of present policy, although their future effect on this policy would be considerable.

The emergence of a different logic is already revealing itself in documents in circulation concerning Cuba. These are distinguishable from earlier ones by the high political convergence of ideologically discrepant perspectives. From the *Inter-American Dialogue* document to those of the Rand Corporation[8] and Washington's CSIS,[9] one can detect, along with other differences, the predominance of a basic logic which can be summarized as follows. Do not modify the policy of external pressure and isolation represented by the blockade and the constant questioning of human rights and democracy issues in Cuba, but at the same time reactivate diplomacy, looking for contacts and exchanges with different sectors in Cuba both within and outside the government, and increase the possibilities for exchange with the island. In place of accenting only the counterrevolution in Miami or groups in the United States, this new focus seeks to communicate, not only with such sectors in Cuba as youth groups or professionals and intellectuals, but also with mid-level political and business officials and even the armed forces. Although these documents all seem to characterize as improbable the possibility of a situation of political crisis and violence in the short term, they also concur on the need for a strategy for avoiding such an occurrence, if only to prevent the complications and risks that it would entail for the United States.

From the above it can be derived that the pace of change in US policy depends, not really on changes implemented in Cuba, but on such factors as the level of priority which the Cuban issue holds within the foreign policy agenda, on the domestic policy factors mentioned above, and on the composition of the new administration. This does not mean, however, that what actually occurs in Cuba will be irrelevant. The principal question is how the United States perceives political stability on the island – that is to say, its perception of the consensus more or less maintained by the Cuban government. The greater the certainty regarding domestic stability and consensus, the less it will be possible for the United States to defend the idea of isolation and pressure as the most efficient means of dealing with Cuba.

American policy towards Cuba could take some time in arriving at a decisive level – perhaps more than we could imagine. However, what is important is that, like a cup, it may have begun to fill, drop by drop, in an almost imperceptible manner.

PREMISES AND PRECAUTIONS FOR 'SOLVING THE CONFLICT'

The logic implicit in the preceding analysis is that of the feasibility of a normalization of relations between the two countries. However, the point of departure of this chapter has been that the two countries must genuinely accept one another's opposing interests and values, beyond the level of diplomatic discourse. This series of opposing variables must be considered in the light of the premises which govern the process of finding a 'solution to the conflict'.

Moreover, counting costs and benefits today is not reducible, as some would imply, to a zero-sum game.[10] Cuba could win without the necessity of the United States losing, and vice versa. The cost–benefit analysis must be based on the analysis of the implications that the different national situations and scales of specific interests have for each country.

The American Angle

The principal premise behind present US policy towards Cuba could be defined as follows: achieving objectives through a more efficient policy in cost–benefit terms than that which has been maintained for the last three decades. This policy seeks (1) to neutralize the effect that the Cuban revolution has had and still has on US national interests, (2) to contain possible Cuban tendencies which could affect these interests in the future, (3) to augment the general US capacity to influence Cuban policy, and (4) to obtain greater benefits in specific bilateral areas. None of these objectives necessarily implies a relationship of animosity with the Cuban regime.

This said, what would the United States win or lose in finding a diplomatic solution to its international agenda with respect to Cuba?

Costs

(1) Confronting conservative groups, including the Cuban community, active in domestic policy concerning Cuba, as well as wrestling with attitudes and predispositions established over more than three decades within the permanent bureaucracy, in the security and foreign affairs departments, and in Congress.
(2) Recognizing de facto the Cuban regime's right to exist, following 30 years of denying it.
(3) Returning the Guantánamo naval base, implying the ceding to Cuban sovereignty of a naval and air resource used by the US navy in the Caribbean for almost a century.
(4) Subjecting radio and television transmissions towards Cuba to a reciprocal accord, in place of the present unilateral formula.

Benefits

(1) Encouraging a constituency of – especially economic – interest groups supportive of open relations with Cuba. Up to the present, these groups have not begun to function as lobbyists owing to the rigidity of US policy. This would include groups representing petroleum, biomedicine, agroindustry, mining and so on. US dialogue with Cuba would particularly liberate a majority within the Cuban community – including business people – that is at present held hostage by traditional conservative policy, allowing it to organize and express itself in favour of the new policy.
(2) Lifting the embargo, completely or partially, would primarily benefit

the private sector. This measure would be in keeping with the original spirit of the embargo itself, given that its principle *constituency* was the corporations affected by the nationalizations of 1960. This would be reinforced by the possibility of bringing up the issue of indemnities for those companies which were originally affected, although this would be above all a symbolic act, rather than a condition based on economic interests. In any event, it is an issue that could only be dealt with within the framework of negotiation.

(3) Returning the Guantánamo base would allow for the improvement of relations, and for exploring forms of constructive coexistence between the armed forces of the two countries. Logically, it would be in the interests of the United States' armed forces to improve relations with an armed force which is the most powerful in the Caribbean, and one of the most professional and experienced in the hemisphere.

(4) Eliminating a point of US discord with Latin America and various industrialized countries, such as Canada, as well as an issue of tension within various international organizations.

(5) Legitimating, maintaining and increasing radio and television emissions to Cuba, on the basis of an agreement.

(6) Establishing, regulating and controlling the flow of people coming from Cuba, avoiding the danger of uncontrolled immigration and preventing counterproductive phenomena like that of Mariel.

(7) Facilitating cooperation with Cuba on issues of mutual interest in the shared areas of the Strait of Florida, such as the interception of drug traffickers, naval and air security, the coordination of coast guards, and so on.

(8) Allowing for agreements making for more efficient communications by telephone, mail and other means which are at present deficient or non-existent.

The Cuban Angle

The Cuban premise could be defined as the preservation of independence, sovereignty and national development. In terms of its relations with the United States, it could be described as reducing the level of hostility which has characterized the last 30 years.

This general objective requires the recognition of a group of realistic/political assumptions: (1) the factors of power and interests which have driven hostile US policy up to the present time will not cease to exist with the negotiation of differences in the bilateral agenda; (2) the activities of those sectors of the executive and Congress pursuing basic changes in the Cuban regime will not cease because the two countries enter into a process of diplomatic normalization; and (3) by agreeing to deal with the Cuban government the United States will not have renounced its goal of holding power and influence within the economic and political system of the country.

It is obvious, however, that Cuba would obtain certain advantages from the reduction of hostilities and a diplomatic agreement with the United States.

Benefits

(1) The reduction of hostilities would favour Cuba's national interests. Receiving the political recognition of the present regime would mean a historic step for the independence and self-determination of the country.
(2) The cessation of the principal pressures on Cuba's foreign relations, including those of an economic nature, as a result of the end of hostilities, would represent a considerable relief and open up new opportunities.
(3) Access to the American market and its capital flows would constitute a valuable resource in itself, beyond the multiplier effect that it would have on Cuba's foreign economic relations.
(4) The return of the Guantánamo naval base would mean the recovery of sovereignty over national territorial integrity, at present limited by the military presence of the United States.
(5) The facilitation of cooperation on bilateral problems deriving from geographic proximity, such as those mentioned above.
(6) The ability to improve Cuban relations with its community in the United States and other countries.
(7) An increase in the amount of contact between the two countries would allow for the construction of alliances and areas of mutual interest with sectors of American society to which Cuba is at present denied access, such as the business community.

Costs

(1) Moving closer to the United States, although seen as necessary by many in Cuba in purely economic terms, causes concerns in political and ideological terms. The most radical sectors of Cuban revolutionary nationalism would support such a policy only up to a certain point, given that it involves a threat to the country's independence.

(2) The impact of a possible flood of American capital into a Cuban economy which has still to complete a process of reform could have a counterproductive effect.
(3) It is possible that the US government will seek to influence its business community with respect to Cuba, advising and directing the flow of capital in order to favour determined political purposes.
(4) If more open relations and more extensive communications come to exist between the two countries, the US government and certain interest groups – including those of the Cuban community – could try to increase their influence over Cuba's internal dynamics, before a process of political reform in Cuba has a chance to be consolidated.
(5) Non-governmental organizations and power structures in the United States, cultural institutions and all types of interest groups – in general, the ideological machinery of American society – will increase their influence over Cuban society precisely as it finds itself in an exposed condition as a result of the economic crisis and its effects.

FINAL COMMENT

Put in its most elemental terms, the problem of the 'solution to the conflict', and of the different political and conceptual approaches to it at the present time, can be reduced to a quotation from Lewis Carroll:

> The question is – said Alice – whether words can have different meanings.
>
> The question is – said Humpty Dumpty – which is master. That's all.[11]

Notes

1. James Baker, 'America in Asia: Emerging Architecture for a Pacific Community', in *Foreign Affairs*, winter 1991–2, pp.15–16.
2. See Rafael Harnández, 'Interests and Values in US–Cuban Relations', in *United States–Cuban Relations in the Nineties* (Boulder, Col.: Westview Press, 1989).
3. Alfred T. Mahan, 'The Relations of the United States to their New Dependencies', in *Engineering Magazine*, January, 1899, *Lessons of the War with Spain and Other Articles* (Boston, Mass.: Little, Brown & Co., 1899) pp.243–7.

4. Joseph Nye, *Bound to Lead: The Changing Nature of American Power* (New York: Basic, 1990).
5. José Martí, 'Congreso Internacional de Washington (II)', *La Nación*, Buenos Aires, 20 December, 1899, *Obras Completas*, vol. 6 (La Habana Editorial Ciencias Sociales, 1975) pp.56–62.
6. 'The manner in which Communism collapses in Cuba could have military implications. Should the United States assist potential insurgent democratic forces by military means? . . . Would the support of democratization be a just cause for the Inter-American community, and by what means?' (F. Woerner and G. Marcella, 'Mutual Imperatives for Change in Hemispheric Strategic Policies: Issues for the 1990s', in L. Erik Kjonnerod (ed.) *Evolving US Strategy for Latin America and the Caribbean* (Washington DC: National Defense University Press, 1992) p.57.
7. The statements of Secretary of State Warren Christopher before the Council of the Americas (3 May 1993) and of Sub-Secretary for Latin America Alexander Watson on the programme 'Worldnet' (August 1993) are interesting for what they were committed to – no discussion of 'Post-Castro Cuba' or of the role assigned to the Cuban community – for what they reiterated – no military threat to Cuba and opposition to violence as a means of change – and for the language that was used. Although it was still a hostile language, it was no longer the language of the Foundation.
8. Edward Gonzalez and David Ronfeldt, *Cuba adrift in a Postcommunist World* (Santa Monica: RAND, December 1992).
9. Ernest Preeg and George Fauriol, 'La transición cubana', *Agenda '93* Washington DC: CSIS, November 1992.
10. See Edward Gonzalez and David Ronfelt, *Cuba a la deriva*, pp.64–76.
11. Lewis Carroll, *Through the Looking Glass*.

12 Clinton and Castro: Pragmatism or Paralysis*

Gillian Gunn

Both Cuba and the United States are undergoing periods of transition. Internally, Cuba is coming to terms with the fact that, in order to salvage the accomplishments of socialism in the absence of Soviet subsidies, the island needs greater economic efficiency. Specifically, in order to finance the programmes that have led to the island's excellent child mortality rate, life expectancy and educational achievement, Cuba needs an economy which produces wealth at a far greater pace than previously. Externally, Cuba needs new, different trade partners and mechanisms. However, entrenched interests and structures related to both the internal and external relationships are threatened by the contemplated adjustments, and resist the reforms. To the outside observer, this situation presents an ambivalent, inconsistent policy course. Naturally, rational economic and political actors interacting with Cuba hesitate to move forward vigorously: they hedge.

Internally, the United States needs more social justice in order to salvage its economic efficiency and the accomplishments of capitalism. Past neglect of health care, education and wealth redistribution has eroded economic efficiency by pushing insurance costs above those of competitors, failing to provide a workforce with modern skills and diverting resources from productive to police activities. Externally, the United States is no longer in a position to make unilateral policy decisions, expecting the rest of the West docilely to follow its lead. The United States is no longer economically dominant in the way it was previously, and needs both new trade and new political allies in order to protect its interests. As in Cuba, old habits die hard, and those whose interests are threatened by the adjustments, or whose outlook is linked to the previous world conditions, resist. Naturally, foreign governments interacting with the United States perceive an ambivalent, contradictory policy course, and they hedge. If they are small and located right next to the United States, as Cuba is, they perceive the cost of error to be extremely high, and become even more cautious.

Consequently, the outsider observing the relationship between the United States and Cuba since President Bill Clinton took office sees two mutually

* Some of the material in this chapter has been adapted from Gillian Gunn, *Cuba in Transition: Options for US Policy* (New York: Twentieth Century Fund Press, 1993).

suspicious entities, each following a contradictory course as it struggles to adapt its own internal and external structures to the new international conditions, each confused by the inconsistency of the other, each burdened by the psychological legacy of over three decades of verbal, and sometimes genuine, sabre rattling. Not surprisingly, the interaction swings between pragmatism and paralysis.

This analysis will primarily focus on the US side of the interaction, though the Cuban side is equally important, and even more complex.

THE CLINTON CAMPAIGN

The responsiveness to conservative opinion can be traced back to the presidential campaign. In 1991, Democratic congressman Robert Torricelli of New Jersey, who recently had become chairman of the House Western Hemisphere Subcommittee, played to his Cuban-American financial supporters by formulating a bill titled the Cuban Democracy Act (CDA). Originally, its drafters wished to enhance communication between the American and Cuban people, focus the damage caused by the embargo on the Cuban government rather than the island's people, provide some incentives to entice the Cuban government to reform, and simultaneously to increase pressure on the Cuban regime.

The political process in Congress – and in particular a well organized lobbying effort by the CANF – removed or reduced many of the 'carrots' and enlarged the 'sticks'. By the time the bill reached its final form, it contained both a prohibition on US subsidiaries abroad trading with Cuba (of dubious international legality because of its extraterritorial reach) and a shipping provision, which forbade ships docking in Cuba from docking in the United States for the following six months. In order for the bill's provisions to be waived, the legislation states that the president must first certify, among other things, that Cuba is 'moving towards establishing a free market economic system'. A few 'carrots' did survive, however. The bill permitted US companies to enhance communication-related trade with Cuba, authorized non-governmental organizations to make humanitarian donations to Cuban NGOs, and slightly broadened the exemptions from the travel ban to include US residents engaged in educational and religious activities.

Originally the Bush administration opposed the CDA on the grounds that the subsidiary provision would damage US relations with important allies. In late April 1992, Bill Clinton, still just one among many aspirants for the Democratic presidential nomination, found his campaign coffers critically low. Though according to a campaign source he had been advised by all his Latin America experts to oppose the bill, in late April 1992 he travelled to Florida and officially endorsed it. 'I think this administration has missed a big opportunity to put the hammer down on Fidel Castro and Cuba,' Clinton said.[1] Shortly thereafter, the candidate raised $275 000 in South Florida. A rueful Democratic campaign official, facing complaints from a Clinton adviser about the consequences of the strategy, remarked that this was a case in which 'good politics makes bad policy'.

President Bush was boxed into a corner and, on 5 May 1992, endorsed the full bill. It subsequently passed both houses of Congress and was signed into law on 23 October two weeks before the elections. The international reaction to the CDA was predictable. On 24 November, barely three weeks after Clinton won the election, the United Nations General Assembly voted to support a non-binding Cuban resolution condemning the embargo. The vote was 59 to three, with 71 abstentions. Important US trade partners, including Britain and Canada, passed blocking legislation prohibiting US subsidiaries from complying with the CDA. The UN vote reflected resentment against Washington's seeking to impose its law on others rather than explicit support for Castro, but the Cuban press went wild, claiming that this showed it enjoyed international support.

CLINTON'S FIRST MONTHS

When President Clinton was inaugurated on 20 January 1993, it was not clear how he would deal with Cuba. He had endorsed the CDA for electoral reasons; nonetheless he did not win the state of Florida. Some observers believed that once in office he would reconsider his approach. Many agreed with the judgement of a Cuban official who, asked in May 1992 about the impact of Clinton's support for the CDA upon Cuban government thinking, remarked, 'US presidents have never felt obliged to carry out each and every one of their campaign promises. If he wins, we will wait and see.'[2]

In its initial months in office, the Clinton administration adopted a contradictory, ambivalent course, displaying hardline tendencies and sensitivity to conservative Cuban-American concerns, interspersed with evidence of 'new thinking'. The first indicator of the new administration's policy confusion was an unseemly fight over the selection of the assistant secretary of state for inter-American affairs. The Clinton transition team initially accepted the suggestion of African-American advisers to name black Cuban American lawyer Mario Baeza to the post. Baeza's supporters knew little of his views regarding his homeland but had a high regard for his knowledge of Latin America as a whole. Conservative Cuban-Americans immediately launched an intensive lobbying effort to get the nomination withdrawn, complaining that Baeza was 'soft on Cuba'. In particular they pointed to his participation in a 1992 conference on business opportunities in Cuba sponsored by the European magazine *Euromoney* and to remarks he had made to journalists that suggested he opposed some provisions of the CDA. The lobbying was successful. The day before the announcement was due to be made, the list of nominees was amended and a line drawn through Baeza's name. Officially the nomination was on 'indefinite hold'. Black Democrats, including the Congressional Black Caucus, complained bitterly, with some protesting that this represented 'racism' by the largely white conservative Cubans. Clinton did not succumb entirely to CANF pressure, however. He resisted suggestions to name the candidate it favoured and eventually selected a career Foreign Service officer, Ambassador Alexander Watson, to the post. In this context, it is worthwhile noting that, when the Clinton administration requested the resignation of all the nation's US attorneys, it specifically exempted Miami-based US attorney Roberto Martínez, a Cuban American, from the list.

While the nomination controversy was being settled, an incident off the coast of Matanzas province reminded observers of the potential for violence within the exile community. In March 1993, a Cypriot oil tanker was sprayed with bullets by men in a small boat. The Miami-based Comandos L organization claimed responsibility for the attack.[3] Earlier, during the US presidential campaign, the same group had sent a boat to strafe the Spanish-Cuban five-star Hotel Melia on Varadero beach with machine-gun fire.

In April, the Clinton administration found itself embroiled in another Cuba-related controversy. The 8 April edition of *The Miami Herald* reported that prosecutors at the Miami US Attorney's Office had 'drafted a proposed indictment charging the Cuban government as a racketeering enterprise and Armed Forces Minister Raúl Castro as the chief of a ten-year conspiracy to send tons of Colombian cartel cocaine through Cuba to the United States'.[4] The evidence in the indictment, some elements of which were deemed inadmissible in court by a congressional source familiar with the material, referred to events preceding the 1989 Cuban trial of General Arnaldo Ochoa Sánchez on drug-smuggling charges. (Ochoa and three alleged collaborators were executed in 1989, following convictions in Cuban show trials. At the time, Fidel Castro maintained that smuggling had occurred without his knowledge – a claim greeted with great scepticism abroad. Whether Castro's claim was valid or not, US federal authorities monitoring smuggling concluded that Cuba played a minor, if any, role in drug trafficking after the 1989 events.)

The leaked indictment caused great controversy, for a similar indictment of strongman Manuel Noriega had preceded the 1989 US invasion of Panama. Many observers feared that, if made official rather than remaining a 'draft', the indictment would be interpreted in Cuba as preliminary to invasion.

The Clinton administration sought to strike a more neutral tone the following month. On 3 May, Deputy Secretary of State Clifton Wharton, Jr., made a major Latin America policy speech to the Council of the Americas. He stressed that the administration would refuse any support for the Castro government, but added, 'Despite what the people of that nation have been told, the United States poses no military threat to their island . . . We hope the Cuban people win their freedom through the kind of peaceful transition which has brought so many other nations to the democratic community. We oppose the attempts to bring changes through violence.'[5]

Three days later, though, Vice President Albert Gore, during a visit to Miami, remarked that the United States remained set on removing Castro from power and bringing free enterprise to Cuba by 'turning up the volume' on TV and Radio Martí. Gore added, 'Castro's chickens are coming home to roost . . . Let us not forget that our principal policy for hastening the departure of Castro is to convince the people of Cuba that his leadership is an abject failure. And our policy is to stay the course . . . There are tremendous opportunities in Cuba if they can just get rid of this dictator.'[6]

Two weeks later, on the occasion of Cuba's independence day (20 May), Washington adopted a slightly more detached posture. President Clinton invited Cuban-Americans to the White House for the celebration and, while the gathering was dominated by conservatives, the CANF was not included. Clinton repeated his support for the CDA but focused most of his remarks on the contribution Cuban-Americans had made to American society.[7]

THE NEUTRALITY ACT

Three weeks later, on 9 June, the Department of State announced that the Neutrality Act applies to Cuba, stating, 'Activities conducted from US territory aimed at overthrowing or otherwise destabilizing the government of Cuba are illegal.'[8] Conservative Cuban-Americans had long claimed that the Neutrality Act did not apply to Cuba, as they consider the Cuban government 'illegal'. Cuban foreign minister Roberto Robaina responded to the 9 June declaration by expressing appreciation that the United States had abandoned its previous 'aggressive language'.[9]

Confrontational rhetoric flared again in early July, however, when Deputy Assistant Secretary of State for Latin America Robert Gelbard told the US press that Cuban marine patrols had shot and killed with grenades Cubans trying to swim to the US naval base at Guantánamo, 'This is the most savage kind of behavior I've ever heard of . . . [It is] even worse than what happened at the Berlin Wall,' Gelbard remarked.[10] Cuba indignantly denied the allegation, and the United States was unable to provide photographs or videotape of the incident. Observers familiar with diplomatic protocol wondered why Washington had not first asked for a Cuban explanation via diplomatic channels.

By the end of July the tone shifted once more, when Washington issued regulations to implement the portion of the CDA that permits US telecommunications companies to improve telephone service with Cuba. It provides for Cuba to receive 50 per cent of the revenue from such calls, in contrast with the previous procedure, which froze Cuba's share of telephone call revenue in a blocked account. (It is not clear whether Cuba will accept the proposal, for it does not release the accumulated funds from the block account, as long demanded.) The administration vacillated, however, in regard to transport links. On 29 July, Washington approved additional charter flights to Cuba, but the very next day, following conservative Cuban-American protests, it rescinded the authorization.[11] Soon afterwards, the administration was back to demonstrating some independence from conservative influence, subjecting Carlos Cancio, a Cuban pilot who had diverted a plane to Miami (after colluding in the forcible subduing of its security officer) to a grand jury hearing with a view to prosecuting him for air piracy. Justice Department investigators arranged with the Cuban authorities to take testimony in Miami from four witnesses who had objected to the plane diversion (and subsequently returned to Havana), provoking energetic street protests by Cuban-American supporters of Cancio.[12]

Throughout the spring and summer of 1993, the Clinton administration also implemented the portion of the Cuban Democracy Act permitting non-governmental organizations to provide humanitarian aid to Cuban NGOs, primarily church organizations. Numerous licences for humanitarian shipments had been issued by August. Humanitarian donations to NGOs had always been permitted under the embargo, but the CDA gave such shipments a right-wing stamp of approval, and the flow consequently increased. Not all forms of aid were deemed acceptable by the government, however. A bus the organization Pastors for Peace wished to donate to a Cuban Sunday school was initially denied export authorization, provoking members of the Pastors delegation to embark on a hunger strike at the US–Mexican border.[13] (The bus was eventually delivered to Cuba.)

During its first seven months in office the Clinton administration was profoundly ambivalent about Cuba. It frequently went out of its way to avoid alienating conservative Cuban-Americans and occasionally used confrontational rhetoric towards Castro. Simultaneously, it made numerous small conciliatory gestures previous administrations had avoided and at times adopted a respectful tone in public pronouncements directed at Cuba. 'New' and 'old' thinking existed uncomfortably side by side. The administration often appeared on the verge of striking out in a new policy direction, only to slip back onto the well-worn path of the Reagan–Bush era when faced with conservative resistance.

DIVERGENT INTERESTS

The contradictions in Clinton's policy towards Cuba reflected divergent interests within his administration. Some of the Latin America specialists Clinton appointed to government posts personally doubt whether continued or increased pressure on Cuba best protects US interests in the Caribbean. Consequently, they are predisposed to implement existing regulations in a more flexible manner than their predecessors. However, they are unwilling to push for a decisive policy shift without explicit authorization from the White House.

President Clinton's political advisers look at the domestic politics involved in a Cuba policy shift and come to this conclusion: if the administration becomes more flexible, it will alienate some Cuban-American campaign donors and voters. Moderate and liberal constituents concerned about the Cuba issue, however, will not shift from the Democratic to the Republican camp simply to protest an ongoing, hardline Cuba policy. Therefore greater flexibility marginally hurts Clinton's electoral prospects, while maintaining a tough stance has a neutral to slightly positive impact. These advisers consequently counsel that Clinton not authorize any policy adjustment likely to annoy conservatives. Clinton's desire to maintain cordial relations with Congress in order to realize his domestic agenda also militates against policy flexibility. Many conservative and moderate legislators, some of whom receive campaign funds from the Cuban American National Foundation, react negatively to any overtures towards Cuba, while only a small number of liberal legislators protest pressure tactics.

The conservatives have their own public relations problems, however, for sharply deteriorating conditions in Cuba undermine their moral stance. Stories of malnutrition and medicine shortages make it harder to justify measures that would render the life of the average Cuban still more difficult. The humanitarian instincts of the American public are vigorous, and conservatives now have to worry about being perceived as 'kicking the Cuban people when they are already down'.

These pressures and interests account for the contradictory policy signals the Clinton administration has issued over the course of its first semester. According to one source close to the White House, 'Cuba' is treated 'as a rude four-letter word', and an adviser wishing to remain in the president's good graces is wise to refrain from referring to the topic. Another source used a twist on popular legend to illustrate the debate: 'The Emperor knows he has no clothes, but he can't decide which ones to put on, so he's still walking around naked.' It is plausible that Cuba policy will continue to drift until some crisis occurs on the island, finally forcing Washington to make decisions. By then, having neglected long-term planning and policy reappraisal in the interest of short-term political expediency, Washington may only be able to choose from among the least of several evils.

WHAT COULD BREAK THE LOG JAM?

Five potential developments could provoke a decisive shift in favour of pragmatism in US policy towards Cuba.

(1) If Cuba makes dramatic improvements in the human rights field, or creates political space for regime opponents, pragmatists in Washington will gain leverage. They will be better able to defend a more flexible policy, without being accused of 'cozying up to a dictator'.

(2) If living conditions in Cuba deteriorate even more significantly, US pragmatists will benefit. The American people have a strong humanitarian streak. If they see Cuban babies dying on television they will demand some form of assistance. The hard line will find that opposition to such demands entails a significant public relations cost.

(3) If Florida is deluged with Cuban refugees fleeing deteriorating economic conditions, the political balance in Miami will shift. As the financial cost of providing social services to the new arrivals erodes local resources, a new constituency for pragmatism will emerge. 'Don't

make the Cuban economy scream quite so hard,' the argument will go, 'so that fewer Cubans feel driven to flee to Miami and soak up our tax dollars with resettlement costs.'

(4) Major, coordinated pressure from allies in Europe and the Americas in favour of a policy shift will be unlikely, in itself, to change the US approach. Such pressure will, however, make it easier for a shift to occur if the administration decides for its own reasons to change course. In that scenario, those pragmatic US officials under fire from the domestic right wing could point to the position of allies to help legitimate their posture.

(5) Increased pressure from the moderate Cuban-American community and from US business for a policy adjustment could have the same effect. These developments, in themselves, would be unlikely to precipitate a policy shift, but they could help legitimate one undertaken for other reasons.

None of these five scenarios is likely to occur in the immediate future, though number two is becoming increasingly plausible. Therefore US policy towards Cuba is likely to remain a classic example of an issue that is so vulnerable to domestic political pressures that it has become difficult for those charged with responsibility for protecting US interests to fulfil their duties. Many US government officials know what the problem is, but until President Clinton provides leadership, or Havana undertakes reforms which provide political protection, paralysis will continue to be punctuated by only intermittent incidents of pragmatism.

CONCLUSION

Just as the contradictory and ambivalent course of Cuban reforms confuses US observers, and complicates the task of those fashioning policy, the reverse is equally true. Rational political actors in Cuba will continue to hedge, they will refrain from taking significant political risks in both the foreign policy and internal field, until they sense pragmatists have gained the upper hand in Washington. They know that major restructuring always entails instability. The question is: when will they feel safe enough to risk that instability? When will they no longer fear that any sign of internal conflict will be seized upon and exploited by the US to destabilize the Cuban system? If US policy continues to drift unpredictably between pragmatism and paralysis, there could be a long wait.

Notes

1. 'Clinton Backs Torricelli Bill; "I Like It," He Tells Cuban Exiles', *Miami Herald*, 24 April 1992.
2. Author's background interview with Cuban MINREX official, Havana, May 1992.
3. 'Oil Tanker in Cuban Waters Attacked', *CubaINFO*, 12 April 1993.
4. 'US Building Cuba Drug Case', *Miami Herald*, 8 April 1993.
5. 'Clinton to Stress Democracy, Human Rights in Latin America Policy', *Washington Post*, 4 May 1993.
6. 'Gore's Comments Fail to Provoke', *CubaINFO*, 21 May 1993.
7. 'Clinton Praises Cuban Exiles at Fete Marking Independence', *Miami Herald*, 21 May 1993.
8. 'Cuba: Participation in Hostile Activities against Cuba', statement by Joseph Snyder, spokesman, US Department of State, 9 June 1993.
9. Notimex, 18 June 1993.
10. 'US Rips Cuba's "Extreme Cruelty"', *Miami Herald*, 5 August 1993.
11. 'Expanded Exile Flights to Cuba Put on Standby', *Miami Herald*, 5 August 1993.
12. 'Justice Department May Use Cuban Witnesses to Prosecute Pilot', *CubaINFO*, 6 August 1993.
13. 'Pastors for Peace Hunger Strike at Border', *CubaINFO*, 6 August 1993.

13 Obstacles to Breaking the US–Cuban Deadlock

Edward Gonzalez

Virtually from the moment Fidel Castro assumed power in 1959, relations between the United States and Cuba became strained. By early 1960, the two nations had become locked in a conflict that would last well over three decades. Although the conflict was to have its ups and down, it seldom subsided, and frequently resumed new forms of intensity.

Today, the collapse of communism, the disappearance of the Soviet Union and the resulting acute crisis being experienced by Cuba would appear to open the way for a possible rapprochement between Washington and Havana. Set adrift in a post-communist world, Cuba is no longer shored up by the Soviet Union; Cuba is no longer a Soviet beachhead in the Western Hemisphere; and Cuba no longer promotes revolution in neighbouring countries or sends combat troops abroad to fight in distant lands. The Cuba of 1993 is different: it is opening up its economy and improving its relations with Latin America, Canada, Europe and other countries.

The United States has also changed. It has ceased to be preoccupied with the Cold War. It is no longer governed by ideologically driven administrations that were visceral in their hostility towards the Castro regime. The Clinton White House is not beholden to the Cuban exile community in Florida because the majority of the Cuban-Americans in the state did not vote Democratic.

Thus, although the president signed an executive order for the implementation of the Cuban Democracy Act, his administration has not moved to bring down the Castro regime by intensifying Cuba's economic crisis. In fact, it appears either less preoccupied by or more flexible on the Cuban issue. For example, although it requested $28 million in funding for Radio and TV Martí, the administration did not mount a full court press campaign to prevent the House Appropriations Subcommittee on Commerce, Justice, State and the Judiciary from deleting the requested funding last June. The State Department has warned Miami-based exiles not to carry out attacks on the island and it has not blocked some forms of humanitarian assistance from being sent to Cuba.

Nevertheless, the resolution of conflict between Washington and Havana does not appear imminent. The Clinton administration's primary focus is domestic, whereas Cuba currently is neither a pressing foreign policy priority nor a winning domestic issue. On the Cuban side, the Castro government ought to see the normalization of relations with the United States as the primary means by which to ease the island's crisis, yet it gives no sign that it is prepared to engage in the kind of system change that would entice the White House to commence negotiations.

What explains this paralysis on both sides, given that the world, Cuba and the United States have changed? I will argue that new as well as old *contradictory* interests continue fundamentally to separate the two governments, which resent major obstacles to normalization. Relatedly, and paradoxically, I will further suggest that Cuba's worsening crisis provides still another impediment to conflict resolution on both sides of the Florida Straits. I will conclude with some remarks on US policy options.

THE PERSISTENCE OF CONTRADICTORY INTERESTS

More than 10 years ago, I distinguished three types of interests in the US–Cuban relationship.[1] There were *congruent* interests in which the countries derived mutual advantage through cooperation in such areas as weather and hurricane forecasting, demarcation of fishing rights, and establishing Interests Sections to facilitate diplomatic communication. There were also *conflicting* interests that derived from the behaviour and stances of the opposing parties, but which were potentially negotiable and thus resolvable within a larger political settlement. Thus the issue of compensation for the nearly $1.8 billion in US claims for nationalized property – and which now may be in the neighbourhood of $6 billion or more – or the issue of the return of Guantánamo Bay to Cuba, constitute examples of conflicting interests that can be negotiated and resolved provided both parties are prepared to work out a political settlement.

What kept the United States and Cuba from either expanding their congruent interests or reaching a compromise over their conflicting interests was that their mutual antagonisms derived from strongly imbedded *contradictory* interests. These stemmed from firm adherence to principles, forms of behaviour and concrete national identity and international role. They could not be abandoned or sacrificed by either without undermining their respective power, status and self-image – at home as well as abroad.

CUBAN INTERNATIONALISM AND THE US REACTION

A clear example of such contradictory interests is seen in the 1970s, in Cuba's active pursuit of 'internationalism' on behalf of two of its allies in Africa – the MPLA, which was fighting for control of Angola following the withdrawal of Portuguese rule, and the Mengistu regime in Ethiopia which was under attack from Somalia – and by the US responses to the two Cuban military incursions in the region. Both events occurred at a time when US–Cuban relations were experiencing a momentary thaw, and both led to renewed strains between the two countries.

In quick succession between 1975 and 1978, the military victories of the Revolutionary Armed Forces in Angola and Ethiopia catapulted Cuba onto the international stage as a world-class actor, heightened its prestige in African and the Nonaligned Movement, and elevated Castro's standing in the Third World. Because its military and political triumphs advanced Soviet interests on the continent as well, Cuba also gained materially by obtaining far higher levels of Soviet economic and military assistance than in the pre-1976 period. In effect, Cuba assumed a special relationship as a privileged 'super-client' of the USSR.[2] This, along with the advantages it gained internationally from its internationalism, clearly outweighed whatever diplomatic or economic gains Cuba might have secured with the United States had it not dispatched troops to Africa.

For their part, neither the Ford nor the Carter administrations could accept either incursion because each was perceived as a strategic gain for the Soviet Union and Cuba, and thus as a setback for the United States in the East–West struggle. And to ignore Cuba's military forays would risk encouraging still more adventurism by Havana and further expansion of the Soviet Union's 'outer empire' under the guise of détente. Thus the Ford administration broke off the secret exploratory talks it had held with Cuban representatives during 1974–5 following the commencement of the Angolan operation in autumn 1975.

The Carter administration reacted similarly to the joint Cuban–Soviet military operation which repulsed the Somalian invasions of Ethiopia in the disputed Ogaden region. To lessen Cuba's dependence on the Soviets, the Carter administration had initially adopted a more conciliatory line towards Havana by working out agreements on fisheries and the establishment of Interest Sections in April 1977. These led to visits to the United States by Cuba's foreign trade minister and other officials to explore the possibility of normalizing commercial relations, with US businessmen also visiting the island for the same purpose. Scarcely three months after the Interests Sections had opened in Havana and Washington, however, the Carter administration dropped its conciliatory stance because of the

Cuban–Soviet intervention in Ethiopia in November 1977. Thereafter, talk of opening up trade relations with Havana ceased, and the administration's posture towards Cuba hardened.[3]

CONTRADICTORY INTERESTS IN THE 'NEW WORLD ORDER' OF THE 1990s

With the end of the Cold War and the disappearance of the Soviet Union, the kinds of contradictory interests that revolved around the East–West struggle and that fuelled the US–Cuban conflict no longer exist or at least have lost much of their saliency. New types of contradictory interests have arisen, however, that now stand in the way of breaking the stalemate between the two countries.

Although it is an exaggeration to speak of a 'unipolar world' in which the United States is the undisputed hegemon, the United States and Western ideals clearly emerged as the victors in the Cold War. There is now almost universal agreement on the superiority of market principles for organizing a nation's economy and on the need for pluralism and political democracy. In this sense, Francis Fukuyama is right to speak of the 'end of history' with respect to the winding-down of the great intellectual battles of the nineteenth and twentieth centuries.

Thus socialist-type or state-centric economies are being replaced in the former Eastern bloc and in Latin America, respectively, by more open market-oriented systems. Though often more present in rhetoric than in practice, there is also a growing realization that pluralism and liberal democracy are required both to counter the potentially oppressive weight of the state and to ensure optimal economic growth and development. Although not necessarily democratic, more liberal orders have thus emerged to replace formerly authoritarian or totalitarian-type systems in most of Latin America and parts of Eastern Europe and the former Soviet Union.

With all its internal blemishes and problems, the United States is the leading champion of this new world order which rests on democratic and market principles, and respect for human rights. Herein lies the source of the new contradictory interests between the United States and Cuba.

THE LIMITS OF CUBAN-STYLE 'LIBERALIZATION'

Despite the fact that under its current transition process Cuba has experienced greater economic liberalization than at any time since 1959, the island falls far short of having a market economy. Socialist forms of ownership and state direction of the economy still predominate. Until mid-1993, liberalization was confined to the external sector of the economy where the island was opened up to foreign investments in the areas of tourism, biotechnology and oil exploration. Even this process of economic liberalization was and remains driven by the Cuban state, however, as Cuban reformers themselves make clear.[4] In the meantime, the market remained absent from the domestic economy save for the rapidly growing informal economy, which remained illegal. The informal economy was tolerated by the government only because it served as a safety-valve for increasingly desperate Cuban consumers throughout the island.

In summer 1993, the government finally took the first steps to liberalize the domestic economy. In July it announced the so-called 'dollarization' of the economy, which permits Cubans legally to possess foreign currency and which is expected to increase the dollar remittances from Cuban exiles in the United States. The reform also eases one discriminatory aspect of 'apartheid tourism' by permitting Cubans to shop in previously off-limits dollar stores that had been reserved for foreigners.[5] In September Cubans were given permission to become self-employed in over one hundred crafts, trades and services that the government cannot provide. Later the same month, new types of cooperative farms were to be granted greater autonomy in hopes of increasing crop and food production.

While these measures aim at easing the economy's severe contraction, they do not necessarily promote or support the transition to the market. They are efforts made by the government to catch up with the illegal market activities already present in the informal economy, and even to exploit these activities to the advantage of the state. In the case of dollarization, for example, the government sought to recapture the hard currency in circulation through immediate price increases at the dollar stores. Meanwhile, the other two decrees are not only grudging concessions to reality but also attempts to constrain market forces.

Thus the scope of the self-employment decree not only confines itself to legalizing the private entrepreneurial activities found in the informal market. It also limits private enterprise to individuals (or families) so long as they do not employ other people; it prohibits university graduates, doctors and company directors and management personnel from engaging in such activities; and it calls upon local authorities to make sure that 'intermediaries and parasites' do not take advantage of the decree.[6] In effect, the decree is more restrictive than the Cuban economic reality of the 1960s, before the 'Revolutionary Offensive' of 1968, and scarcely constitutes a step 'back to the future'. Rather than constituting a significant move towards liberalizing the internal economy, it is reminiscent of the guilds of medieval times.

The agricultural cooperative decree scarcely advances Cuban cooperating beyond the status of the old Soviet collective and state farms. Under the decree, Cuban farmers will enjoy indefinite usage but not legal ownership of the land; and, most critically, they must sell their crops to state purchasing agencies at fixed rather than market prices.[7] As a consequence, increased agricultural production is likely to continue eluding the regime unless and until the government institutes more radical market-oriented reforms – including restoring the peasant free market that Castro abolished in 1986.

Meanwhile, Cuba's policy has been opened up even less than that island's economy. The leadership of one man, one party, remains undisputed. Little political space is permitted outside the regime, and then only within strictly imposed parameters that prohibit political deviation. For example, whereas the constitution that was amended in 1992 provides Cuban citizens with a number of personal freedoms and civil rights, these continue to be granted on a conditional basis as under the original 1976 constitution. Article 62 states that, 'None of the freedoms . . . may be exercised contrary to the stipulation in the constitution and the laws, or contrary to the Cuban people's decision to construct socialism and communism. The infraction of this principle is punishable.'[8] In effect, the state control apparatus – comprising the Ministry of the Interior (MININT), the party-directed Committees for the Defence of the Revolution (CDRs) and the more recently created rapid-reaction brigades directed MININT personnel – is given legal licence to crack down on those Cubans brave enough to openly criticize or oppose the regime.

In the name of preserving revolutionary unity, unanimity and socialism, organized political opposition is thus tolerated even less in Cuba than was the case in such authoritarian systems as pre-Salinas Mexico or Pinochet's Chile. Cuba's civil society remains far weaker and more repressed by the state than its counterparts in authoritarian Mexico and Chile. Although Cuba has not witnessed the brutal repression and widespread political killings found in El Salvador and Guatemala, the Castro regime could well resort to similar forms of heavy-handed repression if the current crisis is not overcome and the populace begins to rebel. Meanwhile, individual human rights continue to be violated, particularly those of political dissidents and critics of the existing order, in part because the regime believes that through tight controls and repression it may prevent a Tiananmen-like confrontation from occurring.[9] At the very least, Cuba remains a 'post-totalitarian' authoritarian state which shows few signs of moving towards a more pluralistic, liberalized order – in contrast to many of its Caribbean and Latin neighbours and much of the world.

POLICY IMPLICATIONS FOR THE UNITED STATES

Cuba's present state of affairs makes it difficult for the United States to seek some kind of settlement with the Castro government because to do so would imply the abandonment of its commitment to the market, democracy and human rights. Of course, such principles did not stop the Bush and Clinton administrations from renewing China's most-favoured-nation status despite the Chinese government's repressive rule – and despite considerable Congressional opposition. Indeed, the Chinese and Cuban cases would appear to be similar. Like Cuba, China is undergoing a transition from communism under the formula of 'market-Leninism' in which the Chinese Communist Party has greatly liberalized the economy while retaining tight political control over society. However, China differs from Cuba in several major respects.

Cuba is not China with its more than one billion people, its enormous and growing internal market and its US investments and economic ties to the West. Having survived Mao's death in 1976, and now presiding over the world's fastest growing economy, the Chinese communist regime remains firmly in power and without any sign of impending collapse or an alternative to its rule. In contrast, the Castro regime may well be a dying regime owing to the island's deepening crisis. Finally, the Chinese community in the United States, which appears less influential than its Cuban counterpart, is not opposed to diplomatic and economic relations with Beijing.

Nevertheless, those advocating a relaxation of US policy towards the Castro government do so on a number of grounds. Diplomatic interests would be served by lifting the US embargo – especially the Cuban Democracy Act – because it would remove a major irritant in US relations with Canada, Western Europe and Latin America. Economic advantage would also be gained because US tourist, commercial and manufacturing interests would be able to invest in or trade with Cuba before the island is locked up by European, Canadian and Latin American competitors. In themselves, however, these diplomatic and economic considerations are not compelling arguments for normalizing relations with a regime that may be in terminal crisis and that, in any event, is not committed to the market, democracy and human rights.

On the other hand, US leftist and liberal critics argue that some form of 'positive engagement' with Havana would advance the political interests of the United States. Lifting the embargo and easing the island's economic crisis, they maintain, would soften the Castro regime's bunker mentality, help open Cuba up, strengthen reform elements in the regime and thereby facilitate the transition towards a more pluralistic, market-oriented society. More importantly, such a step might well head off a potential political explosion that would produce new waves of emigration and lead to possible US armed intervention in Cuba.

The case for 'positive engagement' rests on some questionable assumptions. Cuba's economic predicament has not been caused by the US economic embargo but by the disappearance of its former Communist bloc patrons and by the regime's own failed policies and continued resistance to fundamental system change, which some US critics conveniently ignore.[10] More importantly, there is no certainty that lifting the embargo, whether done conditionally or unconditionally, will strengthen the reformers and facilitate the transition towards a market-based economy and a more open policy as many proponents of policy change assume.[11] In fact, the reverse may occur.

Lifting the US embargo could well freeze or perhaps even retard the reform process, leaving an authoritarian regime in place that would rest, at best, on a more liberalized economic system. It is Castro and the hardliners – not the liberalizing reformers – who hold the sinews of power in the Party, the army and the state's security organs. It is this conservative, authoritarian leadership that resists and limits liberalizing reforms. The infusion of US tourist dollars and investments would remove the incentives for Castro, the hardliners and centrists to accept the necessity of deeper economic and, especially, political liberalization. In this event, US policy would have ensured the regime's survival under some form of 'market Leninism'.

Such a negative Cuban outcome would expose the Clinton administration to sharp attacks not only from conservative Cuban-Americans, but also from Republican, Democratic and human rights circles. Their antipathy towards the Castro regime does not simply reside in the emotional baggage left over from the Cold War, as some critics charge. More fundamentally, it stems from a profound dislike for the type of political–economic order that the Castro leadership has maintained over the past 34 years, that is unlikely to change under the present rulers and that could be prolonged by major US concessions.[12]

Why then, should the Clinton administration take the initiative towards Castro when the Cuban issue is certain to be a political liability at a time when the administration finds itself overtaken by other foreign policy crises and priorities? Why risk President Clinton's newly established stature and authority with Congress following his victory on NAFTA, and his success in meeting Asian leaders, by doing something with Cuba that might well extend Castro's rule rather than hasten his departure?

CUBAN RESISTANCE TO FUNDAMENTAL SYSTEM CHANGE

Meanwhile, Cuba itself appears trapped by the end of the Cold War and by its own leadership, domestic politics and history. Fidel Castro took an enormous gamble in realigning Cuba with the Soviet Union in 1960. For nearly three decades his gamble paid off, but it has now ended in catastrophe because Cuba has been left without an international support system following the collapse of communism and the Soviet Union. As a consequence, Castro's regime has no other alternative but to integrate Cuba into the international system, a Western-led system that is market- and democracy-oriented.

This presents a major problem for Castro and other Cuban leaders of his generation that touches on the very identity of the Cuban Revolution, and that limits the extent to which liberalization may take place on the island. For much of the Cuban leadership, the 'market' is identified with the 'evils of capitalism' and capitalism with the United States and pre-1959 Cuba. 'Socialism' thus became the antidote after 1959: it was the antithesis of capitalism; and it offered national liberation and the means by which to gain a powerful international patron for Cuba. As with other Marxist–Leninists and authoritarians elsewhere, this commitment to socialism reflects a deeply imbedded preference for using institutions, such as the state, the party and the army, to organize and administer the economy, and a profound aversion to reliance on the market.[13]

Thus, while a younger generation of Cuba economists can speak about and even advocate adopting market principles in Cuba, talk of the market is remarkably absent from the political discourse of Castro, Ramón Machado Ventura and other party leaders. Embracing the market would not only virtually erase the revolution's identity, but would also signify that the Cuban leadership had made an enormous historical error. No such error can be admitted, as Castro indicated on 26 July 1993 when he declared, in reference to the former Soviet Union, that 'socialism should have been perfected – not destroyed'.[14]

The very fact that the market is avoided at the level of political symbolism indicates that Cuba's current transition process will stop short of introducing real market reforms, including privatization of major segments of the internal economy. As noted earlier, this has been the case thus far. But the limited character of the reform process is also likely to continue for more practical reasons that go beyond political symbolism and ideology.

The market, like democracy, leads to the state's loss of control over society, something that Castro, the hardliners and even the more moderate, pragmatic centrists are unwilling to allow. The market would wrest economic decision making out of the hands of the regime and place it in the hands of producers, merchants and consumers; and it would promote an entrepreneurial class and a civil society that would be increasingly independent of the state. It would defeat the regime's efforts to imbue society with socialist values.

The market also leads to new winners and losers under a process that is certain to erode the regime's traditional basis of political support. As evidenced by the introduction of the Peasant Free Markets in 1980, the existence of the informal market and the recent dollarization of the economy, the regime's major constituencies are precisely the ones who benefit least from the market and the recent dollarization of the economy. Because only some 3 per cent of the Cuban exile community in the United States is Afro-Cuban, for example, blacks and mulattos on the island will barely benefit directly from the increased remittances that will now flow to Cuba. Party members, government workers, military officers and enlisted personnel, and others living on fixed incomes, are also likely to experience a growing sense of relative deprivation. The reason is that they can see that Cubans who work the market as middlemen and blackmarketeers, ply the tourist trade as taxi drivers, *jineteras* and *jineteros* (prostitutes and pimps), or work in the external sector of the economy are the ones who are getting ahead financially while they, the politically meritorious, must endure acute shortages and a declining standard of living.

Democratic reforms present an even greater threat to the retention of the regime's political hegemony and control over society. As seen by the unravelling of communist rule in Eastern Europe and the Soviet Union, political decompression – especially in the form of democratization – is fraught with risks, all the more so when Cuba is experiencing an acute economic crisis and popular discontent is growing. Whereas political prisoners can be released, political power cannot be shared, much less relinquished. It must remain concentrated in the hands of Castro, the *nomenklatura* and the Communist Party of Cuba (PCC).

In both theory and practice, therefore, Cuba's recently enacted political 'reforms' scarcely conform to democratic principles as the regime continues to tilt the playing field to assure its monopoly of political power.

(1) Although no longer representing the proletariat exclusively, the party nevertheless serves as 'the organized vanguard of the Cuban nation' under the 1992 amended constitution.
(2) A 1992 constitutional amendment calls for the direct election of delegates to the Municipal Assemblies and the National Assembly of People's Power (ANPP). But under the 1992 electoral law, candidates are screened by electoral commissions at the municipal and national levels, while the National Candidacy Commission nominates half the ANPP candidates in order to 'avoid unnecessary improvizations' in the nomination process.[15] As one observer noted afterwards, 'the Communist Party could not tolerate the prospect of even a small number of opposition delegates in the assemblies'.[16]
(3) The electorate in the February 1993 ANPP elections was given a single list of 589 candidates, the same number of seats as in the ANPP, with the regime mounting a major effort to convince voters to approve the entire government list because a partial or no vote, together with spoiled ballots, would be tantamount to treason.[17]

The regime's campaign paid off: although unanimity was not obtained, a reported 88.48 per cent of the voters cast their ballots for the entire list of ANPP candidates, from which the opposition had been excluded.[18]

In sum, Cuba is in transition, but to where? The regime's reforms fall well short of moving the economy and policy towards the market and democratization. Extrapolating from current policies and tendencies, the best that may be expected from the Castro regime is that it will combine economic liberalization with political authoritarianism. If so, Cuba's political economy may come to resemble the post-Maoist Chinese or pre-1982 Mexican models or, more likely, a hybrid system that incorporates elements of the present Cuban model with elements of the Chinese and/or Mexican models. Under any one of these models, the outlook for marketization and democratization remains virtually nil, as does the outlook for the island's economic recovery.[19] Under these circumstances, it is difficult to conceive of the Clinton administration throwing a lifeline to the Cuban government.

THE CRISIS AS A FURTHER IMPEDIMENT TO ACCOMMODATION

The very fact that Cuba remains in a 'lingering crisis', to use Jorge Domínguez's phrase, further lessens the incentives for the US government to work towards a resolution of the Cuban problem. On the one hand, the crisis has not yet assumed such criticality that it compels top administration policy makers to turn their attention to Cuba – particularly when there are more important international issues and flashpoints in the world that consume their time and energy. On the other hand, some American policy makers may assume that the crisis will ultimately lead to the downfall of the Castro government and thus to the realization of US interests in the long run. If so, why should Washington take the initiative and do something that might well enable Castro and his regime to survive at a time when they appear on the ropes?

The crisis also affects the Cuban government in two ways. For the moment, it has enabled the reformers to persuade Castro and hardline circles to begin opening up the economy a little on the grounds that there simply is no other way out of the crisis. In turn, the embryonic character of civil society, the populace's apathy, the lack of viable alternatives to the regime and the state's own political and institutional strengths have thus far enabled the government to enact the limited reforms without the political situation unravelling. But the very fact that the regime remains in control of the streets also weakens the case for further reforms. In the meantime, the weakness of civil society, and especially the absence of an organized private sector, deprives the reformers of outside allies and supporters in pressing for the acceleration and deepening of the liberalization process.

There is another way in which the crisis may affect the regime's behaviour. Against the backdrop of heroism and martyrdom throughout Cuban history, the dominant political culture of Castro and much of the Cuban leadership has been to value struggle, intransigence and defiance. Submitting or surrendering are not part of the leadership's lexicon; death and martyrdom are preferable, as Cuban military officers in Grenada discovered.[20] This culture of heroism and martyrdom thus suggests that the reformers within Cuba cannot press too hard for fundamental changes or concessions lest they be accused of giving in to capitalism and imperialism.

Less obviously, the elite culture suggests that Castro and hardline leaders might prefer a confrontational ending should the crisis become uncontrollable and the regime find itself in a *callejón sin salida* – a dead-end. Faced with such a predicament, the inclination of the leadership would be to halt the reform process and to replace flexibility with renewed intransigence and defiance at home and abroad. At the very minimum, the regime would resort to heightened repression to restore order and remain in power – as exemplified last August by Jorge Lezcano Pérez, PCC Secretary for Havana, when he urged citizens' vigilante groups to act firmly against the increased level of crime and rock-throwing incidents during the city's nightly blackouts.[21] But if tighter controls failed to prevent the internal situation from unravelling, Castro and his like-minded followers might seek a final showdown with the United States in hopes of rallying nationalistic Cubans around the regime and salvaging Castro's place in history, even if this led to a *Götterdämmerung* ending.[22]

In a perverse way, therefore, the crisis appears to act as a brake on both parties: some in Washington may prefer inaction, in part because of their assumptions concerning the eventual outcome of the island's crisis. For their part, the more intransigent circles within the Castro regime may see the crisis as a defining moment for the Cuban Revolution in which there can be no compromise with the United States.

SOME CONCLUDING THOUGHTS ON US POLICY OPTIONS

As indicated by the foregoing analysis, the genesis of the current US–Cuban stalemate continues to reside in history, in the respective international roles and self-images of both parties, and in domestic political considerations for US and Cuban leadership circles. From the perspective of US policy, there are no easy solutions to the current impasse – a point made in our 1992 RAND study, which surveyed the pros and cons of different US policy options.[23]

Since that study was completed, Cuba has undergone some significant changes. The economy has steadily worsened, as has the suffering of the Cuban people. Younger, liberalizing leaders have been elevated to many top positions, and some limited economic reforms have been enacted. But Castro and his provincial first secretaries continue to control the party apparatus; they, along with other hardliners in the army and security forces, remain the dominant forces within the regime. Though still anomic in character, there are some signs of growing restiveness on the part of the populace which could lead to heightened government repression or, if the economic situation worsens and controls break down, to instability and potential civil war on the island.

In the light of these developments and prospects, should US policy be changed in order to try to ease the plight of the Cuban people, influence the outcome of Cuba's current transition process and thereby head off a possible bloodbath on the island? As noted earlier, some critics argue that the US economic embargo ought to be lifted, not only for humanitarian but also for political reasons – to strengthen the hand of the reformers by removing the external US threat and giving them more political space.

This, it is believed, would increase the prospects for greater liberalization in the short run and for a peaceful transition that would move Cuba towards a more market- and democracy-oriented future over the longer run. US policy could thus achieve a 'soft landing' in Cuba.

As was argued earlier, the problem with such reasoning is that Cuba's present economic plight resides in the government's past policies and Castro's continued opposition to full-fledged market reforms. Even were the US embargo to be lifted, his government would still need to obtain US credits in order for Cuba to import US products, which is hardly likely at the present time. The solution to Cuba's economic predicament thus depends less on the lifting of the embargo than on the Cuban government itself moving rapidly towards marketization and privatization of the island's economy. As one specialist on Cuban economic affairs has concluded, what the government must do is 'to insert the global economy *into* Cuba's planned economy'.[24]

In the meantime, Cuba's crisis has thus far led to more economic liberalization than at any time since 1959, with more reforms introduced in 1994. Thus the counterargument can be made that US policy should stay the course in order to maintain the effectiveness of the 'double embargo' – the first the result of US policy, and the second caused by the collapse of the Soviet Union – as a means of assuring still deeper reforms. Conversely, as was pointed out earlier, easing up on the embargo might enable Castro and the hardline leadership to slow down or halt the reform process altogether, thereby leaving an authoritarian regime entrenched on the island.

On the other hand, the interests of the United States and the Cuban people would not be served were the island's crisis to degenerate into political turmoil or, worse yet, civil war. Such a dark Cuban future would most certainly see prolonged political instability, increased racial conflict, massive emigration and the rise of drug trafficking and other criminal activities as a result of the weakening and corruption of state and society. A strife-ridden, devastated Cuba would directly affect the United States.

Clearly, there are risks to US action and inaction, as there are to the United States remaining so fixated on a Cuba under Castro that it loses sight of its more enduring interest in a Cuba after Castro. The 1992 RAND study thus argued against 'humanitarian intervention' except in the most extreme circumstances, not only because of the heavy military and diplomatic costs involved in that option, but also because it would leave a ruinous legacy for both a post-Castro government and future US–Cuban (and hemispheric) relations. Therefore the United States needs simultaneously to pursue short- and long-term objectives. In dealing with Castro, the United States should avoid strengthening his rule, while preparing for the worst possible outcomes from the current crisis, including growing political strife and possible civil war. At the same time, the United States must also prepare the groundwork for a future relationship with Cuba and the Cuban people even though there may be some risk that Castro's position in the short term might be marginally strengthened.

How can these seemingly contradictory US interests, spanning short- and long-term considerations and a Cuba with and without Castro, begin to be reconciled? To begin with, US policy makers should proceed from the assumption that significant liberalization of the Cuban economy and polity is not likely to occur while Castro and the hard-core *fidelistas* remain in power. Nevertheless, Washington could undertake some unilateral short-term initiatives that would avoid giving undue economic or political advantage to Castro, yet lessen the perception of US hostility, including aiding the Cuban people directly. Longer-term initiatives should aim at promoting the eventual emergence of a market economy, civil society and democratic government in a post-Castro Cuba.

The Pentagon's new policy of informing Cuban authorities of impending military exercises at Guantánamo, and the administration's proposed programme for improving telecommunication links to the island, are steps that advance both short- and long-term US policy objectives – the first by lowering Cuban threat perceptions, the second by trying to use increased communication flows to promote elements of civil society in Cuba. Another step would be to relax the embargo's restrictions in order to allow the sale and provision of food, health and other types of humanitarian assistance to Cuba, thereby helping to ease the current plight of the people in the island. Still another would be to encourage ties between US non-governmental organizations (NGOs) with their Cuban counterparts. If over time these initial steps were to lead to the Cuban government's improved observance of human rights, and to clear signs that it is moving towards a market economy and political liberalization, they could be augmented later on by more explicit US concessions, including *selective* lifting of some aspects of the embargo.[25]

Because Castro is no champion of economic and political liberalization, however, the chances are that his government could halt the reform process and heighten state repression. Such regressive policies could occur if he finds that the reforms are going too far, that his regime is losing control, and/or that popular unrest is rising. Were such regression to occur, the United States would have to suspend or rescind its earlier concessions, not only for reasons of domestic US politics, but also because US policy seeks to open Cuba up, not reward an oppressive government.

Such a calibrated approach runs the risk of being overtaken by events on the island. Nevertheless, it resonates with US ideals concerning humanitarian relief, human rights, the free market and democracy. It is also predicated on a more realistic assessment of Cuba's current reality in that it does not rest on the dubious premise that a change in US policy can turn Castro around or, independently of the *líder máximo*, bring about fundamental system change in Cuba. Short of a US invasion or enticing Castro to step down, both of which seem highly unlikely at this juncture, Cuba's fate will probably be decided more by the Cuban people themselves acting on Cuban time than by whatever the United States does in its policy towards Havana.

Notes

1. 'Cuba: The Impasse', in Robert Wesson (ed.), *US Influence in Latin America in the 1980s* (New York: Praeger Publishers and Hoover Institution Press, 1982) pp.198–216.
2. Despite the steep drop in the world market price for sugar, for example, the April 1976 Soviet–Cuban trade agreement stipulated that the higher 1975 price paid by the Soviets for Cuban sugar would constitute the minimum Soviet price under the new agreement. As Jorge I. Domínguez observed, 'the agreement to maintain the 1975 price was, therefore, a substantial Soviet commitment to subsidize Cuban sugar. Moreover, the agreement was signed just as Cuba succeeded in forcing South Africa to withdraw its troops from Angola.' He further noted that, 'beginning in 1976, Soviet sugar subsidies to Cuba (compared with the real world market price) became massive, far exceeding the subsidy level of the 1960s' (*To Make a World Safe for Revolution: Cuba's Foreign Policy* (Cambridge, Mass.: Harvard University Press, 1989) pp.84–5).
3. Wayne S. Smith believes that the Soviets and Cubans were convinced that the United States was behind Somalia's invasion of Ethiopia, which occurred after the Siad Biarre regime had defected to the US side. 'Thus they reacted to what they perceived to be an aggressive move of ours. Brzezinski in turn saw the Soviet reaction as proof that they were testing us. His subsequent portrayal of Soviet and Cuban actions in the Horn as showing contempt for detente had a most deleterious effect on the prospects for SALT and for broader improvement of regions with both the Soviet Union and Cuba' (*The Closest of Enemies* (New York: W.W. Norton, 1987) p.136.
4. 'The impetus for current economic reform policies has come from Cuba's political structures. There is consensus within the Cuban Communist Party . . . for an orderly transition to a different model of social organization in order to effectively reinsert Cuba into today's changed world . . . In Cuba, the choice seems clear: to pursue long-term goals of economic reform *under*

state control' (Pedro Montreal, 'To market, to market . . .', *Hemisfile*, vol. 4, no. 3, May–June 1993, p.11; emphasis added).

5. However, Cubans must still be accompanied by foreigners to enter the restaurants, nightclubs and hotels that are reserved for foreign tourists.
6. Pascal Fletcher, 'Communist-Ruled Cuba Moves Closer to Mixed Economy', Reuter, 9 September 1993.
7. See 'Acuredo de! Buró Político', Para llevar a cabo importantes innovaciones en la agricultural estatal', *Granma*, 15 September 1993, p.1.
8. FBIS-LAT-92-226-S, 23 November 1992, p.7.
9. One high-level Cuban official told Gillian Gunn in 1992 that the government prefers 'to arrest dissidents now rather than have to shoot them later'. Gillian Gunn, speaking on 'The Current Situation in Cuba', at the Americas Society's Conference, 'Cuba at the Turning Point', New York City, 13 March 1992.
10. For example, see Jesse Jackson, 'We May Get Burned by the Cuba Embargo', *Los Angeles Times*, 18 November 1993, p.M5.
11. For recent examples, see Andrew Zimbalist, 'Dateline, Cuba: Hanging On In Havana', *Foreign Policy*, Fall 1993, pp.151–67; and the lengthier study by Gillian Gunn, *Cuba in Transition: Options for US Policy*, A Twentieth Century Fund Paper (New York, 1993).
12. At a joint hearing on Cuba convened by three committees of the House of Representatives on 18 November 1993, Representative Tom Lantos sharply condemned the Castro regime following his return from a week-long visit to Cuba. The Hungarian-born liberal Democrat compared Cuba to Stalinist Eastern Europe and warned that the regime's continued ideological rigidity would make working with it virtually impossible. (*CubaINFO*, vol. 5, no. 15, 24 November 1993, p.2).
13. David Ronfeldt theorizes that Western societies have evolved in terms of hierarchical institutions first, followed later by competitive markets, with multi-organizational networks at present emerging as the next form of societal organization. For reasons of ideology, power and state security, communist regimes remained at the institutional stage of development, making it difficult for them to alter adopt the market. See David Ronfeldt, *Institutions, Markets, and Networks: Toward a New Framework* (RAND, i. preparation). A preliminary summary and application of the theoretical framework appears in David Ronfeldt and Cathryn L. Thorup, *North America in the Era of Citizen Networks*, DRU-459-FF (Santa Monica: RAND, August 1993).
14. FBIS-LAT-93-142, 27 July 1993, p.8.
15. *Trabajadores*, 26 October 1992; FBIS-LAT-108-A, 27 October 1992, p.1.
16. Marifeli Pérez-Stable, 'Vanguard Party Politics in Cuba', in Enrique A. Baloyra and James A. Morris (eds), *Conflict and Change in Cuba* (Albuquerque: University of New Mexico Press, 1993) p.83.
17. *CubaINFO*, vol. 5, no. 3, 26 February 1993, p.5.
18. *CubaINFO*, vol. 5, no. 4, 19 March 1993, p.7.
19. For a comprehensive set of assessments that arrives at similar conclusions concerning Cuba's current political and economic decline, and the island's grim future, see The Cuban Research Institute, *Transition in Cuba: New Challenges for US Policy* (Miami, Florida: Florida International University, 1993).

20. Nelson P. Valdés observes that, 'Death permeates Cuba's historical and political imagination' and that numerous political figures have died 'to show that they have had the best interests of the country in mind and that they held high patriotic and moral standards' ('Cuban Political Culture: Between Betrayal and Death', in Sandor Halebsky and John M. Kirk (eds), *Cuba in Transition: Crisis and Transformation* (Boulder Col.: Westview Press, 1992) pp.221–221). The same point is made by Edward Gonzalez and David Ronfeldt, *Cuba Adrift in a Postcommunist World*, R-4231-USDP (Santa Monica: RAND, 1992) in their discussion of the Cuban tradition of 'resistance and struggle' epitomized by José Martí and Castro himself (p.41).
21. *Los Angeles Times*, 30 August 1993, p.A4.
22. For a further elaboration, see Gonzalez and Ronfeldt, *Cuba Adrift in a Postcommunist World*, pp.54–9. The extensive maze of underground shelters and tunnels that have been constructed underneath Havana and other cities, and that continue to be worked on despite the island's economic crisis, make a *Götterdämmerung*-type showdown or a Numantia (in which the defenders of a Spanish garrison chose suicide rather surrender) less of a far-fetched possibility for a dying Castro regime.
23. Completed prior to the passage of the Cuban Democracy Act, our RAND study rejected the policy alternatives of increasing and decreasing pressures. We recommend instead the option of staying the course, but augmenting it with a communication and information policy: *Cuba Adrift in a Postcommunist World*, pp.60–82. See also Donald E. Schulz, *The United States and Cuba: From a Strategy of Conflict to Constructive Engagement* (Carlisle Barracks, Pa.: Strategic Studies Institute, US Army War College, 1993).
24. Sergio G. Roca, 'The *Comandante* in His Economic Labrynth', in Baloyra and Morris (eds), *Conflict and Change in Cuba*, p.105.
25. Employing a theoretical model, John Arquilla suggests how the United States may try to 'test' the Cuban climate by taking step-by-step initiatives and waiting to see their impact before trying additional concessions. See *A Decision Modelling Perspective on US–Cuban Relations*, MR-377-USDP (Santa Monica: RAND, 1993). For an example of an alternative stratagem in which US concessions are made less contingent on Cuban behaviour, see Gunn, *Cuba in Transition: Options for US Policy*, pp.75–93.

14 Confidence-building Measures and a Cuba–United States Rapprochement

Hal P. Klepak

As détente and talk of détente, and arms control and talk of arms control, waxed and waned in the 1970s and 1980s, the idea of confidence-building measures, surely a very ancient one, came to know new prominence under that name and became the subject of a vast literature in diplomatic and academic circles. First attracting great attention in negotiations of arms control and disarmament agreements in Europe, and more generally regarding nuclear weapons, CBMs, or CSBMs (confidence- and *security*-building measures) were fundamental building-blocks of the process of improved political relations which, it was hoped, would give a strategic environment conducive to major progress on wide security issues between the two main blocs of NATO and the Warsaw Pact nations.

Even this rubric was extended under the Conference on Security and Cooperation in Europe (CSCE) to include non-allied states wishing to join in the construction of a new overarching European security system. CBMs were generally understood to be an approach to security relations containing purposely designed, distinctly cooperative measures intended (1) to assist in clarifying participating states' military intentions; and/or (2) to reduce uncertainties about military activities; and/or (3) to constrain the opportunities for the use of military force.[1] These techniques are designed to lower tensions and are aimed at reducing the danger of conflict occurring as a result of a misunderstanding or miscalculation regarding the actions of a rival.

After the largely successful European experience of recent years, there has been much thought on, and study of, the prospects for transferring the concept, and related activities, to areas of the world outside Europe. Fortunately, this has generally been combined with a widespread understanding that the European context was specific and that it could not serve as a complete 'model' for other regions of the world. Nonetheless, many authors in Latin America, Asia and Africa have tried to draw lessons from the European situation which might be of use in their own or other areas of the world.[2] This trend has gained steam since United Nations Secretary-General Boutros Boutros-Ghali called, in *An Agenda for Peace*, for more energy on the part of regional organizations in peacekeeping, peacemaking and generally in the peaceful settlement of disputes.

Such has been the growth in the employment of these measures within and without Europe that one author has recently referred to their use in the post-Cold War world as 'the preeminent means of preventing accidental wars and unintended escalations in strife-ridden regions'.[3] And while they can be formal or informal, tacit or widely published, they all are the result of the political will in the participating states to move forward in reducing tensions and creating an atmosphere conducive to at least an increase over current levels of mutual trust and cooperation. They must do this without reducing any state's perception of its own achieved level of security.

They must also be seen in a much broader context than just that of CBMs themselves, and as one key element, but only one, in a wide range of tools for enhancing security. Other tools include preventive diplomacy, peacemaking, peace observing, zones of peace, peacekeeping, peace enforcement and what some have called 'conflict avoidance measures', this last often being the first step preceding full-scale CBMs and aiming merely, but importantly, at getting away from conflict and being able then to start the long process of establishing some improved level of mutual confidence.

CBMs need not of course be military but the central role of military considerations in security affairs has tended to give predominance to them in most areas so far. Common approaches to any number of issues can build confidence. Cooperation on trade, health, the environment, foreign policy, scientific research and a myriad of other fields can work to improve confidence between potential adversaries. But the objective is to create an essentially *political* context of improved confidence among political decision makers and thus, while the measures may be many and varied, it is important not to lose sight of the objective which is a political one.[4] Political relations among the parties to a CBM must be improved on a day-to-day basis and this requires a major shift in the way political leaders perceive their new partners, from negative and hostile to positive and less sceptical.

It must be admitted that CBMs have tended to work to greatest effect when they have joined an already moving political process of improvement of the relations between the parties. While CBMs have proved an excellent means to stimulate the acceleration and deepening of that process, they have been much less likely to serve as a catalyst for the whole process from the beginning.

The Canadian Department of Foreign Affairs has a useful breakdown of kinds of CBMs. They are of two types: information and communications CBMs and constraint CBMs. Information and communications CBMs include:

(1) the provision of information about military forces, facilities, structures and activities;
(2) the provision of means of communication;
(3) the provision of advance notification of specified military activities; and
(4) the provision of opportunities to observe specified military activities.

Constraint CBMs include:

(1) provision of opportunities to *inspect* and/or monitor constrained or limited military forces, facilities, structures and activities;
(2) *non-interference* with verification measures;
(3) provision of assurance to avoid or limit provocative military activities;
(4) provision of assurance to avoid or limit the provocative *stationing* or *positioning* of military forces; and
(5) provision of assurance to avoid or limit the development and/or deployment of specified military *technologies*, including systems and sub-systems believed by participating states to have a destabilizing character or impact.

Having introduced the subject of confidence-building measures, it is now possible to begin to set them in the context of current Cuban–US relations in order to then see if there is any utility in searching for CBMs which might be useful in reducing the level of tension in those relations and creating a political atmosphere more conducive to better relations between Havana and Washington. It will also be necessary to look at whether actions short of CBMs can begin a process of rapprochement which future CBMs could then enhance.

CURRENT CUBAN–US RELATIONS

Cuban–US relations are arguably as bad as they have ever been or even at the worst point ever of their frequently stormy story.[5] Despite hopes in some circles that the Clinton administration would bring a fresh approach to those relations, the reality has been that they have actually worsened over the months of the new administration. The Cuban Democracy Act has dealt a savage blow to those anxious to reopen dialogue between the two capitals and both the embargo and the military measures the US deploys against Cuba have been beefed up, not reduced, under President Clinton.

The only real change has been in Havana where the truly desperate circumstances caused by the end of the Soviet and Warsaw Pact connection have forced Cuba to review many of its foreign policy stances and adopt a totally non-provocative stance vis-à-vis Washington on all important issues outstanding between them. This humiliating posture must of course cause great anguish among many of the more ideologically inclined in the government and party, but *realpolitik oblige*.

Havana perceives the United States to be continuing unabated its policy of isolating, weakening and if possible overthrowing the Castro government, despite the fact that Cuba no longer poses anything of a threat to the United States or to US interests more broadly. It believes the United States to be, in Fidel Castro's own words, 'triumphalist' and unwilling to yield on any major issues as it revels in its new-found unipolar world. The word of the day is defence against what is trumpeted as being an ever-growing threat of invasion, subversion or even a combination of both coming from the north.

The United States sees the Castro government as an anachronism hanging on desperately after the collapse of the international communist movement and as a rotten fruit only waiting to fall from the tree. Washington's view of that government is that it is about to reap its just reward for decades of oppression, exploitation and export of revolution and that the United States should help it on its way, if not too directly, because, at least up to this time, there is no requirement to hurry the natural pace of events.

In this context, the security dimension of Cuban–US relations is particularly worthy of revised analysis at the present time. For long the US threat has been used as the primary justification for the enormous efforts Cuba has made to provide a massive defence potential for the island. The Revolutionary Armed Forces, until recent cuts, numbered some 175 000 personnel in the regular services, with the very considerable reserve and paramilitary organizations adding many more through the Youth Labour Army of 100 000, the Civil Defence Force of 50 000, State Security of 15 000, Border Guard Service of 4000 and a huge Territorial Militia of 1 300 000.[6] United States-supported subversion has justified the creation of another huge, internal-oriented security service, including the now rather infamous *Comités por la Defensa de la Revolución* (CDR – Committees for the Defence of the Revolution).[7]

In a similar if less dramatic vein, the United States has used the Cuban 'threat', in tandem with that of the Soviet Union, to justify not only a whole hemispheric security system of vast dimensions, but more specifically the deployment of large-scale forces (and diplomatic initiatives of all kinds) to the Caribbean region.[8] Suggesting that Cuba was a base for communist subversion of all of Latin America, the United States engaged in the reinforcing of the whole inter-American security system and its transformation into an essentially internal security apparatus within the individual Latin American states.[9] Worst-case planning argued that Cuba could provide the USSR, in time of war, with a vital base for operations against US and allied shipping in the Gulf of Mexico and Caribbean and that its own national armed forces could serve as useful adjuncts to Soviet assets striking at Western targets in such scenarios.[10] And while many analyses poured scorn on such interpretations, those anxious to keep US–Cuban relations strained constantly came back to this assessment.[11]

CHANGE

Neither the Cuban nor the US previous strategic assessment of threat appears any longer to hold any validity, if indeed either ever did to any great extent. As mentioned, the Castro government in Cuba is generally seen as about to collapse from its own internal contradictions, and there are few in the United States, outside the very vocal but not really very numerous exile Cuban community, who feel that the process should be sped up through direct US military intervention with all its incumbent risks for US lives and interests. This is especially true of the Pentagon, which seems to hold firmly that operations against Cuba would be ill-advised and almost pointless. While there can be no doubt that Cuba's security analysts would be mad not to take the possibility of invasion or subversion seriously, especially given the increase in US capabilities of late, real threat is made up of both *potential* and *intention* and the latter seems notably lacking in Washington at the moment.

For the United States, the Cuban threat simply can no longer possibly be taken seriously. The Cuban forces are being drastically cut and are largely without fuel, spare parts, ammunition for training or defence, funds for new weapons and prospects. With the end of the Warsaw Pact pillar, their capabilities are waning considerably and will continue to do so, and this is particularly true of offensive potential. US forces, while cut overall, are even more present in the Caribbean region now than during the Cold War, and the Revolutionary Armed Forces are now completely outclassed in every conceivable area of military strength even in the Caribbean area, without considering the vast resources the United States could bring to bear if it actually decided to do something dramatic about the situation on the island.

There is, however, a new security context for both Cuba and the United States and one where there are possible, even probable, problems of importance for both countries. The main 'threat' in the new circumstances is neither direct attack by the other nor foreign complications. It is rather the prospects for change in Cuba getting out of control and leading to widespread violence on the island. That is, there is considerable potential for exiled or even resident Cubans acting to end the political regime through force. It is also possible that the regime will be obliged to turn to force in order to control dissent within the population and that this will radicalize opposition and also lead to further violence.

In this sort of situation, it is not unlikely that there would be a number of highly serious implications affecting the security of both countries. Exiles would be unlikely to remain aloof from such a scenario developing on the island. More importantly, widespread disorder, violence and bloodshed would risk drifting into open civil war and there would inevitably be calls in the United States to intervene to end the fighting and re-establish peace (and no doubt set up a new government). Under circumstances of protracted violence, emigration from the island would no doubt grow by leaps and bounds, a situation with highly significant implications for the United States, doubtless the main target of such emigration and a country with vivid and recent experience in this realm.

Thus it is surely in the interests of both the United States and Cuba to see to it that change of a gradual and controlled kind comes to the island and that bloodshed is avoided. This is not to say that both countries' governments see the current situation in these terms, but simply to suggest that there is much room and reason for consideration of this theme for the benefit of all sides.

CONFIDENCE-BUILDING MEASURES IN THE CURRENT CONTEXT

Before discussing a potential role for CBMs in helping to pave the way for improved relations between Cuba and the United States, it is important to make a point about asymmetries. Cuba is a tiny country, weaker relative to the United States than at any time in decades. The United States is the dominant, perhaps only, *world* power, completely without challengers for political and military leadership not only of the West but of the international community *tout court.*

What this means is that the United States is by far the more *able* to make gestures of importance to move the process of rapprochement along, but that, given its extraordinary and indeed triumphalist situation, it is also by far the less likely to be motivated to do so. Cuba, small and weak, is by far the less able to make gestures of this kind towards the United States but it is obliged to do so if any progress is going to be made in this area. This is doubtless unfair but, as Thucydides remarked, international relations, especially those between great powers and small powers, are nothing if not unfair.

The essential requirement is to make the United States take notice of Cuba during a time when the foreign policy agenda of the Clinton government is, to say the least, quite full. Havana must seek to make it known to Washington that there is little to be lost and something of significance to be gained by addressing the new security situation squarely and attempting jointly to avoid conflict or situations where violence, and therefore population movements and US intervention, are likely. The United States must be shown that the Castro government is indeed changing, in important ways, and that it is in the interest of both governments that this change be achieved without excessive dislocation. In showing the United States this, Cuba must be careful to demonstrate that it is a viable interlocutor in whom confidence can be placed. This sort of move can precede wider CBMs but can even in some ways be seen as the basis on which to build them.

Cuba must be able to use the most effective arrow in the quiver of any country dealing with the United States, that of public opinion. Polls are already suggesting that the vast majority of Americans do not believe force should be used to oust the government in Havana. This sentiment must be capitalized upon through what could be known as initial confidence-building measures of a unilateral kind before moving on to the development of further ones of a bilateral nature.

It is important to note that some real CBMs are already in place between the United States and Cuba. These have been put into place over the years and have worked reasonably well if not with decisive results. Here one refers to agreements on aerial piracy and narcotics interdiction, among others. Even military CBMs have been agreed upon, both for the high seas and with special reference to the US military base at Guantánamo. The small size of that installation and the nature of the harbour entrance to it make some previous notification of maritime traffic essential and the practical nature of the problem has made the US military perfectly willing, indeed keen, to deal with the Cuban armed forces and establish means of reducing potential for conflict through misunderstandings or other mistakes. Neither side has wished to leave room for such misunderstanding and they have moved to remove the most likely causes. This is quite within the normal framework of CBMs elsewhere in the world and shows their flexibility and usefulness.[12]

Cuba should take every effort to make these accords and cooperation much more widely known to the public in the United States. It should show its good will regarding Washington's residual security-related suspicions, however unfounded in reality, by taking measures to reduce offensive capabilities which have in the past been resented by the United States, and should do so with great public relations 'splash'. Some of this can be done with a truly minimal impact on Cuba's defensive capabilities.

For example, the United States has consistently argued that it was concerned about Cuba's potential for mischief in the Caribbean through its amphibious warfare capability. The Cuban navy has two *Polnocny* class amphibious medium landing ships, each with a capacity to transport six tanks and 180 troops, and two battalions of naval infantry whose main tasks in time of war would normally be related to amphibious operations.[13] However, Cuba's road system is much better than most in Latin America and the armed forces' ability to reach most of the island with reasonable efficiency and speed is assured, so that the utility of such ships in any action to defend the island is questionable. Secondly, the overwhelming air and naval superiority the United States would enjoy in the case of an attack on Cuba would be such that it is inconceivable that such ships could put to sea and operate effectively in case of war. Thus little would be lost be scrapping these vessels or, even better, returning them to Russia, and doing so with the loudest fanfare possible.

Much the same could be said of the long-range air transport fleet of the Cuban Air Force, particularly the wide-body Il-76 military cargo aircraft. While it could be argued that short-range air transport could be important in national defence against an invasion (although US air power could well make it impossible to use), surely long-range air transport is less than vital. Many US observers have accused Cuba of continuing to harbour designs on neighbours and far-flung countries of recent ideological interest. If these aircraft are returned to Moscow, much public relations benefit could be obtained as showing Cuba no longer was in the business of exporting revolution or troubling others. There would be little if any impact on Cuba's defensive capability.

Cuba has cut its armed forces massively of late, in the wake of the current economic disasters. This was done quietly and in an almost embarrassed fashion. Surely such cuts should be placed in the context of an attempt to show Cuba is changing, becoming less militarized, uninterested in foreign adventures, and feeling secure that it faces no serious internal problems. The United States knows the extent and effects of those reductions in armed forces size. There should then be no reason not to capitalize on the situation in direct public relations terms. And in doing so, one can emphasize the peaceful nature of Cuba's intentions and the embarrassing (for the Americans) 'David and Goliath' nature of the confrontation and its 'kicking a man while he is down' implications.

Lastly, Cuba has a reasonably good record in anti-narcotics efforts, at least compared to the United States and many of its allies, and despite repeated accusations to the contrary.[14] It can make more of an effort to become involved, and to show publicly that it wishes to become involved, in joint anti-narcotics operations and cooperation in the Caribbean. The armed forces and police of several US allies are active in such operations in the region, and these include the British, French and Dutch as well as most of the Caribbean states. In the waters and skies near Cuba, there is more cooperation needed with neighbours, especially the British (territories in the Turks and Caicos Islands to the north and the Cayman Islands to the south), the Bahamas and Jamaica.[15] While in the light of serious mistakes like the 1980 sinking of the Royal Bahamas Defence Force patrol boat *Flamingo* by Cuban Migs, time and effort must be placed into building confidence with these neighbours. They represent a potential 'end run' to reach another level of indirect security cooperation with the United States which might pay dividends over the long haul.[16] Indeed, as recently as September 1991, Cuba and the Bahamas began discussions on just this sort of cooperation.[17]

Such military measures, some of which could be seen as a kind of CBM, would not be the only ones offering themselves. Diplomatically, Havana has accepted that its policies must now be non-confrontational where the United States is concerned. But surely these things have to become better known. Pro-Cuba groups could be used to help push the new image of Cuban foreign policy in the United States and other Western countries.

Economically, the *apertura* should be carried further, perhaps at a faster pace than so far has been the case. In human rights, Cuba can improve its image and show progress with this thorny problem in a way which reduces anti-Castroists' ability to attack the government. This progress should be shown by making details public and then pushing their circulation.

CONCLUSIONS

It is of course easily argued that Cuba is under no compulsion to make any of the gestures mentioned above. It is a sovereign state perfectly entitled to have the armed forces and foreign policy of its choice, as well as to effect domestic change in the manner its own government decides. There is of course no disagreement with this.

In the interest, of moving forward to a situation where CBMs could become truly bilateral, however, it is difficult not to arrive at a conclusion that involves a greater degree of present-day flexibility on Havana's part than on Washington's. The United States does not as yet see, at least on a public level, the potential problems of not reaching some greater level of cooperation with Cuba. As mentioned, CBMs are much more useful in pushing forward an already established political drive for rapprochement than in starting such a process off. However, in the current circumstances, it does seem that unilateral policy decisions by Havana, costing little but with some degree of promise at least, can follow CBMs already in place and open up the way to possible improvement in the desperate situation now confronting the island and which, if not handled properly, could have the most negative of effects much farther afield.

Notes

1. Definitions in this chapter are those usually accepted within the Canadian Department of External Affairs, and used by that ministry in Canada's efforts in the security field.
2. See the work of the Comisión Sudamericana de Paz, *El Sentido de una tarea* (Santiago: Andros, 1990) pp.1–52; Hernán Patiño Mayer, 'Aportes a un nuevo concepto de seguridad hemisférica-seguridad cooperativa', in *Seguridad Estrategia Regional*, no. 4, September 1993, pp.84–9; Hugo Palma, *América latina: limitación de armamentos y desarme en la región* (Lima: CEPEI, 1986) pp.58–62.
3. Michael Krepon, 'The Decade for Confidence-building Measures', in Michael Krepon *et al.* (eds), *A Handbook of Confidence-building Measures for Regional Security* (Washington: Henry L. Stimson Center) Handbook no. 1, p.1.
4. Edgardo Mercado Jarrín, 'Perspectivas de los acuerdos de limitación y desarme en América latina y el Caribe', in Augusto Varas (ed.), *Paz, desarme y desarrollo en América latina* (Buenos Aires: GEL, 1987) pp.309–11.
5. The evolution of those relations in the first quarter-century of the Castro era is traced in Wayne S. Smith, *The Closest of Enemies* (New York: W.W. Norton, 1987).

6. See International Institute for Strategic Studies, *The Military Balance 1993–1994* (London: Brassey's, 1993) pp.182–3; Adrian English, *The Armed Forces of Latin America* (London: Jane's, 1984) pp.199–218.
7. Andrés Sorel, *Cuba: la revolución crucificada* (Madrid: Libertarias/Prodhufi) pp.117–22.
8. See the excellent work of Lars Schoultz, *National Security and United States Policy toward Latin America* (Princeton: Princeton University Press, 1987); Pierre Queuille, *L'Amérique latine, la doctrine Monroe et le panaméricanisme* (Paris: Payot, 1969) pp.220–36.
9. Alain Rouquié, *L'Etat militaire en Amérique latine* (Paris: Seuil, 1982) pp.148–89.
10. See Jaime Suchlicki (ed.), *The Cuban Military under Castro* (Miami: University of Miami Press, 1989) pp.168–71; Michael C. Desch, *When the Third World Matters: Latin America and United States Grand Strategy* (Baltimore: Johns Hopkins University Press, 1993) pp.120–22.
11. Schoultz, *National Security*, pp.260–65; Abraham Lowenthal, *Partners in Conflict: the United States and Latin America in the 1990s* (Baltimore: Johns Hopkins University Press, 1990) pp.164–7. See also Ivelaw L. Griffith, *The Quest for Security in the Caribbean* (Armonk, New York: M.E. Sharpe, 1993) pp.29, 190–92.
12. For a description of the work of CBMs in a Central American context, and involving interests which the United States considered very important indeed, see the important contribution by Jack Child, *The Central American Peace Process, 1983–1991* (Boulder, Col.: Lynne Rienner, 1992) pp.151–7.
13. International Institute for Strategic Studies, *The Military Balance*, p.183; Suchlicki, *The Cuban Military*, p.168.
14. Peter D. Scott and Jonathan Marshall, *Cocaine Politics: Drugs, Armies, and the CIA in Central America* (Berkeley: University of California Press, 1991) pp.102–3.
15. This issue is discussed in Griffith, *The Quest for Security*, pp.243–71.
16. Ibid., p.200.
17. Ibid., p.270.

15 US Foreign Subsidiary Trade with Cuba: Before and After the Cuban Democracy Act

Donna Rich Kaplowitz

The Cuban Democracy Act (CDA) was signed into law by President Bush on 23 October 1992. The CDA has several facets that shape US policy toward Cuba. They include permitting telecommunication and direct mail services to Cuba, sanctioning countries that provide assistance to Cuba, prohibiting US subsidiary trade and blacklisting ships docking in Cuban ports. The subsidiary trade component of the CDA is examined here. It is one of the most contentious parts of the law.

The CDA turns back the clock on US policy towards Cuba almost 20 years in that it prohibits trade conducted by US subsidiaries based in third countries with Cuba. Direct trade between the United States and Cuba has been impossible for more than 30 years because of the embargo. However, in 1975 the United States amended its embargo to allow US companies located in third countries to trade with Cuba under very specific conditions. This change in policy was primarily the result of pressure from US allies who complained vigorously about the extraterritorial restrictive US trade regulations. For example, Ford Motor Company of Argentina, a subsidiary of a US corporation, campaigned at that time to permit subsidiary trade with Cuba and was subsequently allowed to trade with Cuba under the post-1975 embargo laws. The CDA reverses this opening.

The CDA was passed by the US Congress in the shuffle of 1992 election year politics. The goal of its author – Representative Robert Torricelli (Democrat, New Jersey) – was to speed up the end of the Castro government by tightening the economic noose around Cuba's neck until it is forced to 'cry uncle'. However, this chapter demonstrates that the main impacts of the CDA have been to hurt US competitiveness and help the Castro government gain international support and domestic legitimacy. For the Cubans, the CDA has been an inconvenience at worst, while it has given Castro the political currency he needs to stay in power. It is the US government – condemned by the United Nations, by most of its trade

Table 15.1 Licensed US foreign subsidiary trade with Cuba

	1985	*1988*	*1990*	*1991*	*1992*
Licence applications	256	215	321	285	225
Total exports to Cuba (US$ mn)	162	97	533	383	407
Total imports from Cuba (US$ mn)	126	149	172	335	92
Total exports and imports (US$ mn)	288	246	705	718	499
Export/import ratio	56/44	40/60	76/24	53/47	82/18

Source: Office of Foreign Assets Control, *An Analysis of Licensed Trade with Cuba by Foreign Subsidiaries of US Companies* (Washington DC: US Department of Treasury) July 1991.

partners, Cuban exiles and dissidents, and the religious community – that appears to be the sure loser.

EVOLUTION OF SUBSIDIARY TRADE

Trade between Cuba and subsidiaries of US corporations took place, on a moderate basis, between 1975, when it was first permitted, and 1990. However, when the Soviet Union collapsed in 1990, subsidiary trade jumped almost 300 per cent. Subsidiaries of US corporations in third countries began replacing the Soviet Union as Cuba's trade partners. Some examples of this change in Cuba's trade direction follow.

In 1988, 215 licence applications for trade with Cuba were made to the US Treasury Department. The result was $246 million of subsidiary trade, and the balance of trade in 1988 slightly favoured Cuba (see Table 15.1). This level of trade was typical for the entire 10 year period from 1980 to 1989. During that period, trade between US foreign subsidiaries and Cuba hovered around the $250 million mark and an average of about 200 licences a year were granted by the US Treasury Department for trade with Cuba.[1] Over the 10 year period (1980–89), the export/import ratio for total trade between Cuba and US subsidiaries was more or less balanced.[2]

However, two years later, in 1990, the number of licence applications had increased by 50 per cent to 321. More significant was the increase in the dollar amount and direction of trade. US subsidiary trade with Cuba almost tripled, reaching $705 million in 1990. It rose to $718 million in 1991. By 1990, Cuba had become a net *buyer* from US subsidiaries. Cuban imports accounted for 76 per cent of its total trade with US subsidiaries (see Table 15.1). Thus, the terms of trade changed in favour of US subsidiaries.[3]

In Fiscal Year (FY) 1992, which ended just prior to the signing of the CDA, total trade between Cuba and US subsidiaries dipped slightly, to about $500 million. The 30 per cent drop in total trade from the previous year's level was due entirely to the decrease in imports of Cuban sugar by US subsidiaries. This is not surprising since Cuba's total sugar production fell in 1992 by more than 15 per cent, from an annual average of 8–9 million tons in the 1980s to 7 million tons in the 1991–2 harvest.[4] Despite the decline in total trade between US subsidiaries and Cuba in 1992, US subsidiaries actually exported 6 per cent (roughly $21 million) *more* to Cuba than in the previous year. 1992 saw $407 million worth of goods exported to Cuba from US subsidiaries, which was more than 1991s $383 million.

It is interesting to note that, even at the height of US subsidiary–Cuban trade in 1991, subsidiaries accounted for only 18 per cent of total Cuban trade. Of all trade conducted between US subsidiaries and Cuba, 82 per cent were exports to Cuba and 18 per cent were imports from Cuba (see Table 15.1).

TYPES OF GOODS, US REGULATIONS AND LOCATION OF SUBSIDIARIES

As in past years, consumable goods comprised the great majority of goods traded between US subsidiaries and Cuba. In 1992, consumables accounted for 91 per cent of all trade between US subsidiaries and Cuba. This represented a threefold increase in Cuban food imports from US subsidiaries since 1988, and is a direct reflection of the collapse of the Soviet Union and Eastern bloc and Cuba's activities in the world's markets. Table 15.2 shows the ratio of consumables to durable goods in US subsidiary–Cuba trade. Table 15.3 shows the types of goods sold to Cuba by US subsidiaries during 1985–91.

More than 100 subsidiaries of US corporations have traded with Cuba since such trade was permitted in 1975. Table 15.4 lists those companies that have been licensed to trade with Cuba. US subsidiaries that wished to trade with Cuba prior to the signing of the CDA had to apply for a licence from the Office of Foreign Assets Control (OFAC) of the US Treasury

Table 15.2 Goods exported from US subsidiaries to Cuba (millions of US dollars)

	1985	*1988*	*1990*	*1991*	*1992*
Grain, wheat and other consumables	109	56	500	348	363
Industrial and non-consumables	53	41	33	36	44
Percentage of consumables in subsidiary exports	67.28	57.73	93.81	90.86	89.19
Percentage of consumables in subsidiary trade	37.85	22.76	70.92	48.46	72.75

Source: Donna Rich Kaplowitz and Michael Kaplowitz, *New Opportunities for US–Cuban Trade* (Baltimore: Johns Hopkins University, 1992); US Treasury Department, 'Special Report', 1993.

Department. Usually, a licence was granted if the company complied with all the requirements for licensing. There were three major conditions for licensing: (1) goods sold to Cuba must have been produced in a third country and contain less than 20 per cent US components; (2) US directors of subsidiaries were precluded from dealing with Cuba; and (3) US parent companies had to apply for and receive a licence from the US Department of Treasury before any trade was conducted.

A vast majority – 65 per cent – of the US subsidiaries trading with Cuba were located in Switzerland. This is because several of the largest dealers have subsidiaries headquartered there. For example, the US grain dealer, Cargill Inc., formerly one of the largest traders in the Cuban market, has an affiliate in Switzerland. Offshore companies located in the West Indies accounted for the second largest share (13.6 per cent) of trade between US subsidiaries and Cuba. Trade from subsidiaries located in Canada, Argentina, Mexico and the United Kingdom followed, respectively.

THE CUBAN DEMOCRACY ACT

On 23 October 1992, President Bush signed the CDA precluding all trade between Cuba and US subsidiaries. It took years for the controversial law to wind its way through Congress and the White House. Senator Connie Mack (Republican, Florida) originally introduced similar legislation known

agricultural pesticides	engineering services	passenger cars and	soybean meal
air cleaners	for plastics,	spare parts	spark plugs
aluminium sheets	synthetic leather,	pharmaceutical	sterilizers
asphalt manufacturing	ammonia	products	sunflower seed oil
equipment	eyeglass lenses	photocopy paper	synthetic adhesive
automatic	fertilizer	photographic supplies	telephone exchange
transmissions	flour products	plastic products,	equipment
bottle inspectors	flowmeters	cutlery, toys	telephone pay stations
brake fluid	fluorescent lamps	plumbing equipment	telephone subsets
carbon black	food	plywood	teleprinters – parts
cardboard box mfg.	funeral cars	polyethylene bags	temperature recording
equipment	fuse links	polypropylene ropes	equipment
cardpunch machine	gas pumps & nozzles	polystyrene room	thermostats
and sorter	gear drive mechanisms	dividers	traffic light relays
carpentry tools	gelatin capsules	power boilers	transformers
cement	glass manufacturing	power plant equipment,	truck chassis
ceramic glazes	machinery and	pumps, motors	typewriters
chemical coatings and	parts	steam-generating	tyres
finishes for leather	glass products	pressing machines	underwater equipment,
compressors	hacksaw blades	pressurized cables	masks, snorkels, fins
copper concentrates	hydraulic pumps	processing equipment	valves
corn	ice machines	PVC pipes and fittings	gate, air
detergent alkylate	kerosene lanterns	rice	three-way, globe
feedstock	light bulbs	riveting tools	water system
diesel engines	lubricating oils	rivets	equipment
dry roofing felt	maize	rock-drilling bits	weight scales
electrical connectors	metal warehouses	and rods	wheat flour
electrical fuses	micro switches	roller chain and parts	x-ray equipment
electrical plugs	motors	rubber base adhesive	x-ray film
electrical switches	oats	sausage casings	
elevators	office furniture	sewer system	
enamel glazes	office supplies	equipment	
enamelling furnace	oil additives	sewing machines,	
components	orthopaedic supplies	industrial: parts	

Source: Documents obtained by the authors through a Freedom of Information Act request to the Office of Foreign Assets Control of the US Department of Treasury, 31 March 1992. See also Donna Rich Kaplowitz and Michael Kaplowitz, *New Opportunities for US–Cuban Trade* (Baltimore: Johns Hopkins University, 1992).

Table 15.4 US parent companies of foreign subsidiaries licensed to trade with Cuba, 1985–91

ALCOA	Emhart Industries	Nynex
AM International	Envirotech	Otis Elevator
Aeroquip International	Exxon	Owens Corning Fiber
Analytical Technology	Fischer & Porter	Pfizer
Armco	Ford Motor	Philipp Brothers
BF Goodrich	GK Technologies	Picker International
Baker Hughes	GTE International	Potters Industries
Barry-Wehmiller	General Electric	RCA Global
Beatrice Companies	Genlyte Group	R.J. Reynolds
Bonne Bell	Gilbarco	Raychem
Borg-Warner	Gillette	Reichhold Chemicals
Bridgestone/Firestone	Goodyear Tire and Rubber	Reliance Electric
Buckman Laboratories	H.B. Fuller	Richardson Electronics
Burndy	H.H. Robertson	Rohm & Haas
Butler Manufacturing	Hercules	S.C. Johnson & Son
Campbell Investment	Hoechst Celanese	Joseph E. Seagram & Sons
Carrier	Honeywell	Sigman-Aldrich
Carter Day Industries	Hussmann	Stanley Works
Caterpillar	IBM World Trade	Sybron Acquisition
Central Soya	ITT	TFX Holdings
Champion Spark Plug	Ingersoll-Rand	TRW Teleflex
Coleman	International Multifoods	Tenneco
Combustion Engineering	International Securities	Toledo Scale
Continental Grain	Investment	USM
Cooper Industries	John Fluke Manufacturing	Uarco
Corning	Johnson and Johnson	Union Camp
Crane	Johnson Controls	Union Carbide
Cummins Engine	Joyce International	Vulcan Hart
Del Monte	Litton Industries	Westinghouse Electric
Dow Chemical	Lubrizol	Worthington International
Dorr-Oliver	McGraw Edison	Worthington Pump
Dresser Industries	Manville	
Drew Chemical	Mennen	
Drexel Burnham Lambert	Minnesota Mining & Manufacturing	
E.D.&F. Man International Futures	Monsanto	
E.I. Dupont	Morton International	
Eli Lilly	N.L. Industries	

Source: Documents obtained by the author through a Freedom of Information Act request to the Office of Foreign Assets Control of the US Department of Treasury, 31 March 1992.

as the 'Mack Amendment' in July 1989. The Mack legislation would have precluded all trade between US subsidiaries and Cuba. Foreign governments, US corporations and even the US State Department strongly criticized the Mack Amendment. In 1989, 1990 and 1991, the US State Department, under a Republican president, went on record opposing the legislation. In a 1989 cable from the US State Department to US embassies abroad, the State Department explained the rationale behind its opposition: 'We permit [subsidiary trade] because we recognize that attempting to apply our embargo to third countries will lead to unproductive and bitter trade disputes with our allies.'[5] This reasoning was eventually outweighed by domestic pressure principally from the conservative Cuban American National Foundation (CANF) which generously contributed to the campaign funds of strategic members of Congress and the Bush White House.[6]

Congressman Robert Torricelli first introduced the CDA in 1992. Numerous hearings and much debate took place around this controversial legislation in its many incarnations. The Bush administration flip-flopped on the issue. At first the Republican White House opposed the legislation for the same reasons it had opposed the Mack Amendment. However, President Bush changed his position on the proposed law when it became a victim of US election year politics – in particular, the partisan competition for Florida's electoral votes. In August 1992, then presidential candidate Bill Clinton, while campaigning in Florida for the Cuban American vote, commented on the proposed legislation and said 'I like it.'[7] Those three words were enough to force President Bush to sign the bill into law, lest he appear 'soft on Cuba' and lose the large Cuban American vote in the key state of Florida.[8]

In a highly politicized and publicized move, President Bush signed the CDA into law while visiting Miami on a campaign stop. Bush did not invite Democratic Congressman Robert Torricelli, the bill's sponsor, to attend the signing ceremony. Interestingly, President Bush won the Miami vote by a smaller margin than in any previous election, and had to fight hard for his smaller margin.[9]

OPPOSITION TO THE CDA

The opposition to the CDA has been widespread. It has been expressed and manifested via bilateral formal protests, blocking legislation, regional diplomatic protests and United Nations resolutions. Foreign nations are angered over the extraterritoriality of the legislation. US corporations, dissidents living in Cuba, Cuban exiles in Miami and members of the religious community have expressed their concern about and opposition to the new law.

Even before President Bush signed the bill into law, Canada and Britain had issued blocking orders against the proposed legislation. In October 1990, Canadian Justice Minister Kim Campbell issued an order barring Canadian subsidiaries of US corporations from complying with US measures precluding subsidiary trade, and requiring such companies to report any directives relating to such measures to the Canadian Attorney General. Canadian Foreign Affairs Minister Joe Clark called the proposed legislation 'an intrusion into Canadian sovereignty' in a 1990 letter of protest to US Secretary of State James Baker. Trade between Canadian subsidiaries of US companies and Cuba totalled $34.7 million in 1991.[10]

In September 1991, British Trade Secretary Peter Lilley warned the US Congress that he would use the Protection of Trading Interests Act (PTIA) to block the effects of the Mack Amendment. The PTIA is an act that protects Britain's sovereignty against extraterritorial trade measures invoked by other nations. Lilley noted, 'It is for the British government, not the US Congress to determine the UK's policy on trade with Cuba. We will not accept any attempt to superimpose US law on UK companies.'[11] Shortly before the CDA was signed into law, Britain acted to circumvent the US legislation by invoking the PTIA. British exports to Cuba amounted to $46.2 million in 1991. British imports from Cuba amounted to about $20 million.[12] That same year, US subsidiaries based in Britain conducted $21.75 million worth of trade with Cuba.[13]

US subsidiary companies in Britain and Canada are caught in a quandary: they violate either the US law or their home country's law. On the one hand, the US law carries civil penalties up to $50 000, plus the threat of confiscation of any property involved. On the other hand, host countries' blocking legislation carries heavy penalties. Canada's blocking order, for example, fines Canadian-based subsidiaries up to $8500 or five years' imprisonment for *heeding* the CDA.[14]

After the CDA became law, opposition to the new legislation continued to flood Washington. The European Community's diplomatic protest to the United States warned that 'the extension of [the embargo] has the potential to cause grave damage to the transatlantic relationship'.[15] In mid-September 1993, the European Parliament once again called on the European Community to ignore the CDA. The European Community stands to lose $500–600 million in trade because of the new law.[16]

Mexico and Japan also formally complained to the US government about the new extraterritorial legislation. Mexican Foreign Minister Fernando Solana called the CDA a violation of 'the essential principles of international law, especially non-intervention'. Solana explained that 'the decision of one state to establish commercial links with others is an expression of its sovereignty and is not subordinated to the will of a third ... Commercial activities and exchanges which take place [involving] Mexico or companies based in our country will be conducted exclusively by Mexican law.' On 30 September 1992, the Mexican Congress approved a resolution condemning the Torricelli Bill.[17]

On 22 November 1992, the Mexican Foreign Ministry issued a statement warning US subsidiaries in Mexico not to recognize the new US law. The Mexican statement read: it is unacceptable for companies established in our country to try to place a higher value on foreign legislation in Mexican territory than national legislation'.[18]

Mexican President Carlos Salinas de Gortari risked the wrath of congressional and White House anger when he told his Latin American counterparts in July 1993 that 'The blockade [of Cuba] is completely unacceptable in a sovereign nation.'[19] This is a particularly bold move, given that President Salinas is committed to the North American Free Trade Agreement (NAFTA) and has cautiously avoided ruffling feathers in Washington in order to gain Washington's support for NAFTA. Furthermore, the influential CANF has already condemned Mexican trade with Cuba and has linked CANF's support of NAFTA to the eradication of Mexican–Cuban trade. Nevertheless, Mexican commercial actions have followed its sharp nationalist rhetoric. US subsidiaries located in Mexico quadrupled their level of trade with Cuba between 1991 and 1992.[20] Dr Nobuo Miyamoto, Japanese ambassador to Cuba, said that 'the Japanese government is affected by the law, since it contains articles involving third countries'. Miyamoto went on to state that the 'problem with the law is that [the CDA] constitute[s] the extraterritorial application of US domestic legislation ... which is not permitted in international law'.[21]

Opposition to the CDA also came from Argentina, Bolivia, Chile, Costa Rica, the Dominican Republic, Honduras, North Korea, Uruguay, Venezuela and Vietnam.[22] At a meeting of mayors, municipal officers and legislators of over 20 Spanish-speaking nations, a resolution opposing the Torricelli Bill was issued and sent to the United Nations Secretary General Boutrus-Ghali.[23]

US corporations have quietly and consistently registered their opposition to the CDA for reasons of simple economics. CDA will force US corporations to lose market shares to their competitors. In October 1991, Brendan Harrington, a public affairs attorney at Cargill Inc., said his company leads the fight against efforts by Congress to prevent US subsidiaries in third countries from dealing with Cuba. 'If Cargill is denied access to the Cuban market,' Harrington said, 'European and Japanese traders would be very happy to take up the slack.'[24] Cargill has conducted the largest amount of subsidiary trade with Cuba, primarily through its subsidiary based in Switzerland.

Two other US corporate giants have also taken a public stand against CDA. In August 1992, United Technologies (parent company of Otis Elevator) opposed the CDA in testimony before the US Senate. Otis sold $10 million a year of goods to Cuba through subsidiaries in Mexico and Spain. Daryl Natz, a spokesman for Continental Grain recently pointed out that 'our competitors who aren't subsidiaries of US companies will get the business'. Continental Grain had been selling several million dollars of grain to Cuba annually through its subsidiaries in South America, Canada and Europe.[25]

Even Cubans who have been jailed for their opposition to the Castro government opposed the CDA. Cuban dissident Elizardo Sánchez Santa Cruz wrote a letter to the *New York Times* opposing the tightening of the embargo: 'Continuing economic pressures against the Cuban government will not bring about change,' wrote Sánchez. 'On the contrary, they provide Fidel Castro with excuses for his government's economic shortcomings and civil rights violations.'[26]

Similarly, Eloy Gutiérrez Menoyo, a Cuban exile who spent 22 years in prison in Cuba, recently wrote an essay published in the *Miami Herald*. In it he asks, 'Why not admit that communism has lasted longer wherever an embargo has been imposed? Vietnam, China, North Korea, and Cuba are clear examples. . . . Even under the tightest possible embargo and without significant changes in US policy toward the island, Fidel Castro could shrewdly manage to cling to power.'[27]

There are, of course, those in the exile community who support the CDA. The CANF had a heavy hand in writing the legislation, and in overseeing the bill's passage through Congress and the White House.[28] Apart from the CANF – and of course the pliable members of Congress – one is hard-pressed to find support elsewhere for the CDA.

Also opposed to the measure tightening the embargo were members of the Cuban Catholic Church. The Catholic bishops of Cuba issued a statement declaring their 'rejection of anything that might increase the great economic difficulties which the Cuban people are currently suffering. . . . Total embargoes affecting trade in essential products, including food and medicines, are ethically unacceptable, violate the principles of international law and are always contrary to the values of the Gospel.'[29]

Since the enactment of the CDA, the US group 'Pastors for Peace' have been sending material aid bound for Cuba across the US Mexican border in a direct challenge to the embargo.[30] Most recently, Pastors for Peace sponsored a 24 day hunger strike to release a school bus impounded by the Treasury Department in Laredo, Texas and allow it to be shipped to Cuba.[31]

On 24 November 1992, just one month after the CDA became law in the United States, the United Nations General Assembly resoundingly passed a resolution introduced by the Cuban government against the US embargo of Cuba. The resolution, entitled 'The Need to Terminate the US Economic, Trade and Financial Blockade Against Cuba', expresses concern over the US extraterritorial laws and their impact on the sovereignty of other nations, entities and individuals in other states. The resolution directs UN Secretary General Boutros Boutros-Ghali to prepare a report on the implementation of the resolution calling on all nations to 'refrain from promulgating and applying laws and measures . . . directed at . . . strengthening and extending the economic, commercial and financial embargo against Cuba'.

Until the CDA was passed, President Castro could not gain UN support for his anti-embargo position. When Cuba brought a similar resolution before the UN in 1991, it failed to gain the votes necessary for passage. The CDA was the exact instrument President Castro needed to secure UN support for his anti-embargo position. After the passage of the CDA with its extraterritorial measures, only two countries voted with the United States against the UN resolution: Israel and Romania.[32] Even the US State Department predicted that the impact of the CDA would be to make the US a pariah among its allies. In congressional hearings on the Torricelli legislation held in April 1992 (before the bill became law) then Principal Assistant Secretary for Inter-American Affairs Robert S. Gelbard testified that 'had the embargo applied to US companies in third countries Cuba would have likely won the UN debate' condemning the US trade embargo of Cuba in November 1991.[33] He was correct.

In response to the United Nations vote, the US State Department spokesman Joe Snyder issued a statement which said that the non-binding resolution will not affect US policy towards Cuba or enforcement of the embargo.

ARE COMPANIES COMPLYING?

Before looking at the impact of the CDA on US subsidiaries and on Cuba, an interesting corollary question about it should be examined – are subsidiaries complying? First, it is interesting to note the paucity of available data on the question in the light of the uproar prior to the CDA's enactment. There are no published studies available as of this writing. There are probably two opposing reasons for this lack of data: (1) if companies are heeding the regulations, they may want to do so quietly so as to avoid facing opposition – or blocking orders – in their respective host nations, and (2) if subsidiaries are not heeding the intent of the law, and *are* continuing to trade with Cuba either directly or through intermediaries, they probably want to avoid brazenly confronting US law.

There was some initial speculation in Washington circles that, although *candidate* Clinton publicly supported the CDA, he did so because of domestic politics during a presidential election. Some Cuba analysts have suggested *President* Clinton might choose not to enforce the law once he arrived in the White House.[34] To date, however, despite efforts at toning down the hostile rhetoric from Washington aimed at Havana, the Clinton White House continues to publicly endorse the Act.[35] It has not, however, taken specific action to enforce the law. Neither has it been publicly forced to do so.

The Office of Foreign Assets Control (OFAC) of the US Treasury Department reports that no new licences for subsidiary trade have been granted since 24 October 1992.[36] Moreover, the Treasury Department reports that there have been no enforcement actions taken because companies are 'simply abiding by the law'. Serena Moe, senior counsel to the OFAC noted that 'a lot of companies have found business reasons to avoid trade. Nobody wants to be the test case, so companies are ducking.' Moe added that she expects that if companies are compelled to trade with Cuba because they face a blocking order in their host country they will voluntarily disclose that to OFAC.[37]

Not surprisingly, the US State Department says that there have been no problems getting companies to comply with the new orders. Bob Fretz, a Cuba desk officer at the US Department of State, reports: 'We are always, always, always looking' (for violators of the subsidiary trade laws) and that 'there are no cases that we are aware of' of violations.[38]

Yet one must wonder how assiduously the US Treasury and State Departments are trying to uncover and follow up leads of CDA violations. There seems little doubt that locating, prosecuting and punishing a recalcitrant company will probably create more of a headache for the US government than it is worth. It may simply be easier to avoid looking, or look the other way and confidently report that there are no known violations of the law.

Whether or not one accepts the official US rhetoric at face value, it is clear that the CDA has taken a toll on subsidiaries based in Canada. For example, Eli Lilly of Canada Inc. and H.J. Heinz Co. of Canada Ltd both rebuffed opportunities to sell goods to Cuba this year. Sources at both subsidiaries said that their head offices in the United States refused to permit the trade deals.[39]

Despite its bravado before the enactment of the CDA, the Canadian government has, in effect, 'wimped out' – as one Canadian scholar so aptly put it.[40] According to an article in the Toronto *Globe and Mail*, the Canadian Justice Department has thus far failed to act on about 20 cases of alleged violations of Canada's blocking order against the CDA. Under the Canadian Foreign Extraterritorial Measures Act, the Canadian Department of External Affairs is supposed to refer alleged violations of the Canadian blocking order to the Canadian Justice Department for prosecution. Apparently the Department of External Affairs has done its part in referring the cases to the Justice Department, yet the fact remains that there has never been a single prosecution in Canada under the Foreign Extraterritorial Measures Act.[41]

It is important to keep in mind Canada's particular vulnerability, given its dedication to the success of the North American Free Trade Agreement (NAFTA). Any Canadian challenges to US trade laws at this juncture could be particularly damaging to Canada's NAFTA agenda. Moreover, 80 per cent of Canadian exports go to the United States. Any blemish on this trade partnership would be particularly troublesome for Canada.[42]

The story from Europe is rather muddled. According to a report prepared by the European Parliament in late September 1993, the CDA 'is putting serious obstacles in the way of EC–Cuba trade and could even lead to a secondary embargo imposed on EC exports in the United States'. But, according to David Jessup of the quasi-governmental British West India Committee, the CDA in reality has had 'little direct affect' on subsidiary trade based in Europe. He suggested that US subsidiaries are finding other legal methods of continuing to trade with Cuba: 'Cubans have found creative new ways of doing business abroad – they have changed their buying patterns,' Jessup said. He noted that Cuban trading companies are located and operating around the world, 'even in as obscure a place as Liechtenstein'. He also said that British companies are doing an 'incredible amount of trade' with Panama, the Dominican Republic and Switzerland, among other places. Jessup said that trade between Britain and Curacao, for example, had accelerated in the previous 12 to 18 months. Jessup attributes Britain's increase in trade with these countries to British-based US subsidiaries finding their way around the CDA. 'Companies,' Jessup said, 'find ways of doing business.'[43]

The US based agribusiness conglomerate, Cargill Inc., was one of the most active companies involved in US subsidiary–Cuba trade. Brendan Harrington, of Cargill's Washington office, was more circumspect about whether subsidiaries are complying with CDA. He stated: 'Cargill is an ethical company. We are not going to break US law.' Harrington, however, did criticize the CDA and did not minimize its negative impact on his company. He said quite simply, 'Unilateral sanctions backfire on US companies. All the CDA is going to do is hurt US competitiveness.'[44]

Thus there is contradictory information over whether or not companies are complying with the new regulations. The US government – for obvious reasons – says yes. Subsidiary corporations – also for obvious reasons – say yes. Canada-based subsidiaries do seem to have curtailed their trade, while Europe-based subsidiaries may be getting around the letter of the law. Probably all parties are correct to a certain degree and the compliance question remains somewhat ambiguous.

According to Harrington, Cargill is already feeling the impact of the law. Direct trade between Cargill's subsidiaries and Cuba is clearly prohibited, but Cargill's indirect trade has also taken a blow from the new legislation. Harrington explained that much of the international agricultural commodities trade is contract trade, or 'string trade'. Most of it takes place on paper. Companies buy and sell contracts. A contract to purchase sugar, for example, 'may be bought and sold easily 12 to 15 times'. If Cuba shows up anywhere in that string of trade, the US corporation is now, under the new law, forced to default on the contract, thereby incurring a penalty. (In the past, the US company simply needed to apply for a licence from the Treasury Department.) Cargill may be forced out of the sugar trade because of the CDA. Harrington points out that, because Cuba is such a major factor in the international sugar market, Cargill is hesitant to get involved in contract trade for sugar because it is likely that Cuba will show up in the string trade. If Cuba appears anywhere, Cargill must default – pay – to get out of the contract. Though Harrington refused to confirm it, CDA-based defaults have probably taken place already because shrewd traders can take advantage of Cargill's CDA constraints to get out of losing gambles in the futures market. 'This obviously does not hurt Fidel Castro,' Harrington noted. 'Who gets hurt? The US company.' Harrington concluded, 'It is stupid to sacrifice US market share on the altar of a political gesture.'[45]

IMPACT OF THE CDA ON SUBSIDIARIES

What is clear is that the CDA has already taken a toll on US subsidiaries. Many people, including some US government officials, say the act hurts

US businesses more than it harms Cuba. Serena Moe, at OFAC, laughed when this was put to her. Her response: 'Who do you think the law hurts the most? Of course it hurts US subsidiaries.'[46]

Some subsidiaries – particularly those in the agribusiness sector – engaged in substantial amounts of business with Cuba. Though the figures remain classified, it is safe to assume that the cut-off in trade is being felt by those companies in several ways, including the loss of profits and markets. Although the actual profits earned by the large agricultural traders may have been relatively small, an important part of subsidiary trade was future market potential. As US subsidiaries leave the Cuban market, other foreign companies will fill the vacuum, and US firms will lose not only current business opportunities but also any competitive advantage they may have had when Cuba eventually opens up.[47]

Furthermore, there are some markets with finite resources in Cuba – beach front property, oil and mining rights, for example – that are being divided up now among the United States' principal trade competitors.

Finally, as Cargill has suggested, indirect trade is also affected. Because of the nature of agricultural trade, the mere presence of Cuba in the string of contracts is forcing Cargill out of the sugar trade. Therefore, even if their losses from the absence of direct trade are small in relative financial terms, US subsidiaries are losing future opportunities and current indirect trade markets.

IMPACT OF THE CDA ON CUBA

It is still too early to estimate in quantitative terms the impact of the CDA on the Cuban economy. There are several reasons for this. First, the CDA contains a 'grandfather clause' that allows subsidiaries with underlying contractual obligations to continue to trade with Cuba. The craftily worded language of the law was designed to give the US Treasury Department as much flexibility as possible in order to soften the impact of the act on US subsidiaries and US trade partners. Rather than cutting off all trade between US subsidiaries and Cuba in one fell swoop, the loosely worded language of the grandfather clause has allowed some trade to continue, thereby dampening criticism from US parent corporations and foreign allies. Furthermore, it ultimately delays the impact of the legislation for at least a year, if not several years.[48]

OFAC recently reported that 'because of the contract sanctity provision of the CDA . . . perhaps two dozen licences have been permitted' since the signing of the CDA eleven months earlier.[49] Although the two dozen licences represent a 90 per cent decline from the previous year's number of licences, it is a mistake to assume that it represents an equivalent drop in the level of trade conducted. The licences may have been granted to those companies responsible for large amounts of trade. The names of the companies in this contract sanctity category remain classified, as do the dollar amounts of trade conducted. OFAC did indicate that most of the trade being conducted under the contract sanctity provision fell into the commodity category.[50] Moreover, though more than 100 US corporations formerly conducted subsidiary trade with Cuba, only a handful accounted for most of the trade.[51] Until the grandfather clause runs its course, it will be impossible to quantify precisely the impact of the CDA on the Cuban economy. Because most commodity contracts are issued for two years, it will be sometime before we know the full impact of the trade prohibition in the streets of Havana and the pockets of US subsidiaries.

Adding to the difficulty of quantifying the impact of the law is the fact that some items formerly supplied by US subsidiaries are unique and irreplaceable. Specific medical supplies and replacement parts for US capital goods fall into this category.[52] Despite these obstacles in quantifying the impact of CDA on Cuba, it is safe to assume that Cuba will have a fairly easy time finding new trade partners for most of the trade formerly conducted by US subsidiaries. This is especially so because most of the goods supplied by subsidiaries have been foodstuffs and other fungible goods. Even a US Department of State official recently admitted that Cuba has been successful in finding new markets to replace those previously occupied by US subsidiaries.[53] Cuba may have to pay inflated prices to import these goods, and there might be some interruption in domestic supplies as Cuba finds new trade partners, but the CDA has probably been more of an inconvenience to Cuba than a permanent hardship.

IMPACT OF THE CDA ON COMPANIES NOT UNDER ITS JURISDICTION

The CDA has both inhibited and liberated companies *not* under its jurisdiction from trading with Cuba. Andrew Zimbalist, notes that 'foreign companies afraid of losing unfettered access to the US market might join US subsidiaries abroad in avoiding Cuban products'.[54] Gareth Jenkins, editor of Britain's *Cuba Business* magazine, reports that CDA has had 'a lot of impact scaring people off from trading with Cuba'.[55] Licensing rounds for oil drilling, for instance, may have been a flop because British Petroleum was scared off. Royal Dutch Shell and Clyde Petroleum report that the US State Department 'vigorously discouraged' them from investing in Cuba. Total of France continues to drill for oil off Cuba's coast after allegedly being told that the offshore oil block it was exploring had been sold to US interests before 1959.[56]

There was a dramatic 83.5 per cent decline in British exports to the island for the first two months of 1993 compared to the same period during the previous year.[57] Although there are normally great fluctuations in trade between the two countries, this decline was particularly striking. Part of the drop may be attributable to the impact the CDA has had on wholly foreign companies, although the fragile Cuban economy must certainly be part of the picture.

David Jessup of the British West India Committee explained that until Fidel Castro's July 1993 Cuban dollarization announcement there was a noted decline in European investments in Cuba.[58] He attributes this to the poor performance of the Cuban economy and the pressure – overt or otherwise – from the US government to block trade with Cuba. However, Jessup points out that, following Castro's July announcement, there has been a surge in European interest in investment opportunities in Cuba. Jessup also attributed this attention focused on Cuba and its markets to European sensitivity to 'unofficial signals from Washington that the Clinton administration is beginning to change its policy toward Cuba'. Jessup mentioned, for example, a softening in the anti-Cuba rhetoric coming from Washington.[59]

In an example of renewed British interest, an official British trade delegation visited the island in June 1993. Group leader Baroness Young, a key member of the House of Lords and of the Conservative Party, told reporters in Havana: 'The British government's position is that we have trade relations with Cuba and we are interested in building them up, as we are a trading nation.'[60]

Wolf Grabendorff, director of the Spanish think-tank Institute for European–Latin American Relations (IRELA) also noted increased European interest in Cuba. Grabendorff said that 'in recent years, European enterprises have extended their trade and investment relations with Cuba. In the last two years, for example, European and Canadian firms have established 52 joint ventures with Cuba. . . . French and Spanish enterprises have maintained and even extended their economic relations with the island.'[61]

This may be part of a trend whereby trade formerly conducted with subsidiaries of US corporations is being replaced by foreign concerns. Frank Smeenk, head of Toronto-based MacDonald Mining, noted recently that Washington's efforts to prevent trade with Cuba by Canadian subsidiaries of US firms are helping wholly owned Canadian companies beat their US-owned competitors. Smeenk noted, 'There's been 30 years of waiting. There's lots and lots of business opportunities in that country. It will absorb billions of dollars in capital.'[62] It must be noted that information and data on current business practices relating to Cuba is hard to obtain. Many companies are cautious about releasing information about their Cuban activities for fear of reprisal from certain elements of the Cuban exile community.

Thus it appears that the CDA has had two polar results on companies *not* under its jurisdiction. Some companies are scared off from trading with Cuba simply because the legislation exists, even though it does not pertain specifically to them. Other companies are seeking out markets that were previously dominated by subsidiaries of US companies.

CONCLUSION: WHO LOSES THE MOST?

One must wonder, who in fact, loses the most from the CDA – Cuba or US subsidiaries. As has been pointed out, it is probably fairly easy for Cuba to find alternative suppliers for most, if not all, of the goods it previously purchased from US subsidiaries. Granted, it may cost Cuba in terms of time and money to switch trade partners, but, in the long run, the new law is probably more of an inconvenience to the Cubans than a permanent hardship.

Additionally, there are those who argue that the CDA actually aids the current Cuban government politically. Domestically, President Castro can continue to blame the economic hardships facing the island on the United States. Furthermore, the CDA has enabled the Castro government to gain unprecedented international support in the United Nations.

US subsidiaries have probably suffered, perhaps to a greater extent than Cuba, under the new legislation. Even if their corporate losses are small in relative financial terms, US subsidiaries are losing today's indirect trade markets and tomorrow's opportunities.

So I posit that the surest loser is the US government. The goal of toppling the Castro government through economic strangulation has not been accomplished. Furthermore, the United States' current Cuba policies have subjected the US government to international condemnation in the United Nations and by nearly all of its trading partners. Worse yet, it seems that a US policy aimed at speeding up the demise of Fidel Castro is instead legitimizing his rule. The US government appears obviously the worse for wear.

Notes

1. 'Special Report, An Analysis of Licensed Trade with Cuba by Foreign Subsidiaries of US Companies', April 1990, Office of Foreign Assets Control, US Department of the Treasury, Washington DC. These figures all come from the US Treasury Department 'Special Report'. They are probably inflated. According to Brendan Harrington, a public affairs attorney for Cargill Inc., only about 15 per cent of the licensed trade is actually carried out. Harrington explained that there is no penalty for overestimating the amount of trade that may take place while there is a penalty if a company underestimates. Therefore nearly all companies request licences for more trade than they actually expect to conduct. (Telephone interview with Brendan Harrington, public affairs attorney, Cargill, Inc., Washington DC, 15 September 1993.)
2. The average export import ratio for 1980–89 was 51/49. This number was calculated from the US Treasury Department 'Special Report', 1990.
3. In 1992, the balance of trade evened out a little but continued to favour US subsidiaries by a ratio of 53 per cent to 47 per cent.
4. See *CubaINFO*, vol. 5, no. 9, 16 July 1993, p.9.
5. 'Cuba Sanctions Amendment in the State Authorization Bill', from US State Department to US embassies in Brussels, Paris and Ottawa, September 1989.
6. Andrew Zimbalist notes: 'As in previous US Cuba policy maneuvers over the past decade, it is clear that the chief aim for American politicians in the Cuban Democracy Act was to appease the rich and influential members of the Cuban American National Foundation (CANF)'. See Andrew Zimbalist, 'Dateline Cuba: Hanging on in Havana', *Foreign Policy*, no. 92, Fall 1993, p.151. See also Wayne Smith, 'The End of the Cold War? US–Cuban Relations Remain Unchanged', *Los Angeles Times*, 13 September 1992, p.M2.
7. See *CubaINFO*, vol. 4, no. 9, 24 August 1992, p.1.
8. Peter Slevin, 'Bush Signs Law Aimed at Castro: Duking it out for Voters in Miami', *Miami Herald*, 24 October 1992, p.1A.
9. Former President Bush won 75 per cent of the Cuban American vote and President Clinton won 20 per cent of that vote. In 1988, Michael Dukakis received only 7 per cent of the Cuban American vote, thus making Clinton's 20 per cent substantially higher than the Democratic share in previous years. See *Miami Herald*, 11 November 1992, p.2B; *Miami Herald*, 5 November 1992, p.22A; *New York Times*, 31 October 1992, p.6.
10. Helen Simon, 'US Allies Angered by New Cuba Bill', *Business Latin America*, 26 October 1992.
11. British Embassy Press Secretary Michael Price stated, 'We made clear that there will be provisions within the legal system which will prevent subsidiaries operating out of Britain from complying [with Torricelli].' See *CubaINFO*, vol. 4, no. 11, 2 October 1992, p.1; *Wall Street Journal*, 1 November 1991, p.A19; *Globe and Mail*, 31 October 1990, p.A1; *Globe and Mail*, 1 November 1990, p.A1.
12. Reuters, 'Britain Acts to Circumvent US–Cuba Trade Ban', The Reuter European Community Report, 21 October 1992. See also *CubaINFO*, vol. 5, no. 8, 18 June 1993, p.5.

13. US Treasury Department, 'Special Report', 1993.
14. See *CubaINFO*, vol. 4, no. 12, 27 October 1992, p.2.
15. The Cuban Democracy Act affects $625 million of the $750 million in annual EC–Cuban trade. See *The Financial Times*, 9 October 1992; *The Gazette*, 9 October 1992; *Agence France Presse*, 8 October 1992; *CubaINFO*, vol. 4, no. 12, 27 October 1992, p.2.
16. Helen Simon, 'US Allies Angered by New Cuba Bill', *Business Latin America*, 26 October 1992.
17. *Nuevo Herald*, 1 October 1992, p.1A; *CubaINFO*, vol. 4, no. 12, 27 October 1992, p.2–3.
18. *Washington Times*, 22 November 1992, p.A14; *CubaINFO*, vol. 4, no. 14, 4 December 1992, p.3.
19. David Schrieberg, 'Anti-US Winds Blow from the South', *Sacramento Bee*, 17 July 1993, p.A12.
20. According to the US Treasury Department, US subsidiaries located in Mexico increased their trade from $5.3 million in 1991 to $21.93 million in 1992. Other locations showing an increase in trade with Cuba include France, Germany, the Netherlands and Spain. See 'US Treasury Department, Special Report', 1993.
21. *Granma International*, 22 November 1992, p.13. See also *CubaINFO*, vol. 4, no. 14, 4 December 1992, p.3.
22. See *CubaINFO*, vol. 4, no. 13, 13 November 1992, pp.3–4.
23. Foreign Broadcast Information System, Latin America, 14 October 1992, p.3.
24. 'US Companies Sidestep Embargo on Cuba', *Chicago Tribune*, 21 October 1991, p.5.
25. Helen Simon, 'US Allies Angered by New Cuba Bill', *Business Latin America*, 26 October 1992.
26. Elizardo Sánchez, 'Let Fidel Castro Lead the Way', *New York Times*, 26 August 1993. Sánchez has spent 10 of the past 13 years in Cuban prisons.
27. Eloy Gutiérrez Menoyo, 'To the Exile Community, The Whole World Dialogues, So Why Not Cubans?', *Miami Herald*, 27 August 1993, p.17A.
28. Alfonso Chardy, 'Torricelli Bill Backer Urged Exile Unit', *Miami Herald*, 25 September 1992, p.21A.
29. *CubaINFO*, vol. 4, no. 12, 27 October 1992, p.3.
30. See *CubaINFO*, vol. 4, no. 14, 4 December 1992, p.4; *CubaINFO*, vol. 4, no. 15, 18 December 1992, p.2.
31. See *CubaINFO*, vol. 5, no. 11, 3 September 1993, pp.2–3. The US Treasury Department had permitted all but one of the 95 vehicles loaded with goods bound for Cuba to cross the border. They forbid the export of buses because they are not considered 'humanitarian goods'. Pastors for Peace stated that the bus will be used to bring children to Sunday school and to church services. See also *CubaINFO*, vol. 5, no. 10, 6 August 1993, p.1.
32. Fifty-nine countries voted in favour of the resolution, 71 abstained and 42 did not appear for the vote. Among those voting in favour of the resolution were Canada, France, Mexico, Venezuela, Brazil, Chile, Colombia, Ecuador, China, India, New Zealand, Indonesia, Spain and Uruguay. Among those abstaining were Britain, Germany, Belgium, Denmark, Greece, Ireland, Italy, Luxemburg, the Netherlands, Portugal and Russia. See *CubaINFO*, vol. 4, no. 14, 4 December 1992, p.2.

33. Statement by Robert S. Gelbard before the Committee on Foreign Affairs, House of Representatives, 8 April 1992.
34. Jorge Domínguez said, 'One alternative is that [the subsidiary trade laws] will get lost in the bureaucratic maze and not be enforced de facto.' See Helen Simon, 'US Allies Angered by New Cuba Bill', *Business Latin America*, 26 October 1992.
35. Some of the Clinton administration's small steps to ease tension between the two countries include: (1) new efforts to conclude a telecommunications deal with Cuba that would expand phone links with the island and allow US companies to pay tens of millions of dollars to Cuba each year; blocked accounts, however will remain blocked; (2) public statements indicating that Washington has no hostile intentions toward Cuba, advising Cubans in advance of military manoeuvres, and pledging to crack down on anti-Castro terrorism in the United States; (3) easing restrictions on travel and humanitarian aid; (4) ceased funding for Television and Radio Martí. See Christopher Marquis, 'US Policy Toward Cuba Softening', *Knight-Ridder*, p.A26; 'New Telecommunications Policy toward Cuba Nearing Completion', *Communications Daily*, 12 July 1993, p.1.
36. Telephone interview with Clara David, Office of Foreign Assets Control, US Treasury Department, 31 August 1993.
37. Telephone interview with Serena Moe, US Treasury Department, 13 September 1993.
38. Telephone interview with Bob Fretz, US Department of State, 7 September 1993.
39. Jeff Sallot, 'Don't Let Washington Call the Shots', *Globe and Mail*, 16 July 1993, p.A17.
40. Telephone interview with Dr John Kirk, 9 September 1993.
41. Jeff Sallot, 'Don't Let Washington Call the Shots', *Globe and Mail*, 16 July 1993, p.A17.
42. Telephone interview with Jeff Sallot, Foreign Affairs Correspondent for the Toronto *Globe and Mail*, 14 September 1993.
43. Telephone interview with David Jessup, 14 September 1993.
44. Telephone interview with Brendan Harrington, public affairs attorney at Cargill's Washington office, 15 September 1993.
45. Interview with Brendan Harrington, 15 September 1993.
46. Telephone Interview, Serena Moe, 13 September 1993.
47. Helen Simon, 'US Allies Angered by New Cuba Bill', *Business Latin America*, 26 Ootober 1992.
48. Telephone interview with Michael Krinsky, lawyer representing Cuba, 9 September 1993; telephone Interview with Clara David, Office of Foreign Assets Control, US Treasury Department, 31 August 1993.
49. Telephone interview with Clara David, 31 August 1993.
50. Telephone interview with Clara David, 13 September 1993.
51. Documents obtained by the author through the Freedom of Information Act from the US Treasury Department show that Cargill and Continental Grain, large US grain concerns, occupied a substantial percentage of the total subsidiary trade market.
52. Telephone Interview, Serena Moe, senior counsel at the Office of Foreign Assets Control in the US Treasury Department, 13 September 1993.

53. Telephone Interview with Bob Fretz, US State Department, 7 September 1993.
54. Andrew Zimbalist, 'Dateline Cuba: Hanging on in Havana', *Foreign Policy*, no. 92, Fall 1993, p.161.
55. Telephone Interview with Gareth Jenkins, editor of *Cuba Business*, 7 September 1993.
56. Andrew Zimbalist, 'Dateline Cuba: Hanging on in Havana', *Foreign Policy*, no. 92, Fall 1993, p.159.
57. British exports to Cuba totalled 1.4 million pounds for January–February 1993, compared with 8.3 million pounds in 1992: '1992 Foreign Trade Statistics – United Kingdom', *Cuba Business*, vol. 7, no. 5, June 1993, p.2. Telephone interview with David Jessup, British West India Committee, 14 September 1993.
58. In President Fidel Castro's 26 July speech, he announced that it would be legal for Cubans to have foreign currencies and to use them for local purchases.
59. Interview with David Jessup, British West India Committee, 14 September 1993.
60. *Miami Herald*, 14 June 1993, p.10A. See also *CubaINFO*, vol. 5, no. 8, 18 June 1993, p.5. Baroness Young has not, however, followed up by attempting to obtain export credits for companies interested in the Cuba trade. Until this happens, it remains doubtful that there will be a significant increase in British trade with Cuba.
61. Faxed letter from Wolf Grabendorff to Donna Rich Kaplowitz, 10 September 1993.
62. Peter Benesh, 'Canadian Trade with Cuba Growing, US Embargo is Helping by Pushing Business Opportunities North', *Star Tribune*, 16 August 1993, p.8D.

16 The Compensation Issue in Cuban–US Normalization: Who Compensates Whom, Why and How?*

Archibald R.M. Ritter

INTRODUCTION

An issue which will likely be complex and contentious in any process of normalization of relations between Cuba and the United States concerns 'compensation'. The United States government has been insistent in requiring compensation from countries which have expropriated properties of US nationals. It has formalized its claim against Cuba through the Foreign Claims Settlement Commission (FCSC). On the other hand, the US embargo on Cuba was meant to damage the Cuban economy and succeeded, so that a Cuban case can be made for compensation for the effects of the embargo. An even more contentious issue relates to the claims of Cuban-Americans who were not US citizens in 1959 and perhaps, in future, Cuban citizens whose properties were confiscated. Some of these are adamant on ultimately obtaining redress through restitution or compensation. These issues will require resolution if future legal imbroglios over asset ownership are to be avoided so as to minimize uncertainty and the economic paralysis to which such uncertainty would contribute.

This chapter begins with some brief comments on the historical context of the compensation issue, though a full review of the deterioration and break in US–Cuban relations in 1959–61 is beyond the scope of the present study. Next, the specifics of the US claims on Cuba are outlined and one unofficial Cuban estimation of losses imposed on Cuba by the

* This chapter draws in part on materials included in a study entitled 'Financial Aspects of Normalizing Cuba's International Relations: The Debt and Compensation Issues', prepared for the Cuban Research Institute, Florida International University study, *Transition in Cuba: New Challenges for US Policy.*

US embargo is presented. Ethical and legal aspects of the compensation conundrum are presented in separate sections, which are followed by a brief exploration of alternative approaches to resolving the compensation issue. In the penultimate section, the question of compensation payments to Cuban-Americans who were not US citizens in 1959–61 and to Cubans is commented upon briefly, but not analysed in depth. Finally, the essential argument of the essay is summarized and some conclusions are presented.

THE HISTORICAL CONTEXT

The compensation issue was at the heart of the 1959–61 conflict between the United States and Cuba, which led to the cancellation of Cuba's sugar quota, the economic embargo and the break in diplomatic relations. A detailed reanalysis of Cuban–US relations in the 1959–61 period cannot be presented in the time or space available here.

On re-examining this period, I am led to the conclusion that neither Cuba nor the United States was blameless in the process of economic and political rupture. Both parties engaged in provocation, retaliation and brinkmanship, so that the rupture was the result of a complex action–counteraction sequence. On the US side, the policy makers seemed to think that Cuba could be 'brought into line' by threats and coercive actions. Indeed, Eisenhower approved what might be labelled a 'second track' policy towards Cuba on 15 March 1960. This approach included possible sabotage, economic sanctions and military action, while US officials were simultaneously conducting reasonably correct diplomacy.[1] The second track approach – of which the Cubans were aware – helped to poison the atmosphere of US–Cuban relations. On the Cuban side, the leadership appeared to be ready to 'pick a fight'. It seemed to view the cut in the sugar quota and the economic embargo as desirable means of ending the ties to US imperialism, which was viewed as a source of Cuba's economic problems.[2]

In sum, neither side can claim virtue in the rupture of relations. The US was not simply responding to Cuban expropriation without appropriate compensation but was campaigning to influence the course of events within Cuba and was ready to use 'dirty tricks'. Cuba was not simply the innocent and passive victim of unprovoked US unilateral aggressions but was a participant in an escalation of hostilities leading to the rupture.

Table 16.1 Claims awarded under the Cuban claims programme of the Foreign Claims Settlement Commission.

	To corporations	*To individuals*	*Total*
Total value, July 1972	$1 578.5 million	$221.0 million	$1 799.6 million
Number of awards			
by value (dollars)			
5 000 or less	258	2 953	3 211
5 001–25 000	234	1 233	1 467
25 001–100 000	140	536	676
100 001–500 000	133	219	352
500 001–1 000 000	41	33	74
Over 1 000 000	92	39	131
Total	898	5 013	5 911
Total value, July 1994	$4 986.1 million	$698.1 million	$5 685.0 million

Note: The mid-1994 values were calculated by compounding annually the 1972 values with the customary FCSC interest rate of 6 per cent.

Source: Foreign Claims Settlement Commission of the United States, *Final Report of the Cuban Claims Program* (Washington, DC, July 1972); Reprinted from the 1972 Annual Report to the Congress.

US CLAIMS ON CUBA AND POSSIBLE CUBAN COUNTERCLAIMS

The value and validity of claims on Cuba from a US perspective were determined by the FCSC under the authorization of Public Law 88-666, signed into law by the President of the United States in October 1964. Following this, the FCSC commenced a programme for the determination of such claims by US corporations and citizens. This involved (1) inviting potential claimants to present their claims under procedures and regulations made public in November 1965, (2) adjudicating the claims and holding hearings over the next few years, and (3) issuing decisions on some controversial, or precedent-determining aspects of its Annual Report of 1972.[3] Of the claims which were filed, 5911 were accepted by the Commission, including 898 corporate and 5013 personal claims.[4] A distribution of the number of awarded claims by size is presented in Table 16.1. The total value of the claims came to about $US 1.8 billion in 1972. If this were compounded with the 6 per cent interest rate used by the FCSC to update claims, the mid-1994 value would be about $US 5.7 billion (see Table 16.1).

The claims which were ultimately awarded by the FCSC involved a good deal of adjudication, as there were a variety of grey areas in interpretation of the appropriate values and many of the claims lacked unequivocal evidence and documentation. Among the types of losses which were deemed to be justifiable and which were awarded compensation (if proved appropriately) were the following:

(1) Death or disability of US citizens (executed by firing squad after 1 January 1959).
(2) Business properties confiscated, nationalized, intervened, expropriated or inflicted with administrative controls and obstacles which were impossible to comply with. This included:
    business and industrial premises and real estate;
    machinery, equipment and capital equipment;
    inventories;
    financial assets and cash.
(3) Personal properties confiscated, including:
    housing and furnishings;
    jewelry;
    paintings;
    cash and financial assets;
    shares or stock interests.

A variety of major US businesses were expropriated or confiscated under the laws mentioned above. The largest such claims are listed in Table 16.2. Of these claims, the relative magnitudes of Cuban Electric, ITT, US-owned sugar interests, oil refining and the mining sector are striking. Some corporate and individual claimants obtained tax benefits on losses arising from the seizure of their Cuban properties. Such claimants would have to reimburse the US Inland Revenue Service (IRS) appropriately from any compensation received.

The government of Cuba has not made an official response to the compensation claims produced by the FCSC, nor has it indicated how it might approach any possible future negotiations with the United States with respect to this issue. However, it is not unlikely that the current or a prospective government would approach compensation negotiations with a set of its own claims against the United States for various types of damages. Carlos Rafael Rodríguez, for example, indicated to a visiting US delegation in 1975 that the compensation issue would have to include consideration of US payment for damages arising from the embargo, the Bay of Pigs and the attacks by exile groups. Similar assertions were made by President Castro in 1977.[5]

Table 16.2 Claims over US$ (1994) 10mn awarded to corporations under the Cuban claims programme of the Foreign Claims Settlement Commission

Corporation	*Amount US$ (1994)*	*Corporation*	*Amount US$ (1993)*
Cuban Electric	845	Pan American Life Insurance	31
ITT	413	United States Rubber	30
North American Sugar	344	F.W. Woolworth	29
Moa Bay Mining	279	Havana Docks	28
United Fruit Sugar	269	Continental Can	28
West Indies Sugar	268	Firestone Tire and Rubber	26
American Sugar	256	International Harvester	26
Standard Oil	226	Owens-Illinois	25
Bangor Punta	169	General Motors	24
Francisco Sugar	166	Chase Manhattan	23
Texaco	158	IBM World Trade	20
Manati Sugar	153	First National City Bank	20
Nicaro Nickel	104	Swift	19
Coca-Cola	87	First National Bank, Boston	19
Lone-Star Cement	80	General Electric	19
New Tuinueu Sugar	74	Libby	18
Colgate Palmolive	45	Goodyear Tire and Rubber	16
Braga Brothers	40	Sears Roebuck	12
Broise Cascade	37	Reynolds Metals	11
American Brands	33	Lykes Brothers	11
Atlantic Richfield	32	Sherwin Williams	11
Burns Mills	31		

Note: The mid-1994 values were calculated by compounding annually the 1960 values using the customary FCSC simple (not compounded) interest rate of 6 per cent.

Source: Business International Corporation, *Developing Business Strategies for Cuba*, New York, March 1992, p.76.

At present one can only speculate as to what might be included in a possible Cuban counterclaim. However, some analysts in the Instituto Nacional de Investigaciones Económicas (INIE), the research institute affiliated with the Junta Central de Planificación (Juceplan) produced estimates of the costs imposed by the economic embargo (see Table 16.3).[6] The IIE obtained estimates of the value of damages to the Cuban economy from the various relevant ministries, and seems to have produced its own estimates for some of the categories. A set of somewhat more speculative estimates for indirect costs of the embargo were also made. Unfortunately,

Table 16.3 Costs to Cuba of the US economic embargo: a Cuban estimate

Category		*Cost US$mn*
1 Loss of preferential US sugar market		4 676
2 Increased inventory requirements		1 990
3 Monetary and financial costs		3 128
Blocked assets	230	
US$ exchange rate changes and impacts	2 383	
on debt and trade	515	
4 Geographical reorientation of trade: transport costs		5 921
5 Losses to the tourist sector		3 508
6 Losses to specific economic sectors		9 224
sugar agroindustry	5 000	
other agriculture	319	
basic industry	632	
transport and communications	809	
commerce and services	844	
fisheries	20	
lack of replacement parts	1 600	
7 Other losses		234
public health	105	
culture and sport	129	
Total		28 681
Additional indirect costs		
8 Additional infrastructure investments required		1 732
9 Loss of access to US technology		2 318
10 Loss of human capital through emigration		1 779
doctors	508	
others	1 271	
11 Blockage of attempts to renegotiate the debt (to 1990)		3 303
12 Obstacles to financing through unconventional channels		84
Total		9 216

Source: A. Aguilar Trujillo and M. Fernández Font, 'El Bloqueo Económico a Cuba por los EE. UU', *Compendio de Investigaciones: Estudios Recientes sobre la Economía Cubana* (Havana: Instituto Nacional de Investigaciones Económicas, September 1992).

there is no analytical detail as to the calculation of the estimates in the IIE study, so their realism cannot be ascertained. A few of the categories are curious. For example, the alleged impact of $US exchange rate changes on the value of the Cuban hard currency debt and of primary commodity exports merely reflects changes in the 'measuring rod' function of the US dollar as it underwent appreciation and devaluation vis-à-vis the main currencies in which Cuba's debt is denominated (the mark, yen and Swiss franc). Two items on which there is some agreement are blocked Cuban assets, that is the value of assets belonging to Cuba or Cubans held in the United States since the embargo, and blocked fees from telephone traffic between the United States and Cuba. The latter amounts to some $US 40 million, and is not contentious. The former is placed in the Cuban study at $US 230 million, while the US valuation of this category is $US 140 million.

ETHICAL DIMENSIONS

Should Cuba pay compensation to US citizens for properties seized without payment in 1959–60? Should the United States pay compensation to Cuba in view of the damages to the economy and the harm to the material welfare of Cubans which resulted from the embargo? These questions do not have quick or easy answers.

There are a number of reasons why Cuba should pay compensation for the expropriated properties. First, in most countries, governments are legally required to protect citizens and businesses from damages arising from the arbitrary actions of that government or to refrain from imposing such damages in the first place. Thus, while governments are entitled to acquire properties for the well-being of society, it is considered appropriate that they indemnify the original owners of these expropriated properties. Second, the government of Cuba did compensate the citizens and businesses of other countries such as Canada, Spain and Switzerland. Cuba also allowed for some compensation – though it was not paid – to landowners whose lands were being nationalized under the first agrarian reform law of May 1959, which affected the large holdings of some US companies. Third, the government of Cuba initially agreed to compensate US nationals for some of the major nationalizations of properties.

On the other hand, there are grounds on which one might argue that compensation for the expropriation of US properties should not be paid. First, if the properties had been acquired fraudulently in the first place through theft or corrupt practices, then compensation would not be appropriate. (The owners of properties seized in February 1959 from Batista and his close associates and which were allegedly acquired illegally did not receive compensation. This was widely viewed as being reasonable.) Were the expropriated US properties acquired illegally? There were no allegations that this was the case at the time and, to my knowledge, this argument has not been made recently.

Second, it might be argued that the US enterprises which were expropriated had paid adequate or more than adequate returns to their owners through profit repatriation or other means (transfer pricing or expatriate employee remittances). This *may* have been the case but it would now be difficult to determine if it indeed was. But would this justify non-payment of compensation?

Third, should current and future generations of Cubans be liable for the actions, policies or errors of the leadership of Cuba in the 1959–60 period? Here one would think that, just as we do not hold children responsible for the actions of their parents, so too Cubans today should not have to pay for the actions of their government in 1959–60. While this appears to apply in criminal law and everyday life, it does not seem to apply to finance and economics (or the environment) where future generations in fact do assume responsibility for domestic fiscal debts and external debts (as well as environmental damages) incurred by earlier generations.

Fourth, it might be argued that the failure to provide compensation must be viewed within the historical context of 1959–61, that is the process of the deterioration of relations with the United States leading ultimately to the embargo and the rupture of diplomatic ties. Presumably, if the United States had not been applying pressure on the government of Cuba at various times in order to influence the design of public policy and to defend the economic and strategic interests of the United States, or to destabilize or overthrow that government, perhaps the embargo and the diplomatic break, and the radicalization of the revolution, would not have occurred. In this case, a more reasonable compensation arrangement might have been proposed, negotiated and accepted.

If the rupture of economic and political relations had been purely the result of unilateral US actions, perhaps one could argue that the non-payment of compensation was a natural and reasonable response. However, as noted earlier, the rupture of relations was not simply the result of unilateral action by the United States to which Cuba responded by non-payment of compensation. Instead, it was an action–counteraction phenomenon, with Cuba and the United States each responding to the actions of the other, characterized on both sides by miscalculation, provocation, brinkmanship, and recklessness. The government of Cuba bears a shared responsibility for the course of events in the relationship with the United States at this time. Indeed the revolutionary leaders welcomed the cancellation of the sugar quota and the economic embargo, in their official statements at least. They seemed to participate willingly in the escalation of economic animosity between the two countries. Thus it would be difficult to argue that Cuba should be freed from an obligation to pay compensation on the grounds that it was the victim of purely unilateral action on the part of the United States. On the other hand, the United States was an active participant in the course of events, which made it difficult for Cuba to negotiate at first and which made it impossible to negotiate or to pay compensation after the diplomatic rupture.

A fifth argument is that, while under an obligation to pay compensation, Cuba has in effect already paid a number of times over through the damages caused by the embargo. Such damages were inflicted intentionally, they were genuine and they were serious. The value of such damages is probably impossible to determine, and the estimates mentioned earlier may be overstated or understated. Should the United States be liable for the damages caused to another country through imposition of an embargo on that country? Again this is a difficult question. Are countries under a moral or legal obligation to trade with each other or is this merely a matter of mutual convenience? To my knowledge, no analyst, philosopher or policy maker has proposed that when a country imposes tariff or non-tariff barriers to trade or investment there should be compensation for the foreign enterprises or countries which are damaged by such action. Nor was it argued that the OPEC countries should compensate the oil-importing low-income countries for the oil embargo and then the higher oil import prices. But when a very large country imposes an embargo on a small country the economy of which is closely integrated into that of the large country, is the former liable in some ethical senses for the damages inflicted on the latter? Perhaps. From a legal standpoint, however, there would appear to be no such liability. Can similar arguments be made for the Bay of Pigs invasion or other covert actions?

Sixth, should Cuba be asked to make compensation when its foreign exchange earnings have fallen precipitously in real terms, when its internal economy has been in turmoil as a result of the disruption of relations which Eastern Europe and the former Soviet Union, and when the difficulties of the economic transition are intensifying? Under these circumstances, should Cuba under *any* government be asked to make compensation payments involving real net resource transfers out of the country? Probably not. On the other hand, there are some types of arrangements which would not involve a net real resource out-transfer but in fact could promote technological transfer or foreign investment (see pp.272–5).

LEGAL DIMENSIONS

International law and established precedent seem to be reasonably clear on the issues of compensation for nationalization. Indeed, the government of Cuba appears to have agreed with the principle and practice of compensating enterprises and individuals whose properties were nationalized for all countries except for the United States. On the other hand, there appears to be no body of international law or established set of precedents concerning compensation payments to a country which has faced economic sanctions, embargoes or covert destabilization imposed by a large neighbour. The established corpus of law thus appears to favour the compensation claims of the United States.

The standard approach to nationalization and compensation in 1959–60 and continuing to the present is that nationalization is acceptable when carried out for purposes of legitimate public purpose, when implemented in a non-discriminatory and non-retaliatory way and when provision is made for the payment of compensation which is 'prompt, adequate and effective'. Most countries have bodies of law which incorporate these essential elements, and this has been the case in Latin America.[7] Cuba's constitution of 1940 and the Fundamental Law of the Revolution (Article 24) adopted by the Revolutionary Government in 1959 were consistent with international law. The Fundamental Law, Article 24, permitted nationalization 'for duly established reasons of public utility or social interest, and in every case after payment in cash of proper compensation, the amount of which will be determined by the court'.[8] In more detail, international law concerning nationalization and compensation might be described generally as follows.

First, nationalization was and is legitimate when undertaken for purposes of public interest. This may include general processes of social and economic reform, and specifically nationalization of large-scale land holdings or latifundia when this is appropriate for the installation of more equitable land tenure patterns in order to achieve a more equitable pattern of income distribution, reduced poverty and social justice. Thus Cuba's First Agrarian Reform, and land reform generally in Latin America, has been considered an acceptable rationale for nationalization in terms of public interest. Second, nationalization is supposed to be non-discriminatory and non-retaliatory. It is supposed to focus on target groups equitably rather than being directed specifically against a particular ethnic, religious, racial, or national group. Also it is not supposed to be undertaken in retaliation for actions of another party or government. Third, compensation must be paid, and the compensation is supposed to be 'prompt, adequate and effective'. There has been some disagreement over the terms of compensation. Immediate payment of cash for the market value of a nationalized property would be highly 'prompt, adequate and effective'. The 'promptness' criterion can be stretched out considerably, to 20 years or more, with payment in instalments or the issuing of bonds payable in the future, presumably earning a reasonable interest. There is greater controversy over what constitutes 'adequate' compensation. Should this be the market value of the property, before or after expropriation is proposed? Should it be the tax assessed value? How is 'effective' compensation to be defined? Does this require payment in convertible foreign currency or can a local inconvertible currency be employed?

Did Cuba's nationalization law and processes conform to the commonly accepted international law and precedent? The First Agrarian Reform Law seems to have been largely acceptable and accepted: it was undertaken for a purpose of legitimate public interest; it was not passed in retaliation against the policies of a foreign government; it was not implemented discriminatorily against specific ethnic, national, racial or religious groups.

The compensation provisions of this law – payment through the issuance of bonds serviced in Cuban currency – were dubious with respect to the 'effectiveness' criterion, because the Cuban peso was not convertible and the exchange controls would have made the transfer of funds out of Cuba difficult. As it turned out, the relevant lands, buildings, equipment and cattle were often seized without court order, appraisal or receipt, making a systematic and equitable payment of compensation difficult. No compensation bonds were issued or, apparently, printed; no formal valuations of the affected properties for compensation purposes were made public; and no compensation was ultimately paid.

The seizures or interventions of other US enterprises were initially considered to be temporary rather than full nationalizations, so that the compensation issue did not arise. However, the interventions in time became full nationalizations, occurring mainly after Nationalization Law 851 of 6 July 1960. Law 851 appears to be questionable with respect to its implementation and compensation provisions. First, the law was of an explicit retaliatory nature, aimed at properties owned by US nationals and in direct response to the action of the US Congress authorizing the president to cut Cuba's preferential sugar quota. It was discriminatory in that it affected only properties owned by US citizens. The compensation provisions of Law 851 appeared to be designed so as to be unacceptable, although it is also possible that the Cubans thought that this might be a good position from which to begin negotiations on compensation. The provisions called for:

(1) payment in 30 year bonds, with a 2 per cent interest rate payable on unamortized balances;
(2) amortization and interest to be paid with 25 per cent of the proceeds from US sugar purchase in excess of 3 million *long* tons (2240 lb per

ton) and with revenues accruing when the price exceeded 5.75 cents per lb;

(3) annual interest which could not be paid when the previously cited conditions did not occur would be considered cancelled.

It would have been difficult for the United States to accept these compensation provisions. Cuba's quota in the preferential US market – where price was a good deal higher than the world price – averaged about 2.6 million short tons (of 2000 lb per ton) from 1952 to 1959. To increase Cuba's quota further in order to permit compensation to be paid, the United States would have had to reduce the quota shares of other foreign suppliers or of its own beet and cane sugar producers in order to make space for increased imports from Cuba.

The United States responded to Law 851 by cutting the sugar quota, though only for a three-month period, beginning in October. Cuba did not back down but accelerated the nationalization process. With the imposition of the embargo (19 October 1960), the elimination of the sugar quota and the diplomatic rupture, Cuba argued that the United States had made it impossible – as well as unjustifiable – for it to pay compensation. Thus there was never a serious negotiation or discussion of the compensation proposals of Law 851. This is where the issue remains to this day.

Should the United States Compensate Cuba?

In contrast to the existence of the reasonably well elaborated body of law dealing with compensation for nationalization there appears to be no international law on compensation for the impact of embargoes, economic sanctions, boycotts or any refusal of a country to trade or to have economic interaction, on another country. Embargoes or sanctions are usually imposed on one country by another country or group of countries in order to pressure the country to desist from certain actions, to change certain policies or to comply with certain internationally accepted standards of behaviour. The countries subject to such sanctions obviously have no resource to compensation, the sanctions having been imposed in the first place in order to enforce international law or internationally accepted codes of behaviour.

In other cases, countries have imposed embargoes in order to effect changes in the policies of other countries and/or to exercise collusive oligopoly power to increase export revenues. The OPEC oil embargo of 1973 is an obvious case in point. There is no law which says that a country or countries imposing an export embargo for whatever reason then has to compensate the losing countries for the higher prices of their imports. Furthermore, countries may impose import restrictions or prohibitions for a variety of reasons. There is a considerable body of trade law, codified under the General Agreement on Tariffs and Trade (GATT) which attempts to limit the imposition of tariff or non-tariff barriers to trade. However, there again is no recourse to compensation for countries damaged by such actions. Retaliation by the aggrieved party is the only possible response if appeals through the GATT fail. In this situation, small countries which are highly dependent on a trade or broader economic relationship (including capital flows, tourism, workers' remittances and so on) are vulnerable to the unilateral action of the larger economic partner. Only the mutual acceptance of fair 'rules of the game' as interpreted and ruled upon by a multilateral agreement such as the GATT or a formal bilateral trade agreement can constrain economic policies on the part of a large country which severely damage the economy and material well-being of a small trading partner. There appears to be no recourse in international law for compensation for the economic damages imposed on one country as a result of the trade or other economic policies of another country. Thus international law does not provide much, if any, support or encouragement to Cuba if it should try to obtain recognition, valuation and compensation for any of the damages imposed upon it by the embargo and the break of virtually all economic relations with the United States. However, international law and fairness or equity are not necessarily the same thing. It is possible that the ethical ambiguities of the issues relating to the embargo and its impacts on Cuba will be of influence in determining how the compensation issue is resolved ultimately.

Should Cuba Compensate the United States?

On the issue of whether Cuba 'should' pay compensation to US nationals (through the US Federal Claims Settlement Commission), law and ethics provide contradictory answers. International law is particularly one-sided: it supports the right of property owners to receive compensation for properties expropriated by a foreign government, but it says nothing about the right of one country to claim compensation for the damages inflicted by a hostile neighbour through the imposition of a trade boycott, economic embargo, political destabilization or even through invasion.

A basic sense of equity, on the other hand, does not support the right of a large country to damage a neighbour – and a small neighbour at that – by taking hostile economic, political, military or clandestine actions. Furthermore, because Cuba has already paid through the damages of the embargo, not to mention the other US actions, it would be unfair for Cuba alone to have to pay compensation to the United States while the latter paid no compensation for the damages it imposed on Cuba. Finally, owing to its current and prospective economic difficulties, Cuba will be unable to pay any compensation involving real net out-transfers of resources for many years to come.

Arguably, therefore, little or no net real compensation should be paid by Cuba to US nationals (via the FCSC). Perhaps a 'symbolic' payment could be made, though this would have to be in a 'non-compensation' form, such as 'generalized vouchers' that could then be used for purchase of equity in properties being privatized (that is a 'compensation for equity swap').

EVALUATING ALTERNATIVE COMPENSATION APPROACHES

The Cuban–US compensation issue might be dealt with in a variety of ways. The possible approaches include restitution or the return of properties to the original owners, actual compensation payments involving net financial transfers out of Cuba, cancellation or 'mutual forgiveness' (partial or complete), 'compensation-for-equity swaps', a 'generalized voucher system' or hybrid combinations of all of the above approaches.

Mutual Forgiveness

The United States and Cuba could cancel or forgive each other's claims. Despite the formality and ostensible inevitability of the US claims process under the FCSC, the president is empowered to determine the magnitude of the settlement of a claims case – in terms of the 'cents on the dollar' agreed upon for claimants. Indeed, the president is able to nullify and block claims for compensation if other circumstances warrant it, as where a major foreign policy dispute requires it, so that claimants in fact could receive zero compensation. (This was decided by the Supreme Court, 1 July 1980 in the Dames and Moore versus Regan, Secretary of the Treasury Case).[9]

Mutual forgiveness would be of obvious benefit to Cuba. It also would be viewed by many observers as being 'fairer', in that Cuba has already suffered the damages of the embargo. Mutual forgiveness would 'wipe the slate clean' regarding US–Cuban relations. On the other hand, the claimants of other nations did receive satisfactory compensation, so that non-payment of US claimants appears discriminatory, though some are likely to have received tax write-offs for some of the losses arising from expropriation.

Financial Compensation

Direct financial compensation is simply not feasible now or in the near future (to the year 2000?) owing to the current and prospective problems of the Cuban economy problems which were well known by 1994. Moreover, Cuba faces a commercial debt of about $US 7.8 billion which will also have to be renegotiated. (The $US 28 billion debt to Russia has evaporated, being denominated in rubles, although Russia may be hoping to collect some proportion of this.)

Restitution

The return of expropriated properties partly or completely to their original owners would avoid the financial disbursements required for compensation. This approach might lead to valuable and rapid transfers of technology and managerial knowhow to local enterprises (for example, in telephones) but could also contribute to a reconcentration of ownership and social inequity. This approach also faces logistic problems: some properties may no longer exist; some properties may have been run down or improved; housing has been occupied by other people for over 30 years; and valuation difficulties could be severe.

A Generalized Voucher System

Under this arrangement, certified claimants would be issued with vouchers equal to some agreed proportion of their compensation claim in US dollars. The vouchers could then be used to purchase any assets which were being privatized in Cuba. Such vouchers could be exchanged on a 'secondary market', so that claimants who merely wanted cash could sell their vouchers – and presumably convert the revenues to convertible currency. Other claimants could then acquire additional vouchers for purchases of assets the value of which exceeded their original voucher allotment. Other possible foreign investors could perhaps participate in the secondary market as well.

Compensation Swaps

The generalized voucher approach would permit claimants to exchange their compensation vouchers for equity ownership in some real asset within Cuba. As such, it could be labelled a sort of 'compensation for equity swap', somewhat analogous to a 'debt for equity swap'. The advantages of this approach are that no net transfer out of Cuba would be required; claimants would receive an asset which would be highly flexible.

This approach could permit highly creative resolutions of the compensation issue which could be mutually satisfactory or even beneficial to both Cuba and the United States. For example, the generalized compensation vouchers could be placed in Cuban venture capital funds or mutual funds for investment lending, or they could be invested directly in technological transfer institutions similar to the *Fundación Chile*,[10] or they could be used for the purchase of assets being privatized. One could also envisage a variety of types of 'compensation swaps' similar to 'debt swaps', such as the following:

(1) 'Compensation for Nature Swaps': foreign environmental organizations could purchase discounted compensation claims from claimants, and would swap the claims for lands which then would be included in Cuban nature reserves, national parks or forest reserves.
(2) 'Compensation for Land Swaps': foreign investors could purchase discounted compensation claims which could be used for land purchase for housing developments, commercial developments or tourist hotels.
(3) 'Compensation for Equity Swaps': foreign investors could acquire discounted compensation claims from claimants and then use the claims for the local currency costs of investment projects or for purchase of assets being privatized.

These swap arrangements using generalized compensation vouchers would avoid real resource transfers out of Cuba and could encourage new resource inflows, technological transfers or direct foreign investment in Cuba.

Hybrid Arrangements

The above elements – and some others – could be combined in a variety of ways, some of which might be advantageous to Cuba. Both Cuba and the United States would have to be willing to think creatively, however. For example, one might imagine the following arrangements:

(1) partial forgiveness, for 75 per cent of total;
(2) partial restitution for some major corporate claimants where technical transfer was likely;

(3) provision of compensation vouchers to other claimants, for use in Cuba;
(4) compensation voucher swaps;
(5) no net resource transfers out of Cuba.

Various emphases could be placed on these elements. Ultimately, it is likely that the Cuba–US compensation problem will be resolved using a hybrid mix of the above methods. Especially attractive would be a mix which combined major forgiveness with a 'generalized voucher' system which would permit some partial restitution arrangements, cash claims for some claimants, or compensation for equity swaps.

NON-FCSC CLAIMS OF CUBAN-AMERICANS AND CUBANS

More vexing and contentious than the US governmental claims on Cuba are the claims on the part of some Cuban-Americans. A common view in the exile community is that all properties nationalized in Cuba were previously owned by somebody. With a change in government, their intention is to reclaim such properties following the East German and some other East European examples.

The threat that such claims may be made in the future is serious for Cuba now. It means that some potential foreign investors face the risk that the joint ventures or sole-ownership projects they establish may be challenged. Such possible ownership disputes are likely to be a disincentive to investment in Cuba.

A reclamation of assets in Cuba by their previous owners would recreate much of the economic and social inequity which existed prior to 1961 and which was a major reason for the Cuban Revolution in the first place. (Restitution of urban properties, for example, would force many people out of homes which they now own.) Such a regression to pre-1959 social structures and economic inequities would be undesirable as well as politically unviable in Cuba. On the other hand, is it fair that foreigners received compensation for expropriation but those who were Cuban citizens at the time did not? (The nationalization of the properties of the Batistianos under Law 78 of February 1959 would not be included here.)

There may be the possibility of a compromise, however. For example, Cuban claimants of urban properties might be awarded their family's house or part thereof if they had lived there themselves and if they returned to live in it or part of it again. Or they might be awarded generalized vouchers for a portion of the value of the properties up to a specific low maximum. Likewise, owners of stores, rural properties or enterprises might be awarded generalized vouchers up to a specific low maximum which, exchanged on a secondary market, could be used to invest in properties being privatized, or mutual funds, for example.

Resolving this difficult issue will have to balance the need for continuing social equity and a defence of the beneficiaries of the revolution with some recognition that pre-1960–68 shop owners, house owners and so on are no less deserving with respect to compensation for their expropriated assets than foreigners. This will be a hard balance to reach. To my knowledge, no one has analysed alternative compromise arrangements. Instead, some in the exile community claim 100 per cent compensation/restitution while many analysts and the Cuban government consider the case closed, at 0 per cent.

SUMMARY AND CONCLUSION

In this chapter, the issue of the claims assumed by the government of the United States (specifically the Federal Claims Settlement Commission) for properties of US citizens expropriated by the government of Cuba in 1959–60 has been analysed. Resolution of this issue will have to be one element in the process of the normalization of US–Cuban relations.

Law and ethics appear to provide contradictory answers to the question of who should compensate whom. International law is quite clear in supporting the rights of property owners to receive compensation for properties nationalized by a foreign government. It does not seem to support the claims of countries which have been damaged by the trade policies or embargoes of other countries even if the damaged country is small and vulnerable and the damaging country is large and powerful. On the other hand, basic ideas of fairness would lead to the conclusion that the severe damages inflicted on Cuba and the Cuban people by the US embargo should not be ignored in the determination of a just compensation settlement.

Of the many possible approaches to resolving the compensation issue, *financial compensation* requiring net real resource transfers out of Cuba is out of the question at the present time and in the near future because of the problems faced by the Cuban economy generally and the export sector in particular. Cancellation or mutual forgiveness of compensation claims is a possible approach which not only would relieve Cuba of difficult obligations while in desperate economic circumstances but would be simpler and fairer in the view of many. While complete forgiveness is unlikely, partial but significant forgiveness is probable, largely in tacit recognition of the confusion and dual responsibility for the US–Cuba rupture and of the damages inflicted by the embargo.

Restitution, or the return of properties to former owners, was seen to have limited applicability. A *generalized voucher system* in which certified claimants were awarded vouchers for part of their claims which could be used for the purchase of other assets is especially attractive. This system could in fact be adopted to promote 'compensation swaps' so that foreign investment and technological transfer could be promoted. In sum, creative approaches to the resolution of the issue are possible, and could promote the mutual benefit of Cuba and the United States.

Resolving the claims for compensation of those who were Cuban citizens at the time of expropriation will be particularly difficult. However, a compromise solution involving some form of compensation, also in the form of generalized vouchers, up to a certain low maximum and subject to other limits, may be possible.

Notes

1. P. Sigmund, *Latin America: The Politics of Nationalization* (Madison, Wisconsin: University of Wisconsin Press, 1980) p.105.
2. See T. Draper, *Castroism: Theory and Practice* (New York: Praeger, 1965) pp.142–4; E. Guevara, *Guerrilla Warfare*, 20 June 1960.
3. Foreign Claims Settlement Commission of the United States, *Final Report of the Cuban Claims Program* (Washington, DC, 1972).
4. Ibid., p.412.
5. P. Sigmund, *Latin America*, p.126.
6. Alejandro Aguilar Trujillo and Mario Fernández Font, 'El Bloqueo Económico a Cuba por los EE. UU', *Compendio de Investigaciones* (Havana: Instituto Nacional de Investigaciones Económicas, September 1992).
7. Andreas F. Lowenfeld (ed.), *Expropriation in the Americas: A Comparative Law Study* (New York: Dunellen, 1971).
8. Michael W. Gordon, T*he Cuban Nationalizations: The Demise of Foreign Private Property* (Buffalo, New York: W.S. Hein and Company, 1976) p.125.
9. United States Supreme Court, *Dames and Moore* v. *Regan*, October Term, 1980, pp.654–91.
10. F. Meissner, *Technology Transfer in the Developing World: the Case of the Chile Foundation* (New York: Praeger, 1988).

Select Bibliography

Aguilar Trujillo, Alejandro and Mario Fernández Font, 'El Bloqueo Ecónomico a Cuba por los EE. UU', *Compendio de Investigaciones* (Havana: Instituto Nacional de Investigaciones Económicas, September 1992).

Añe, Lía and Nélida Pérez, 'El proceso de cooperativación en Cuba', *Temas de Economía Mundial*, no. 26, 1989, pp.91–145.

Association for the Study of the Cuban Economy, *Cuba in Transition* (Miami: Latin American and Caribbean Center, Florida International University, 1992).

Baloyra, Enrique A. and James A. Morris (eds), *Conflict and Change in Cuba* (Albuquerque: University of New Mexico Press, 1993).

Bunck, Julie Marie, *Fidel Castro and the Quest for a Revolutionary Culture in Cuba* (University Park, Pennsylvania: Pennsylvania State University Press, 1994).

Business International Corporation, *Developing Business Strategies for Cuba* (New York, March 1992).

Cardoso, Eliana and Ann Helwege, *Cuba after Communism* (Cambridge, Mass.: MIT Press, 1992).

Carranza Valdés, Julio, 'Cuba: los retos de la economía', *Cuadernos de Nuestra América*, no. 19, 1993.

Carriazo Moreno, George, 'Las relaciones económicas Cuba–Estados Unidos: una mirada al futuro', *Estudios Internacionales*, XXVI: 103, July–September 1993.

Casanova Montero, A. and G. Pedro Monreal, 'Cuba and the United States: The Potential of their Economic Relations', *Cuban Foreign Trade*, 1993.

Castañeda, Jorge G., *Utopia Unarmed: The Latin American Left After the Cold War* (New York: Alfred A. Knopf, 1993).

Cuban Research Institute, *Transition in Cuba: New Challenges for US Policy*, (Miami: Florida International University, 1993).

Deere, Carmen Diana and Mieke Meurs, 'Markets, Markets Everywhere? Understanding the Cuban Anomaly', *World Development*, 20:6, June 1992, pp.825–39.

Díaz-Briquets Sergio, 'Collision Course: Labour Force and Educational Trends in Cuba', *Cuban Studies*, vol. 23, pp.91–112.

Dilla, Haroldo, 'Cuba: la crisis y la rearticulación del consenso político', *Cuadernos de Nuestra América*, no. 20, July–December 1993, pp.20–45.

Domínguez, Jorge, *To Make a World Safe for Revolution: Cuba's Foreign Policy* (Cambridge, Mass.: Harvard University Press, 1989).

Erisman, H. Michael and John M. Kirk, *Cuban Foreign Policy Confronts a New International Order* (Boulder, Col.: Lynne Rienner, 1991).

Feinsilver, Julie M., *Healing the Masses: Cuban Health Politics at Home and Abroad* (Berkeley: University of California Press, 1993).

Figueras Miguel, *La industrialización en Cuba* (Havana: Editorial de Ciencias Sociales, 1991).

Fogel, Jean-François and Bertrand Rosenthal, *Fin de Siècle à la Havane: Les Secrets du Pouvoir Cubain* (Paris, Editions du Seuil, 1993).

Geldof, Lynn, *Cubans: Voices of Change* (New York: St Martin's Press, 1991).

Gonzalez, Edward, *Cuba Adrift in a Post-Communist World* (Los Angeles: RAND Corporation, 1992).

Gunn, Gillian, *Cuba in Transition: Options for US Policy* (New York: Twentieth Century Fund, 1993).

Halebsky, Sandor and John M. Kirk (eds), *Cuba in Transition: Crisis and Transformation* (Boulder, Col.: Westview Press, 1992).

Hennessy, Alistair and George Lambie, *The Fractured Blockade: West European–Cuban Relations During the Revolution* (London: Macmillan, 1993).

Hernández, Rafael and J. Domínguez (eds), *US–Cuban Relations in the Nineties* (Boulder, Col.: Lynne Rienner, 1991).

Interamerican Dialogue, *Cuba in the Americas: Reciprocal Challenges* (Washington, DC: 1992).

Kirk, John M., *Between God and the Party: Religion and Politics in Revolutionary Cuba* (Gainsville: University of Florida Press, 1989).

Krinsky, Michael and David Golove (eds), *United States Economic Measures Against Cuba* (Northampton, Mass.: Aletheia Press, 1993).

Léon Delgado, Francisco, 'Cuba y la economía internacional', *Estudios Internacionales*, XXVI: 103, July–September 1993.

Luque Escalona, Roberto, *The Tiger and the Children: Fidel Castro and the Judgement of History* (New Brunswick, New Jersey: Transaction Publishers, 1992).

Martínez, Fernando, 'Desconexión, reinsérción y socialismo en Cuba', *Cuadernos de Nuestra América*, no. 20, July–December 1993, pp.46–64.

Martinez, Osvaldo, 'Desarrollo humano: La experiencia cubana', *Revista Cuba Economica*, April–June 1991, pp.16–36.

Mesa-Lago, Carmelo, A*re Economic Reforms Propelling Cuba to the Market?* (Miami: University of Miami Press, 1994).

Meurs, Mieke, 'Popular Participation and Central Planning in Cuban Socialism: The Experience of Agriculture in the 1990s', *World Development*, 20:2 February 1992, pp.229–40.

Morley, M.H. *Imperial State and Revolution: The United States and Cuba, 1952–86* (Cambridge: Cambridge University Press, 1987).

Oppenheimer, Andres, *Castro's Final Hour: The Secret Story Behind the Coming Downfall of Communist Cuba* (New York: Simon & Schuster, 1992).

Paterson, Thomas G., *Contesting Castro: The United States and the Triumph of the Cuban Revolution* (New York: Oxford University Press, 1994).

Pérez-López, Jorge F., *Cuba at a Crossroads: Politics and Economics after the Fourth Party Congress* (Gainesville Florida: University of Florida Press, 1994).

Pérez-Stable, Marifeli, *The Cuban Revolution: Origins, Course and Legacy* (London: Oxford University Press, 1993).

Rabkin, Rhoda P., *Cuban Politics: The Revolutionary Experiment* (New York: Praeger Publishers, 1991).

Rich Kaplowitz, Donna, *Cuba's Ties to a Changing World* (Boulder, Col.: Lynne Rienner, 1993).

Ritter, Archibald R.M., 'Exploring Cuba's Alternate Economic Futures', *Cuban Studies*, vol. 23, 1993, pp.3–32.

Rodríguez, José Luis, 'The Cuban Economy in a Changing International Environment', *Cuban Studies*, vol. 23, pp.33–48.

Smith, Wayne S., *The Closest of Enemies* (New York: W.W. Norton, 1987).

Suárez Salazar, Luis, 'Crisis, reestructuración, y democracia en Cuba', *Cuadernos de Nuestra América*, no. 20, July–December, 1993, pp.65–82.

Valdés, Nelson, 'Cuban Political Culture: Between Betrayal and Death', in Halebsky and Kirk (eds), *Cuba in Transition: Crisis and Transformation* (Boulder, Col.: Westview Press, 1992) pp.207–28.

Index

All references are to Cuba unless otherwise indicated.